Warwick the Kingmaker

Richard Neville, Earl of Warwick.

Steve Williams

Also, by Steve Williams

History

Richard III A Man of his Time

Richard III The Sources

William Hastings Lord Chamberlain of England

House of York 'History with Dialogue & Character' Series

The Rising Sunne of York… Edward IV becomes King

The Sunne of York in Splendour… Edward IV is King

John Smith Crime Detective Series

Things could be worse… but I very much doubt it

Things could be better… but I'm not hopeful

Copyright © 2023 Steve Williams
All rights reserved.
ISBN: 9798876731548

"Is there any other man in English history so well-known and so little known about?"

Warwick the Kingmaker

By Paul Murray Kendall
George Allen & Unwin 1957

"The Earl of Warwick was the most powerful noble in our history. He was the central figure in the War of the Roses, and at one time he held two Kings of England as his prisoners."

Warwick the Kingmaker

A Ladybird History Book
Wills & Hepworth 1966

"The Earl of Warwick… was a wise man and a courageous warrior, and of such strength, what with his lands, his allies, and favour with all the people, that he made Kings and put down Kings almost at his pleasure… and it were not impossible for him to have attained (the throne) himself if he had not reckoned it a greater thing to make a King than to be a King."

Sir Thomas More

Simon Webb
Langley Press 2015

Warwick the Kingmaker

Richard Neville, Earl of Warwick

Richard Neville, Earl of Warwick, was born to a distinguished noble family with royal blood in his veins. Warwick became the pre-eminent English Lord of his time and earned the sobriquet Kingmaker for his exploits. He is often portrayed as a legendary figure in English history… a maker and breaker of Kings, who was the real power behind the throne in those turbulent times known to us as the Wars of the Roses.

Contemporaries speak of someone who was "like another Caesar in these parts" and was "everything in this kingdom". Warwick was considered "as astute a man as ever was Ulysses" who "was ever had in great favour of the commons of this land" and made Edward IV "King and was responsible for deposing King Henry".

Sir Thomas More considered him to be "a wise man and a courageous warrior, and of such strength, what with his lands, his allies, and favour with all the people, that he made Kings and put down Kings almost at his pleasure."

Warwick clearly merits his own *Ladybird Adventure Book of History*, but Warwick had his critics too. Yorkist, Lancastrian and Burgundian writers had good reason to speak ill of someone so damaging to their interests. Warwick was a mighty, some say over-mighty, subject. It is no wonder that foreign observers talked of Edward and Warwick ruling England together.

Warwick lived and died by the sword, but there is so much more to his life. The true picture is complex. Warwick was influenced by his background but mostly by the times in which he lived. Warwick, like many in those days, rode the roller coaster that was the medieval wheel of fortune. It is a great story. Enjoy!

Steve Williams

Contents

England in the 1460's Map

Richard Neville Timeline

Views through the Years

    Born into Royalty and Nobility

    Fortune lends a hand…

    Troubled Times

    From Lancaster to York

    St Albans 22nd May 1455

    Captain of Calais

    Love Day

    The Road to Ludford

    The Parliament of Devils

    The Lords of Calais

    Northampton 10th July 1460

    Wakefield 30th December 1460

    St Albans 17th February 1461

    Towton 29th March 1461

    Everything in this Kingdom

The Winning of the North

The Falling Out

The Commons of the North Rebel

A Rebellion in Lincolnshire

The Return of Warwick

Barnet 14th April 1471

Epilogue

Bibliography – Primary Sources

Bibliography - General

The Battlefields Trust

Northamptonshire Battlefield Society

Richard III Society

About the Author

Other Books by the Author

England in the 1460's

Richard Neville Timeline

Monday 22nd November 1428 Birth to Sir Richard Neville and Alice Montagu

1436 Betrothal / Marriage to Lady Anne Beauchamp

23rd July 1449 Recognised as Earl of Warwick

5th September 1451 Birth of Daughter, Isabel Neville, future Duchess of Clarence

22nd May 1455 1st Battle of St Albans

May 1455 Appointed Captain of Calais

11th June 1456 Birth of Daughter, Anne Neville, future Queen of England

23rd September 1459 Battle of Blore Heath

13th/14th October 1459 Battle of Ludford Bridge & Flight to Calais

10th July 1460 Battle of Northampton

30th December 1460 Death of Richard, Duke of York and Richard, Earl of Salisbury, at or after the Battle of Wakefield

2nd/3rd February 1461 Battle of Mortimer's Cross

17th February 1461 2nd Battle of St Albans

4th March 1461 Edward IV proclaimed King

29th March 1461 Battle of Towton

28th June 1461 Coronation of Edward IV

February 1463 Reburial of Richard, Earl of Salisbury, and Thomas Neville, at Bisham Priory

1st May 1464 Marriage of Edward IV and Elizabeth Woodville

11th July 1469 Marriage of Isabel Neville to George, Duke of Clarence

24th July 1469 Battle of Edgcote

July 1469 Imprisonment of Edward IV

September 1469 Edward IV allowed to go free…

12th March 1470 Battle of Empingham (Losecote Field)

25th July 1470 Ceremony of Betrothal between Anne Neville and Prince Edward of Lancaster

13th September 1470 Warwick and Clarence land at Dartmouth

2nd October 1470 Edward IV flees to Flanders

6th October 1470 Warwick enters London and kneels before Henry VI

28th November 1470 Henry VI's Readeption Parliament

14th March 1471 Edward IV lands at Ravenspur

14th April 1471 Battle of Barnet / Death of Richard Neville

Views through the Years

"He had what today are called charisma and leadership qualities. He also cultivated celebrity... he had the temerity to put himself on a par with Kings and to outshine them. For so doing he was at first greatly admired and later roundly condemned by posterity." [1]

Richard Neville was a huge character in his lifetime. Views have differed through the centuries, yet this should not be a surprise. Contemporaries were also quite divided depending upon their perspective and interests. Views changed.

Disputes over inheritances did not endear Warwick to those who lost land and entitlements. Lancastrians came to view the Earl as their main opponent who was responsible for the death of many of their leading lights and the ascent of the Yorkists. The Burgundians came to dislike his favourable disposition to France. Yorkist views changed as he turned against them and sought to reinstate the Lancastrian King. No-one, though, could ignore Warwick.

Yorkist propaganda praised "that noble knight and flower of manhood, Richard, Earl of Warwick, shield of our defence" in a manifesto posted on the doors of Canterbury Cathedral heralding the return of the Lords from Calais in June 1460. [2]

A celebratory Poem in the early part of Edward IV's reign praised Warwick "born of a stock that ever shall be true" as a "guiding star" for his help in subduing rebellious "castles, towns and towers" and thus helping and rescuing King Edward. [3]

---

[1] *Warwick the Kingmaker Politics, Power and Fame* by A.J. Pollard. Continuum Books 2007. Conclusion Page 200.
[2] *Edward IV* by Charles Ross. First Published 1974. Yale University Press 1997. The Yorkist Triumph Page 25. *The English Chronicle* edited by Davies. Camden Society 1856. Pages 91-94.
[3] *Warwick the Kingmaker Politics, Power and Fame* by A.J. Pollard. Continuum Books 2007. Page 168. *Political Poems and Songs relating to English History* edited by T. Wright. 1861. Page 270.

Warwick "was named and taken in all places for the most courageous and manliest knight living… as famous a knight as was living." according to the author of **Bale's Chronicle**. [4]

Warwick was almost larger than life… "like another Caesar in these parts" according to the Milanese ambassador, **Antonio de la Torre**. [5] Other reports in the **Milanese State Papers** talk of Warwick being **"everything in this kingdom"** [6] and that he "has made a new King of the son of the Duke of York." [7] Warwick was "as astute a man as ever was Ulysses." [8]

The **Governor of Abbeville** wrote about England to his King, Louis XI of France, perhaps in jest but not necessarily so… "They have but two rulers, M. de Warwick and another whose name I have forgotten." [9]

Commynes who served Duke Charles of Burgundy and then as counsellor to Louis XI of France, was in no doubt of the importance of Warwick. "The leading supporter of the House of York was the Earl of Warwick… a very great man, for in his own right he was already a great lord and besides that he held extensive lordships at

---

[4] *Warwick the Kingmaker Politics, Power and Fame* by A.J. Pollard. Continuum Books 2007. Conclusion Page 167.
[5] *Calendar of State Papers* Milan 1461 Letter of 24th January 1461 Antonio de la Torre, English Envoy to the Papal Court and to the Duke of Milan to Francesco Sforza, Duke of Milan.
[6] *Edward IV From Contemporary Chronicles, Letters and Records* by Keith Dockray. Fonthill Media Limited 2015. Page 131. Milanese State Papers Newsletter from London, 31st July 1461.
[7] *Edward IV From Contemporary Chronicles, Letters and Records* by Keith Dockray. Fonthill Media Limited 2015. Page 131. Milanese State Papers Newsletter from London, 17th April 1461.
[8] *Edward IV From Contemporary Chronicles, Letters and Records* by Keith Dockray. Fonthill Media Limited 2015. Page 131. Milanese State Papers Newsletter from London, 16th August 1469.
[9] *Warwick the Kingmaker* by Michael Hicks. Blackwell Publishers 1998.

the King's gift, both from the crown lands and from confiscations, as well as being captain of Calais and holding other great offices." [10]

Commynes wrote that Warwick "could almost be called the King's father as a result of the services and education he had given him… he governed King Edward in his youth and directed his affairs. Indeed, to speak the truth, he made him King and was responsible for deposing King Henry." [11]

The Flemish monk, **de But**, wrote in 1478-88 that he considered Warwick as the "third King" of England because "his reputation was so great that having deposed Henry VI, he made King in his place Edward of York, Earl of March, and then again by his doing Edward was chased away and Henry VI restored." [12]

Warwick had the common touch. The Chronicler **Jean de Waurin** wrote of him… "The Earl of Warwick had in great measure the voice of the people, because he knew how to persuade them with beautiful soft speeches; he was conversible and talked familiarly with them – subtle, as it were, in order to gain his ends. He gave them to understand that he would promote the prosperity of the kingdom and defend the interests of the people with all his power, and that as long as he lived, he would never do otherwise. Thus, he acquired the goodwill of the people to such an extent that he was the prince whom they held in the highest esteem, and on whom they placed the greatest faith and reliance." [13]

Waurin explained how Warwick gained his favour… "I went to see the Earl of Warwick, and he kept me nine days in all honour and

---

[10] *Memoirs - The Reign of Louis XI 1461-83* by Philippe De Commynes Translated by Michael Jones Penguin Classics 1972 Pages 180-181
[11] *Memoirs - The Reign of Louis XI 1461-83* by Philippe De Commynes Translated by Michael Jones Penguin Classics 1972 Pages 413
[12] *Warwick the Kingmaker Politics, Power and Fame* by A.J. Pollard. Continuum Books 2007. Page 172. *Warwick and Waurin* by L. Visser-Fuchs University of London PHD thesis 2002. Page 85.
[13] *Edward IV From Contemporary Chronicles, Letters and Records* by Keith Dockray. Fonthill Media Limited 2015. Page 87. Jean de Waurin Chronicles of the Wars of the Roses. Edited by E. Hallam Page 244.

kindness, when I took leave of him, he paid all my expenses and gave me an excellent saddlehorse." [14]

Warwick knew how to position himself well. **Robert Fabyan** the author of the **Great Chronicle of London** tells us how Warwick gained his popularity… "The Earl of Warwick was ever had in great favour of the commons of this land, by reason of the exceeding household which he daily kept in all counties wherever he sojourned or lay; and when he came to London, he held such a house that six oxen were eaten at a breakfast, and every tavern was full of his meat, for whoever had any acquaintance in that house should have as much as he might carry on a long dagger." [15]

For the Burgundian **Chastellain,** writing in the mid 1460's, Warwick was to be counted amongst "the great men of the world." However, Burgundian writers only 5 years later became more influenced by continental politics and the threatened invasion of their country by France, allied with England. "Where else but to death are you rushing?" asked **Jean Mielot** for whom Warwick was a traitor breaking the alliance between Edward IV and Duke Charles "through strife, deceit, by vice and fraud and snares." **Monstrelet's chronicle** referred to "his cunning treason and diabolic deception." For **Chastellain**, Warwick was now a "low born criminal Englishman". **Molinet** pointed out his "thirst for blood." **Basin** called him "that perfidious man." Even De Waurin changed his view of Warwick in shock at the lack of chivalry of the crude and cunning traitor. [16]

---

[14] *Edward IV From Contemporary Chronicles, Letters and Records* by Keith Dockray. Fonthill Media Limited 2015. Page 87. Jean de Waurin Chronicles of the Wars of the Roses. Edited by E. Hallam Page 244.
[15] *Edward IV From Contemporary Chronicles, Letters and Records* by Keith Dockray. Fonthill Media Limited 2015. Page 84
[16] *Warwick the Kingmaker Politics, Power and Fame* by A.J. Pollard. Continuum Books 2007. Pages 168-169.

A **Burgundian Ballad** praises the downfall of Warwick at Barnet Field.

"Now time his schemes have eaten
And his coin, yes, there's the sting
For Warwick's dead and beaten
Ha! What a sly dog is the King!

Frenchmen, one to another,
Rain tears and drip alarms,
For Warwick, your sworn brother,
Is crushed by force of arms." [17]

Livia Visser-Fuchs has extensively reviewed the Burgundian literature and sums up what they thought of Warwick ... "he was proud, a trickster and a coward who was a hero in his own thoughts and a child in his actions; a poor idiot whose hands were unable to hold all that he tried to grasp; a fool and a traitor rushing towards his end; and as a crowning insult he is made to say of himself that we must not regard him as one of the Nine Worthies, but rather as a character from Bocaccio, a conceited but helpless victim of Fortune's wheel." [18]

Not all English chroniclers praised him. The seemingly pro Yorkist **Hearne's fragment** records that... "His (Richard Neville) insatiable mind could not be content, and yet before him was there none in England of the half possessions that he had..." [19]

---

[17] *Warwick the Kingmaker* by Paul Kendall. George Allen & Unwin 1957. Page 323. Leroux de Lincy Pages 159-173

[18] *Warwick the Kingmaker* by Michael Hicks. Blackwell Publishers 1998. Page 2. *Edward IV's Memoir on Paper to Charles, Duke of Burgundy* by L. Visser-Fuchs. NMS xxxvi 1992.

[19] *The Chronicles of The White Rose of York: A series of Historical Fragments, Proclamations, Letters and Other Contemporary Documents relating to the Reign of Edward IV* Edited by James Bohn. Published London 1845. Paperback Version Reprint 2012. Page 23, Hearne's Fragment.

Yorkist accounts from 1470-1471 such as **The Arrival**, of course, speak ill of Warwick as a "traitor and rebel" yet even they acknowledged that "right many were towards him". Warwick was popular and that was why "the King commanded that the bodies of the dead lords, the Earl of Warwick, and his brother the Marquess, should be brought to St Paul's Church and openly showed to all the people…" [20] Warwick needed to be dead and people needed to see that he was no more.

The Battle of Barnet was a short Yorkist poem. It urged those who supported Warwick to "Turn away and fear your King…" for "Warwick is dead" but the author wrote more in sorrow than in anger and mourned his loss…

'Allas!' may he sing that caused all this,
Sorrow and care caused many a day.
Pray for his soul, that he may come to bliss
You that are his friends, you Priests, to pray." [21]

John Rous, still chaplain to the Countess of Warwick, wrote in 1483-5 of the fame of his sponsor's late husband… "A famous knight and excellent, greatly spoken of throughout the most part of Christendom… He had all England at his leading and was dreaded throughout many lands. And though fortune deceived him in the end, yet his knightly acts had been so excellent that his noble and famous name could never be put out of laudable memory." [22]

In Tudor times, it no doubt helped that Warwick had died fighting for the Lancastrians against the Yorkists for writers during this

---

[20] *History of the Arrival of Edward IV in England and the Final Recovery of the Kingdoms from Henry VI* Transcribed by John Stowe. Edited by John Bruce. Camden Society 1838. Kessinger Publishing 2007. Written 1471. Page 21.
[21] *Historical Poems of the Fourteenth and Fifteenth Centuries* edited by R.H. Robbins. New York 1959. Pages 226-227.
[22] *Warwick the Kingmaker* by Michael Hicks. Blackwell Publishers 1998. Page 3. *Rous Roll* Numbers 56 & 57.

period typically spoke well of the Earl. In 1521 the Scot **John Major** in his History of Britain wrote that "of him it was said that he made Kings and at his pleasure cast them down." [23] Major has been called out for his use of the words *regum creator*. Warwick is a maker of Kings. In truth Commynes and other contemporaries credited him with the same. "Warwick the Kingmaker" did not become commonly used until centuries later.

Sir Thomas More in the same period talked of Warwick making and putting down Kings… "The Earl of Warwick took out of prison and set up again King Henry VI, who was before by King Edward deposed, and that mostly by the power of the Earl of Warwick. This same Earl was a wise man and a courageous warrior, and of such strength, what with his lands, his allies, and favour with all the people, that he made Kings and put down Kings almost at his pleasure." [24]

Polydore Vergil, the Tudor writer, spoke of Warwick in particularly glowing terms… "He was a young man, not only marvellously adorned with virtues indeed, but also had a special gift… for his wit was so ready and his behaviour so courteous, that he was wonderfully beloved of the people. He was also liberal to all men… the people were fully persuaded that there was no matter of so great importance which the said Richard was not able to undertake." [25] Warwick "resisted valiantly" at Barnet and died a true noble's death.

Another Tudor writer, **Edward Hall,** echoed much of what Virgil wrote. For Hall, Warwick had a "stout stomach and invincible courage" and at least death at Barnet gave him "rest, peace,

---

[23] *A History of Great Britain* by John Major. Edited by A. Constable. Scottish History Society 1892.
[24] *Edward IV From Contemporary Chronicles, Letters and Records* by Keith Dockray. Fonthill Media Limited 2015. Page 87. Sir Thomas More, Pages 65-66.
[25] *Three Books of Polydore Vergil's English History* by Camden Society. Edited by Sir Henry Ellis. Published by Forgotten Books 2012 Originally published 1844. Written 1510. Pages 94-95.

quietness and tranquillity" which he never had in life. Warwick is a great noble, a man of honour and pride. [26]

Shakespeare has Warwick as a "Proud setter-up and puller-down of kings" who raises Edward to be crowned King but then infuriated with Edward's marriage, seeks to bring him down "not that I pity Henry's misery but seek revenge on Edward's mockery." [27]

In 1559 the popular book *The Mirrour for Magistrates* considered good and bad behaviour of those in power through the eyes and words of men of renown and fame. Anthony, Earl Rivers describes Warwick as a "Prancing courser" who would not be the King's ward, his "rancour was extreme" and he wouldn't stop until he was slain. Warwick himself speaks of his greatness and declares that actions must match words.

"I never did nor said, save what I meant
The common weal was still my chiefest care…
…For upright dealing, debts paid and poor sustained,
Is the means by which hearts are thoroughly gained." [28]

The Elizabethan **Samuel Daniel** in 1609 in his *Civil Wars between the Houses of Lancaster and York* focused on Warwick's popularity with the commons "Warwick had their hearts." [29] Another Elizabethan

---

[26] *Hall's Chronicle: Containing the History of England During the Reign of Henry the Fourth, and the Succeeding Monarchs, to the End of the Reign of Henry VIII* by Edward Hall - Published by Forgotten Books 2018. Originally published by Richard Grafton 1548. Page 296.
[27] *Henry VI Part 3 Act 1 Scene 3 & Act 3 Scene 3* Shakespeare www.folger.edu/explore/shakespeares-works/download/
[28] *The Mirrour for Magistrates* edited by L.B. Campbell. Cambridge University Press 1938.
[29] *Warwick the Kingmaker* by Michael Hicks. Blackwell Publishers 1998. Page 4.
The Civil Wars between the Houses of Lancaster and York by S. Daniel. 1609 Page 185.

Thomas Habington though believed that Warwick's "mighty spirit" was "consumed in his own fire." [30]

Around 1620, **Thomas Gainford** wrote the first real biography on Warwick entitled the *Unmatchable Life and Death of Richard Neville Earl of Warwick in his time the darling and favourite of Kings*. Warwick was "great, by reason of his hospitality, riches, possessions, popular love, comeliness of gesture, gracefulness of person, industrious valour, indefatigable, painstaking and all the signatures of a royal mind and generous spirit." [31]

In 1743, the French historian **Paul Rapin de Thoyras** in his *History of England* declared that Warwick was the most outstanding Lord in England who "had the honour of restoring Henry to the throne, after having deposed him, and of pulling down Edward, who had been raised entirely by his means. Wherefore he was commonly called The King-Maker." [32]

Thomas Carte in his *General History of Britain* in 1750 saw Warwick as "the most popular man of the age, universally beloved and esteemed" who was "undoubtedly the greatest subject in England for power and estate and deserved all the popularity he enjoyed." [33]

Times and attitudes change. In 1761 **David Hume** in his *History of England* wrote that Warwick was "the greatest as well as the last of those mighty barons that formerly overawed the crown and

---

[30] *Warwick the Kingmaker* by Michael Hicks. Blackwell Publishers 1998. Page 5. *History of Edward the Fourth King of England* by his son William Habington 1640 Page 85.
[31] *Warwick the Kingmaker* by Michael Hicks. Blackwell Publishers 1998. Page 4. *Unmatchable Life and Death of Richard Neville Earl of Warwick in his time the darling and favourite of Kings* by Thomas Gainford 1618-24
[32] *The History of England* by Paul Rapin de Thoyras. Translated by N. Tindal 1743 Volume 1 Page 596.
[33] *Warwick the Kingmaker* by Michael Hicks. Blackwell Publishers 1998. Page 4. *General History of Britain* by Thomas Carte 1750.

rendered the people incapable of any regular system of civil government." [34]

Sharon Turner in 1823 believed Warwick to be "too powerful to be a peaceful subject to any sovereign yet compelled always to remain one." [35]

There was still some who saw Warwick as some heroic figure. In 1834 **James Raine** wrote that he was "the greatest subject that ever lived." No exaggeration there! Warwick's "valour and extraordinary energy, combined with his profuse liberality and fascinating manners, rendered him the idol of the multitude. He was, in good truth, the setter up and putter down of Kings." [36]

Lord Lytton's novel *The Last of the Barons* in 1843 found Warwick praiseworthy. He "stood colossal... the greatest and the last of the old Norman chivalry... kinglier in pride, in state, in possessions, and in renown, than the King himself." [37]

James Gairdner in *The Houses of Lancaster and York* was highly critical of Warwick in 1874... "the last great feudal nobleman who ever made himself dangerous to the reigning King... his policy throughout seems to have been selfish and treacherous and his removal was an unquestionable blessing to this country." [38]

Charles Oman, the military historian, believed that Warwick did not compare unfavourably with other leading men of the time and praises his "industry and perseverance, his courage and courtesy, his

---

[34] *The History of England* by D. Hume. 1871 Pages 160-161.
[35] *History of England during the Middle Ages* by Sharon Turner. 1823 Pages 290 and 337.
[36] *Warwick the Kingmaker* by Michael Hicks. Blackwell Publishers 1998. Page 4. *Testamenta Eboracensia* edited J. Raine Surtees Society xxx 1834 ii Page 242.
[37] *The Last of the Barons* by EGEL Bulwer-Lytton. London 1843. Volume 1 Page 8.
[38] *The Houses of Lancaster and York* by James Gairdner. 1874 Page 186.

liberal hand and generous heart". Oman's biography *Warwick the Kingmaker* in 1891 was wholesome in its praise for the many good leadership qualities he displayed. Warwick's once-in-a-life sin of treason and treachery is excused due to dire provocation. [39]

Perhaps the most unique historical reference to Warwick is by **Ian Duncan Colvin** in *The Germans in England 1066-1598* written in 1915 which lauds Warwick as a "terrible enemy" of the Hanseatic League and as such one of the few patriotic heroes who tried to see off Germany for its interference in English affairs for political and commercial gain. [40]

"Warwick deserves credit for the forbearance he showed in his days of power' believed **Cora Scofield** in her extensive and detailed biography of *Edward IV*. "Whether he proved himself a wise statesman is another question, and unfortunately the answer in this case cannot be favourable to him, as it is evident from the course he essayed to take with reference to France and Burgundy that he either lacked understanding of England's needs and real desires or else allowed his ambition and resentment and the ties with which he had bound himself to the king of France to override his judgement, even his common sense." Warwick promised much that he could not deliver including peace, lower taxes and the restoration of lost possessions in France. [41]

Paul Murray Kendall in his very readable biography *Warwick the Kingmaker* in 1957 writes of a turbulent age and of the warrior who bestrode it. Kendall bemoans that we know so much about his

---

[39] *Warwick the Kingmaker* by Charles W. Oman. Originally Published 1891. iThink books. Page 214.
[40] *Warwick the Kingmaker Politics, Power and Fame* by A.J. Pollard. Continuum Books 2007. Pages 195. *The Germans in England 1066-1598* by I.D. Colvin National Review 1915 Pages xi-xii, 94, 103-18, 214.
[41] *The Life and Reign of Edward the Fourth King of England and of France and Lord of Ireland* by Cora L. Scofield. Volumes One and Two. Fonthill Media 2016. First Published 1923. The Struggle with Warwick Page 548.

deeds but so little about the Kingmaker himself. Warwick is "one of the great vitalities of the fifteenth century and Kendall is almost in awe of "the combat he waged with the shape of things in his time." Warwick's career was a "gigantic failure" in that he "poisoned his character" in "reaching higher than he could grasp." Warwick was a "consequence of the family into which he was born, the marriage his father made for him, and the time of violence in which he was bred."

Warwick's standing in English History is perhaps best evidenced by him being chosen as one of twenty-one individuals covered by the **Ladybird Adventure from History** series. *Warwick the King maker* was published in 1966. Warwick "was the most powerful noble in our history. He was the central figure in the War of the Roses, and at one time he held two Kings of England as is prisoners." [42]

In 1974 **Charles Ross** in his biography *Edward IV* wrote very unfavourably on Warwick… "The impression (is) that Edward was excessively generous and Warwick excessively greedy. For the Earl was already by far the richest of Edward's subjects in his own right. Yet he appropriated for himself a disproportionately large share of the most valuable offices at the King's disposal and continued to acquire more as the reign wore on… Even by the standards of an acquisitive age Warwick appears exceptionally grasping." [43]

Michael Hicks in 1998 published his excellent and illuminating "fuller not full" biography *Warwick the Kingmaker*. Hicks is clear that Warwick is a big subject being "the greatest nobleman of his age, the heir to four great families, their estates, connections and traditions." Warwick was "an emotional, charming, and popular man with a strong sense of family loyalty" and his "whole career

---

[42] *Warwick the Kingmaker* by L. Du Garde Peach. Ladybird History Book. Wills & Hepworth 1966.
[43] *Edward IV* by Charles Ross. First Published 1974. Yale University Press 1997. The Establishment of the Yorkist Regime Page 71.

should not be judged by the *bouleversement* of his last years." A very well-travelled individual of almost limitless energy with an "indefinable popularity that made him much more than the greatest of subjects." [44]

Warwick was a "great gleaming star… exceptional in his defiance of the crown" argues **Antony Pollard** in 2007 in his scholarly *Warwick the Kingmaker Politics, Power and Fame*. "Warwick did indeed act as though he was at the head of a state within the state…he enjoyed wealth and exercised influence on a scale arguably never matched before or since by a nobleman who was not directly of the royal blood." Warwick was a charismatic leader of men who liked to portray himself as a Prince above Princes, and Kings. Posterity has both admired and condemned him. [45]

Warwick strode though this turbulent period "like a colossus" wrote **K.L. Clark** in *The Nevills of Middleham* in 2016, "determined to hold on to power forged in the white heat of civil war and rebellion." Warwick "turned against the King he had helped to the throne, dying in a hopeless attempt to change the world." Clark declares that "our admiration for him must always be tempered by a recognition of his faults and failings. [46]

Admiration is not for all. Warwick was an "unconstrained ego" and a "pioneer of mass propaganda" according to **Hugh Bicheno** in his 2016 book *Blood Royale, The Wars of Lancaster and York 1462-1485.* [47] "The case for Warwick's defence is that he was denied the honour due to him and acted to prevent a clearly signposted attack on his sources of power" argues Bicheno but this "hypothesis can

---

[44] *Warwick the Kingmaker* by Michael Hicks. Blackwell Publishers 1998. Page 6.
[45] *Warwick the Kingmaker Politics, Power and Fame* by A.J. Pollard. Continuum Books 2007. Conclusion Pages 197-200.
[46] *The Nevills of Middleham* by K.L. Clark. The History Press 2016. Introduction Page 11.
[47] *Blood Royale; The Wars of Lancaster and York 1462-1485* by Hugh Bicheno. Head of Zeus 2016.

only be sustained if taken in isolation from Warwick's no less clearly signposted desire to dominate." Bicheno is not a fan of Warwick.

Wikipedia provides the following summary… "Warwick's historical legacy has been a matter of much dispute. Historical opinion has alternated between seeing him as self-centred and rash, and regarding him as a victim of the whims of an ungrateful king. It is generally agreed, however, that in his own time, he enjoyed great popularity in all layers of society, and that he was skilled at appealing to popular sentiments for political support." [48]

Whatever your view, Warwick left his mark on history, like few others.

---

[48] https://en.wikipedia.org/wiki/Richard_Neville,_16th_Earl_of_Warwick

Born into Royalty and Nobility

...born of a stock that shall ever be true... [49]

Richard Neville was born to Sir Richard Neville and Alice Montagu on 22nd November 1428 on St Cecilia's day, the patron saint of music and musicians. Richard was their third child but their eldest son. His pedigree was beyond reproach, and he could trace his lineage back many years to at least three of the leading English families of that age.

Richard was related on his paternal side to Edward III and on his maternal side to Edward I. He was not just a noble but a son of royal blood. *He was born of a stock that shall ever be true.* Richard was born into privilege and entitlement, and he would not forget his background. Nature gave him a good start in life. Nurture would see him become the leading noble of his age.

Richard was born at a time when England was unsure of itself. Henry V and Agincourt were glorious memories. War in France was not going well. Joan of Arc was helping to break the siege of Orleans. Charles VII was to be crowned King. Henry VI was a child King of just seven years old. England was divided and weak. *Woe to thee, O land, whose king is a child.* [50]

Richard's father, Richard Neville, married Alice Montagu the daughter and heiress of Thomas Montagu, 4th Earl of Salisbury around 1420. Thomas died in 1428 and not long after, Richard was confirmed as 5th Earl of Salisbury and Alice, the Countess of Salisbury.

The elder Richard Neville, or Salisbury as he became known, came from a royal and noble family background. Salisbury's maternal

---

[49] *Warwick the Kingmaker Politics, Power and Fame* by A.J. Pollard. Continuum Books 2007. Page 168. Celebratory Poem in early reign of Edward IV. *Political Poems and Songs relating to English History* edited by T. Wright. 1861. Page 270.
[50] *Ecclesiastes* Chapter 10 Verse 16. The Bible.

grandfather was John of Gaunt, son of **Edward III**. Salisbury's mother Joan Beaufort was stepsister to **Henry IV**.

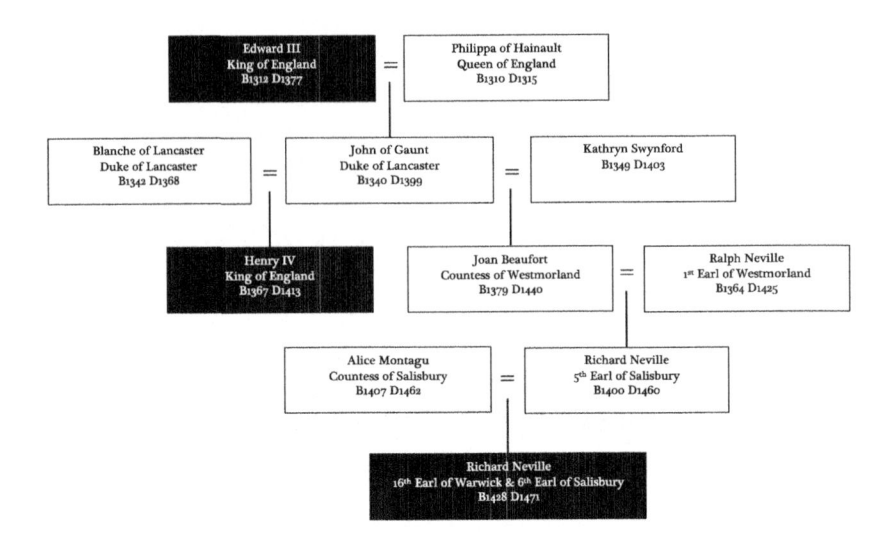

```
                    ┌─────────────────────┐       ┌─────────────────────┐
                    │    Edward III       │       │ Philippa of Hainault│
                    │  King of England    │ = │   Queen of England  │
                    │    B1312 D1377      │       │    B1310 D1315      │
                    └─────────────────────┘       └─────────────────────┘

┌──────────────────┐     ┌──────────────────┐     ┌──────────────────┐
│Blanche of Lancaster│    │  John of Gaunt   │     │ Kathryn Swynford │
│ Duke of Lancaster │ = │ Duke of Lancaster │ = │   B1349 D1403    │
│   B1342 D1368    │     │   B1340 D1399    │     │                  │
└──────────────────┘     └──────────────────┘     └──────────────────┘

            ┌──────────────┐   ┌──────────────────┐     ┌──────────────────┐
            │  Henry IV    │   │  Joan Beaufort   │     │  Ralph Neville   │
            │King of England│   │Countess of Westmorland│ = │1st Earl of Westmorland│
            │ B1367 D1413  │   │   B1379 D1440    │     │   B1364 D1425    │
            └──────────────┘   └──────────────────┘     └──────────────────┘

                        ┌──────────────────┐     ┌──────────────────┐
                        │  Alice Montagu   │     │ Richard Neville  │
                        │Countess of Salisbury│ = │5th Earl of Salisbury│
                        │   B1407 D1462    │     │   B1400 D1460    │
                        └──────────────────┘     └──────────────────┘

                                ┌──────────────────────────────────┐
                                │        Richard Neville           │
                                │16th Earl of Warwick & 6th Earl of Salisbury│
                                │         B1428 D1471              │
                                └──────────────────────────────────┘
```

Alice Montagu's maternal grandfather was the stepbrother of **Richard II**, and her maternal 2nd great grandfather was Edmund of Woodstock, the son of **Edward I**.

Page 25

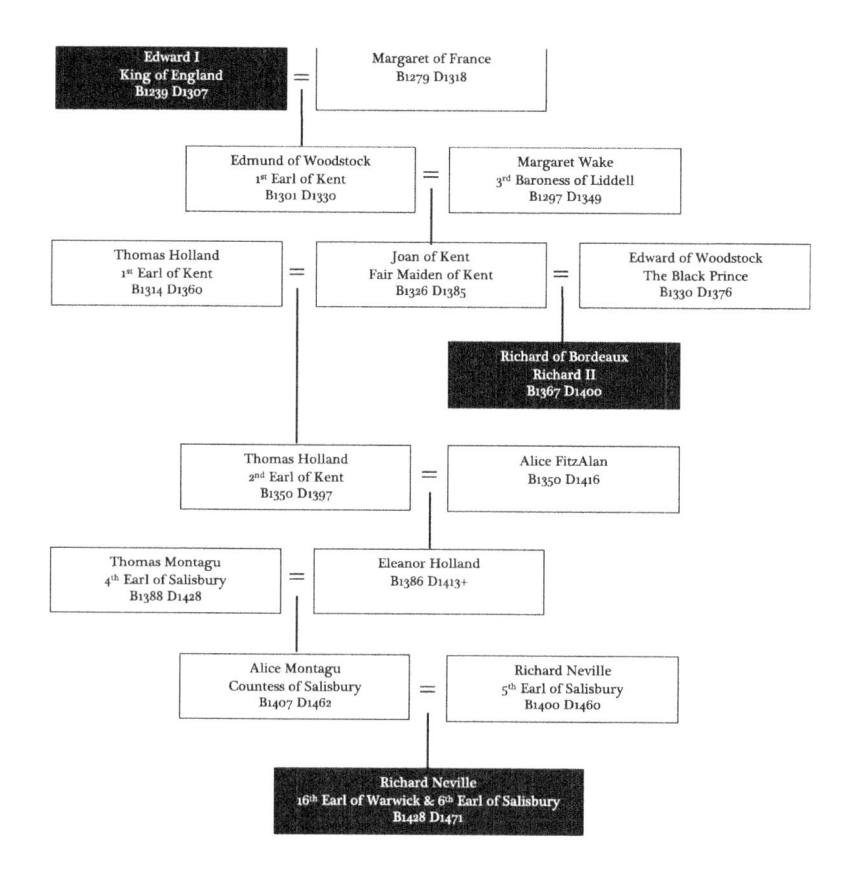

```
Edward I                    Margaret of France
King of England      =      B1279 D1318
B1239 D1307

         Edmund of Woodstock          Margaret Wake
         1st Earl of Kent        =    3rd Baroness of Liddell
         B1301 D1330                  B1297 D1349

Thomas Holland        Joan of Kent              Edward of Woodstock
1st Earl of Kent  =   Fair Maiden of Kent  =    The Black Prince
B1314 D1360           B1326 D1385               B1330 D1376

                          Richard of Bordeaux
                          Richard II
                          B1367 D1400

         Thomas Holland              Alice FitzAlan
         2nd Earl of Kent       =    B1350 D1416
         B1350 D1397

Thomas Montagu        Eleanor Holland
4th Earl of Salisbury =   B1386 D1413+
B1388 D1428

         Alice Montagu               Richard Neville
         Countess of Salisbury  =    5th Earl of Salisbury
         B1407 D1462                 B1400 D1460

                  Richard Neville
                  16th Earl of Warwick & 6th Earl of Salisbury
                  B1428 D1471
```

Alice Montagu's paternal great grandmother was the granddaughter of Joan of Acre, the daughter of **Edward I**.

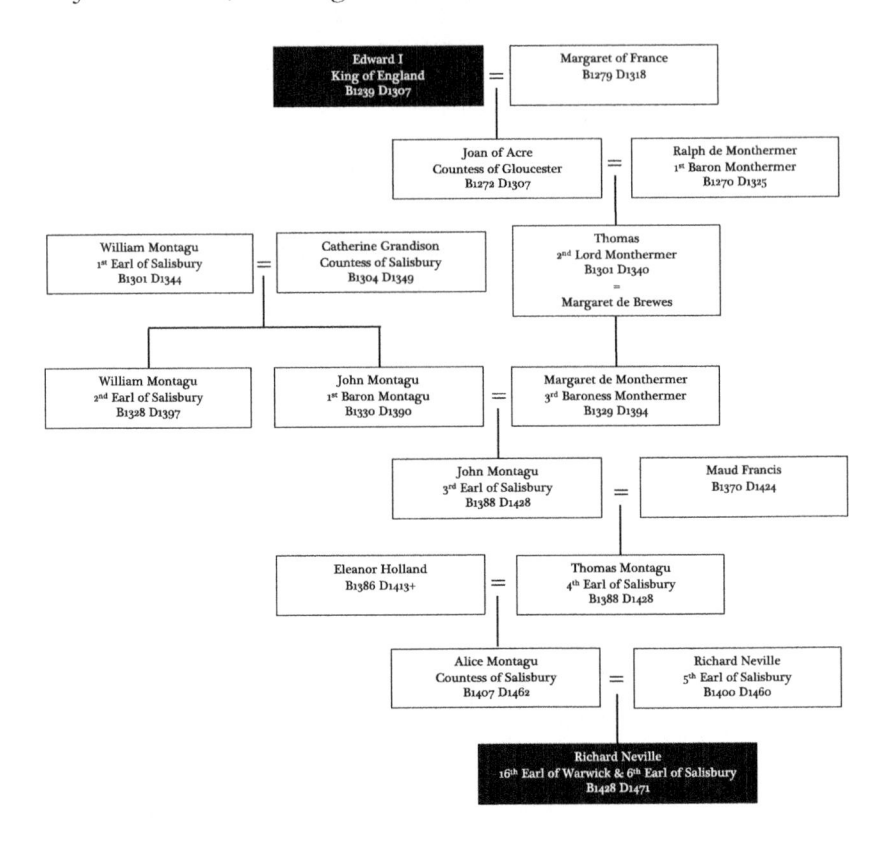

```
                    ┌─────────────────────┐   ┌─────────────────────┐
                    │     Edward I        │ = │ Margaret of France  │
                    │  King of England    │   │    B1279 D1318      │
                    │   B1239 D1307       │   └─────────────────────┘
                    └─────────────────────┘
                              │
                    ┌─────────────────────┐   ┌─────────────────────┐
                    │    Joan of Acre     │ = │ Ralph de Monthermer │
                    │ Countess of Gloucester│ │  1st Baron Monthermer│
                    │    B1272 D1307      │   │    B1270 D1325      │
                    └─────────────────────┘   └─────────────────────┘
                                                        │
┌──────────────────┐   ┌─────────────────────┐   ┌─────────────────────┐
│ William Montagu  │   │ Catherine Grandison │   │      Thomas         │
│ 1st Earl of Salisbury│=│ Countess of Salisbury│ │ 2nd Lord Monthermer │
│   B1301 D1344    │   │    B1304 D1349      │   │   B1301 D1340       │
└──────────────────┘   └─────────────────────┘   │         =           │
                              │                  │ Margaret de Brewes  │
                                                 └─────────────────────┘
                                                        │
┌──────────────────┐   ┌─────────────────────┐   ┌─────────────────────┐
│ William Montagu  │   │   John Montagu      │   │ Margaret de Monthermer│
│ 2nd Earl of Salisbury│ │ 1st Baron Montagu │ = │ 3rd Baroness Monthermer│
│   B1328 D1397    │   │   B1330 D1390       │   │    B1329 D1394      │
└──────────────────┘   └─────────────────────┘   └─────────────────────┘
                              │
                    ┌─────────────────────┐   ┌─────────────────────┐
                    │   John Montagu      │   │    Maud Francis     │
                    │ 3rd Earl of Salisbury│ = │    B1370 D1424      │
                    │    B1388 D1428      │   └─────────────────────┘
                    └─────────────────────┘
                              │
                    ┌─────────────────────┐   ┌─────────────────────┐
                    │   Eleanor Holland   │   │   Thomas Montagu    │
                    │    B1386 D1413+     │ = │ 4th Earl of Salisbury│
                    └─────────────────────┘   │    B1388 D1428      │
                                              └─────────────────────┘
                              │
                    ┌─────────────────────┐   ┌─────────────────────┐
                    │   Alice Montagu     │   │   Richard Neville   │
                    │ Countess of Salisbury│ = │ 5th Earl of Salisbury│
                    │    B1407 D1462      │   │    B1400 D1460      │
                    └─────────────────────┘   └─────────────────────┘
                                      │
                          ┌─────────────────────────────┐
                          │      Richard Neville        │
                          │16th Earl of Warwick & 6th Earl of Salisbury│
                          │       B1428 D1471           │
                          └─────────────────────────────┘
```

The royal bloodline was important. Richard Neville was related to Henry VI and Edward IV and many of the leading Lancastrian and Yorkist nobles. He was first cousin once removed to Gloucester and Bedford, and Cardinal Beaufort was his grand uncle.

Richard Neville was second cousin to Henry VI and first cousin to Edward IV. Somerset (3rd Duke) was his second cousin. Buckingham (1st Duke) was his second cousin once removed.

The War of the Roses is not for nothing known as *The Cousin's War*.

Salisbury was first cousin to **Henry V** through his mother, Jean Beaufort, stepsister to Henry IV. He was first cousin once removed to **Henry VI**.

Richard Neville was second cousin to **Henry VI**.

= = = = = = = = = =

Salisbury was the brother-in-law to **Richard, Duke of York**, through his sister Cecily Neville.

Richard Neville was first cousin to **Edward IV**.

= = = = = = = = = =

Salisbury was first cousin to the Lancastrian **Edmund Beaufort, 2nd Duke of Somerset**.

Richard Neville was second cousin to the Lancastrian **Henry Beaufort, 3rd Duke of Somerset** and second cousin once removed from the future **Henry VII**.

= = = = = = = = = =

Salisbury was second cousin to the Lancastrian **Humphrey Stafford, 1st Duke of Buckingham**. Stafford married Salisbury's sister, Anne Neville, and was also his brother-in-law.

Richard Neville was second cousin once removed to the Lancastrian **Humphrey Stafford, 1st Duke of Buckingham**.

```
                              Edward III
                              King of England
                              B1312 D1377
```

| Lionel of Antwerp, 1st Duke of Clarence B1338 D1368 | Edmund of Langley 1st Duke of York B1364 D1402 | Kathryn Swynford B1349 D1403 | John of Gaunt Duke of Lancaster B1340 D1399 = Blanche of Lancaster B1342 D1368 | Thomas of Woodstock 1st Duke of Gloucester B1355 D1397 |

- Philippa of Clarence B1355 D1382
- Roger Mortimer B1374 D1398
- Ann Mortimer B1388 D1411 = Richard, 3rd Earl of Cambridge B1385 D1415
- Joan Beaufort Countess of Westmorland B1379 D1440 = Ralph Neville 1st Earl of Westmorland B1364 D1425
- John Beaufort 1st Earl of Somerset B1371 D1410
- Henry IV B1367 D1413 = Anne of Gloucester B1383 D1458 = Edmund Stafford 5th Earl of Stafford
- Henry V B1386 D1422
- Humphrey Stafford B1402 D1460 1st Duke of Buckingham
- Richard 3rd Duke of York B1411 D1460 = Cecily Neville Countess of York B1415 D1495
- Richard Neville 5th Earl of Salisbury B1400 D1460
- John Beaufort 1st Duke of Somerset B1404 D1444
- Edmund Beaufort 2nd Duke of Somerset B1406 D1455
- Henry VI B1421 D1471
- Humphrey Stafford Earl of Stafford B1425 D1458
- Edward, Earl of March, EDWARD IV B1442 D1483
- Richard Neville 16th Earl of Warwick B1428 D1471
- Margaret Beaufort
- Henry Beaufort 3rd Duke of Somerset B1436 D1464
- Henry Stafford 2nd Duke of Buckingham B1455 D1483
- Henry Tudor HENRY VII B1457 D1509

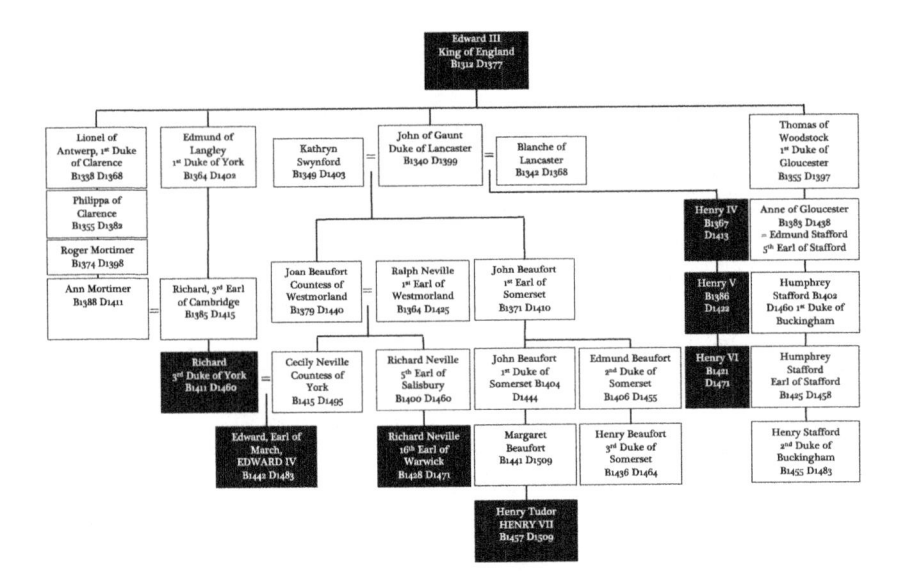

Richard Neville grew up as a family member of this extensive, prestigious and powerful elite who ruled and governed England. He was no parvenu. Yet it was his direct Neville family that had the earliest influence on the young Richard Neville.

The Neville family traced their lineage back to the Normans and were significant Barons in the North. They served their King and country well in holding the north against the plundering Scots.

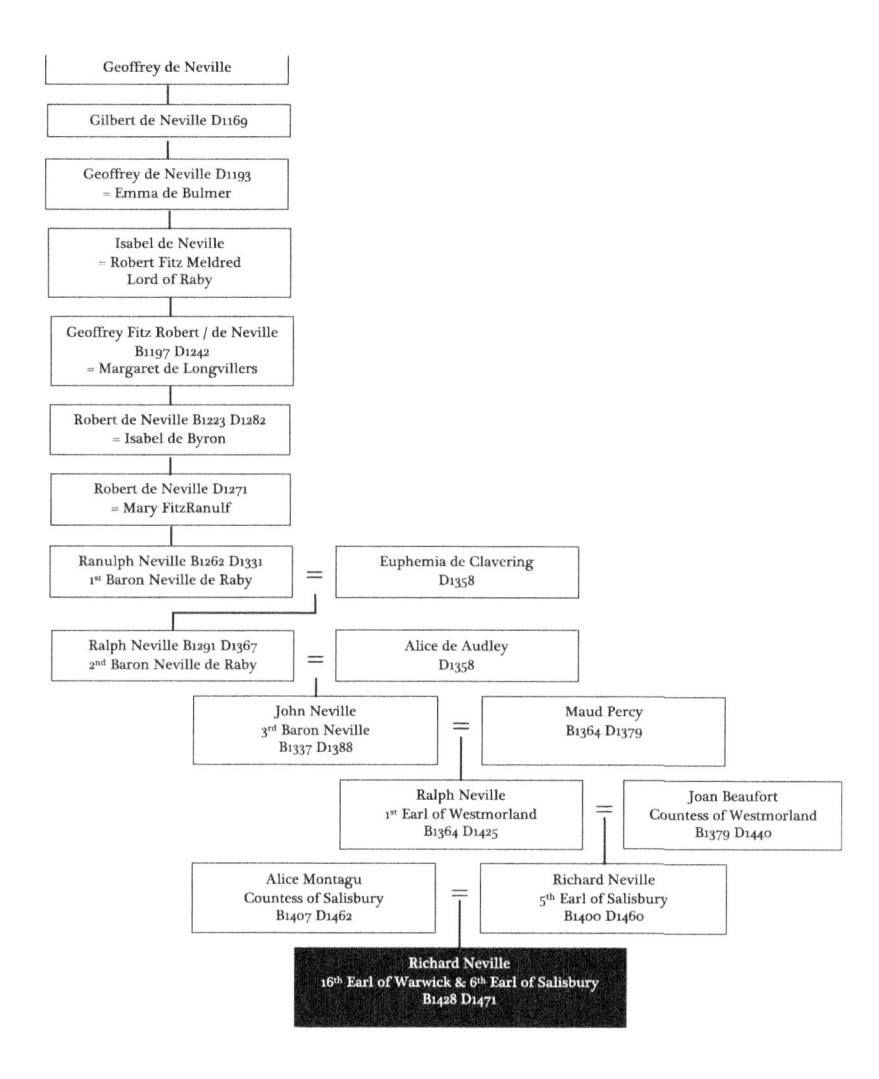

```
Geoffrey de Neville
        |
Gilbert de Neville D1169
        |
Geoffrey de Neville D1193
   = Emma de Bulmer
        |
Isabel de Neville
 = Robert Fitz Meldred
     Lord of Raby
        |
Geoffrey Fitz Robert / de Neville
        B1197 D1242
  = Margaret de Longvillers
        |
Robert de Neville B1223 D1282
     = Isabel de Byron
        |
Robert de Neville D1271
   = Mary FitzRanulf
        |
Ranulph Neville B1262 D1331   =   Euphemia de Clavering
1st Baron Neville de Raby              D1358
        |
Ralph Neville B1291 D1367     =   Alice de Audley
2nd Baron Neville de Raby              D1358
        |
   John Neville           =   Maud Percy
   3rd Baron Neville           B1364 D1379
   B1337 D1388
        |
   Ralph Neville          =   Joan Beaufort
   1st Earl of Westmorland    Countess of Westmorland
   B1364 D1425                B1379 D1440
        |
Alice Montagu              =   Richard Neville
Countess of Salisbury          5th Earl of Salisbury
B1407 D1462                    B1400 D1460
        |
   Richard Neville
16th Earl of Warwick & 6th Earl of Salisbury
        B1428 D1471
```

Robert de Neville lived in the mid thirteenth century. He was the eldest son of Geoffrey fitz Robert, who later took his mother's name and called himself Geoffrey de Neville, and the grandson of Robert fitz Meldred, Lord of Raby. Robert was Sheriff of Northumberland and Yorkshire and was entrusted with the defence of all England north of the river Trent. He held much of the north for Henry III

Page 30

through the difficult times of the Second Baron's War and went on to serve Edward I for ten years before his death in 1282.

Robert's heir, Robert the younger, pre-deceased his father in 1271. Robert was thus succeeded by his grandson **Ranulph** who became the first Baron Neville of Raby by writ of Parliament in 1295.

Ranulph's eldest son Robert the "Peacock of the North" died in 1319 fighting with the Scots. **Ralph Neville** became 2nd Baron Neville of Raby on Ranulph's death in 1331. Ralph led the English to victory against King David II of Scotland at the Battle of Neville's Cross in 1346.

Ralph's son **John Neville**, 3rd Baron Neville, was a Captain at Neville Cross but made his name in France and was knighted near Paris in 1360 fighting for Edward III. John Neville served as Admiral of the North, Warden of the North and Lieutenant of Gascony. He died in 1388.

Ralph Neville was grandfather to Richard Neville although he died three years before his grandson's birth. Ralph served in Brittany and was created Earl of Westmorland in 1397 by Richard II as reward for his support for the King against Thomas Woodstock and the Lords Appellant.

Ralph's first wife Margaret Stafford died in 1396. Ralph at the age of thirty-three married the eighteen years old widow Joan Beaufort becoming son-in-law to John of Gaunt, Duke of Lancaster, son of Edward III.

Ralph chose to change his allegiance and support his brother-in-law, Henry Bolingbroke, against Richard II who had taken over the Lancastrian inheritance upon the death of Gaunt in early 1399. Ralph's interests and those of his young Beaufort wife were more clearly aligned with the future Henry IV. *Warwick was not the first in his family who had to choose between Kings.*

Ralph carried the sceptre at the coronation of Henry IV in 1399 and helped the new King put down the rebellions by Henry Percy, Earl of Northumberland in 1403 and 1405. He looked after the North for Henry V and was appointed a member of the Council of Regency for the child King Henry VI.

Ralph Neville had two sons and six daughters by his first wife, Margaret Stafford.

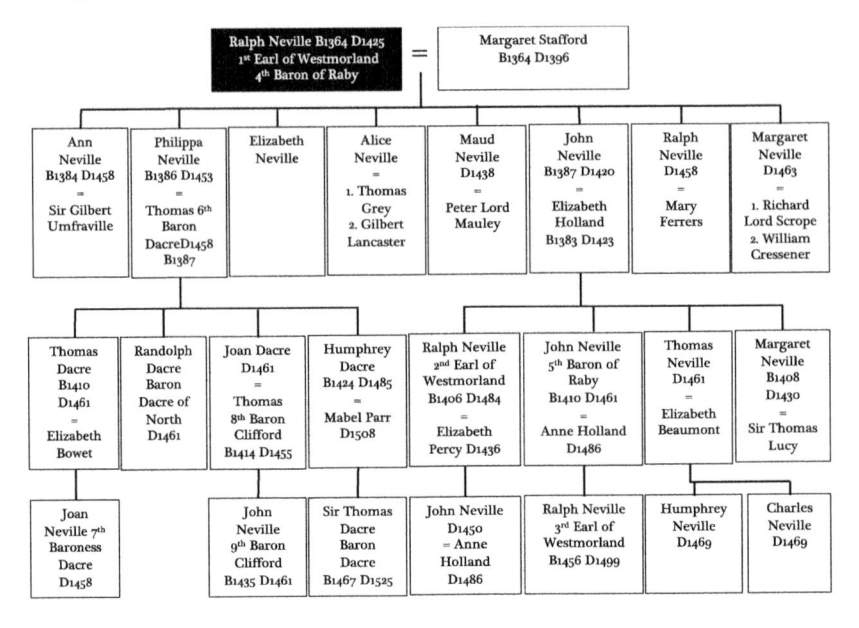

```
                    Ralph Neville B1364 D1425        Margaret Stafford
                    1st Earl of Westmorland    =     B1364 D1396
                    4th Baron of Raby
```

| Ann Neville B1384 D1458 = Sir Gilbert Umfraville | Philippa Neville B1386 D1453 = Thomas 6th Baron Dacre D1458 B1387 | Elizabeth Neville | Alice Neville = 1. Thomas Grey 2. Gilbert Lancaster | Maud Neville D1438 = Peter Lord Mauley | John Neville B1387 D1420 = Elizabeth Holland B1383 D1423 | Ralph Neville D1458 = Mary Ferrers | Margaret Neville D1463 = 1. Richard Lord Scrope 2. William Cressener |

| Thomas Dacre B1410 D1461 = Elizabeth Bowet | Randolph Dacre Baron Dacre of North D1461 | Joan Dacre D1461 = Thomas 8th Baron Clifford B1414 D1455 | Humphrey Dacre B1424 D1485 = Mabel Parr D1508 | Ralph Neville 2nd Earl of Westmorland B1406 D1484 = Elizabeth Percy D1436 | John Neville 5th Baron of Raby B1410 D1461 = Anne Holland D1486 | Thomas Neville D1461 = Elizabeth Beaumont | Margaret Neville B1408 D1430 = Sir Thomas Lucy |

| Joan Neville 7th Baroness Dacre D1458 | | John Neville 9th Baron Clifford B1435 D1461 | Sir Thomas Dacre Baron Dacre B1467 D1525 | John Neville D1450 = Anne Holland D1486 | Ralph Neville 3rd Earl of Westmorland B1456 D1499 | Humphrey Neville D1469 | Charles Neville D1469 |

Page 33

Ralph surpassed this by having nine sons and five daughters by his second wife, Joan Beaufort, albeit four sons died in childbirth or as infants.

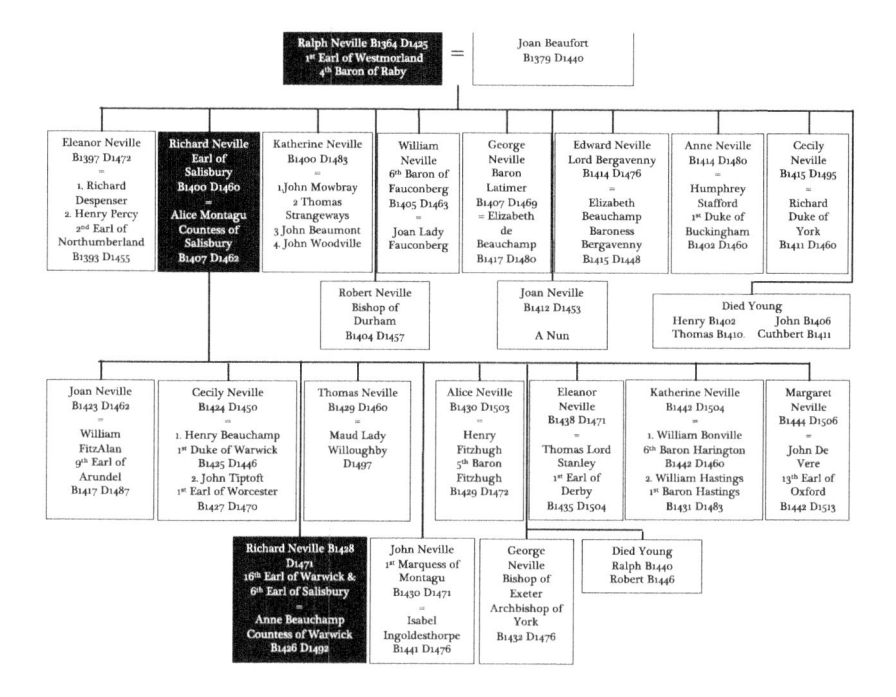

```
                    Ralph Neville B1364 D1425
                    1st Earl of Westmorland      =    Joan Beaufort
                    4th Baron of Raby                 B1379 D1440
```

| Eleanor Neville B1397 D1472 = 1. Richard Despenser 2. Henry Percy 2nd Earl of Northumberland B1393 D1455 | **Richard Neville Earl of Salisbury B1400 D1460 = Alice Montagu Countess of Salisbury B1407 D1462** | Katherine Neville B1400 D1483 = 1.John Mowbray 2 Thomas Strangeways 3.John Beaumont 4. John Woodville | William Neville 6th Baron of Fauconberg B1405 D1463 = Joan Lady Fauconberg | George Neville Baron Latimer B1407 D1469 = Elizabeth de Beauchamp B1417 D1480 | Edward Neville Lord Bergavenny B1414 D1476 = Elizabeth Beauchamp Baroness Bergavenny B1415 D1448 | Anne Neville B1414 D1480 = Humphrey Stafford 1st Duke of Buckingham B1402 D1460 | Cecily Neville B1415 D1495 = Richard Duke of York B1411 D1460 |

| | Robert Neville Bishop of Durham B1404 D1457 | Joan Neville B1412 D1453 A Nun | Died Young Henry B1402 John B1406 Thomas B1410 Cuthbert B1411 |

| Joan Neville B1423 D1462 = William FitzAlan 9th Earl of Arundel B1417 D1487 | Cecily Neville B1424 D1450 = 1. Henry Beauchamp 1st Duke of Warwick B1425 D1446 2. John Tiptoft 1st Earl of Worcester B1427 D1470 | Thomas Neville B1429 D1460 = Maud Lady Willoughby D1497 | Alice Neville B1430 D1503 = Henry Fitzhugh 5th Baron Fitzhugh B1429 D1472 | Eleanor Neville B1438 D1471 = Thomas Lord Stanley 1st Earl of Derby B1435 D1504 | Katherine Neville B1442 D1504 = 1. William Bonville 6th Baron Harington B1442 D1460 2. William Hastings 1st Baron Hastings B1431 D1483 | Margaret Neville B1444 D1506 = John De Vere 13th Earl of Oxford B1442 D1513 |

| **Richard Neville B1428 D1471 16th Earl of Warwick & 6th Earl of Salisbury = Anne Beauchamp Countess of Warwick B1426 D1492** | John Neville 1st Marquess of Montagu B1430 D1471 = Isabel Ingoldesthorpe B1441 D1476 | George Neville Bishop of Exeter Archbishop of York B1432 D1476 | Died Young Ralph B1440 Robert B1446 |

Ralph through service, and marriage to Joan Beaufort, had risen to be one of the most senior nobles around the Lancastrian Kings. Letters patent for Henry IV describe Earl Ralph as "the King's brother".[51] Royal Genealogies of the time treat them, and their offspring, as members of the royal family.[52] Ralph was therefore able to secure the very best marriages and careers for his children.

Eleanor married Richard Lord Dispenser and upon his early death, Henry Percy, Earl of Northumberland. Salisbury married the heiress Alice Montagu, Katherine married the Duke of Norfolk, William

---

[51] *Calendar of the Patent Rolls CPR 1401-1405*. Page 227.
[52] *Warwick the Kingmaker* by Michael Hicks. Blackwell Publishers 1998. Page 15. *Handbook to the Maude Roll*. Edited by A. Wall. Auckland 1919.

married the Fauconberg heiress, George married the daughter of Richard Beauchamp, Earl of Warwick, Edward married the Beauchamp of Bergavenny heiress. The best marriages were to Dukes of royal blood. Anne married the Duke of Buckingham and Cecily married Richard, Duke of York.

Robert was appointed Bishop of Salisbury and then Bishop of Durham in 1437. George became Baron Latimer. Joan became a nun. Ralph would not live to see it, but five sons and their four brothers-in-law would sit in the House of Lords. Salisbury, Fauconberg, Northumberland, Buckingham and York would all receive the order of the Garter. When Joan Beaufort died in 1440, she was the mother to an Earl, three Barons, a Countess, three Duchesses, a Bishop and a Nun.

It was to this second successful and influential family by Joan Beaufort that Ralph directed his lands and estates, and they were named as the major beneficiaries in his will. Ralph's eldest son John Neville died in 1420. It was left to John's son Ralph Neville, who inherited the title of 2nd Earl of Westmorland, to contest the settlement upon the elder Ralph's death five years later in 1425. Joan Beaufort and her eldest son, Salisbury, led from their side.

The *Neville-Neville* dispute was vicious and sometimes violent. At York on 18th August 1430, Countess Joan and the Westmorland were ordered to maintain the peace. They were not to trespass on each other's lands nor cause "hurt or harm". They were bound by a bond of £2,000. The bond was increased to £4,000 and renewed on 16th May 1431 and 6th November 1434. [53] Further trouble ensued around the finding of a will in support of young Ralph's claims. Beaufort family pressure ensured the will did not see the light of day.

A truce was agreed in the presence of the King on 28th February 1436. Salisbury and his brother William would fight in France. Earl Ralph promised not to distress the countess and her lands whilst they were away. This only worked to a limited extent. Westmorland

---

[53] *Calendar of Close Rolls CCR 1429-1435*. Page 67.

had married Margaret Cobham and his new brother-in-law, Humphrey of Gloucester, perhaps encouraged him due to his feud with Cardinal Henry Beaufort. Joan Beaufort and Westmorland were summoned before the young King Henry VI on 28th December 1438 to explain themselves. Once more they were bound over to keep the peace. [54]

The dispute was not settled until after Joan's death in 1440. The younger Ralph secured the Lordship and Castle of Raby, and Brancepeth. Salisbury kept the rest of his inheritance including Middleham, Sheriff Hutton and Penrith. Joan's brother, Cardinal Beaufort, was an influential royal counsellor. Salisbury was the King's cousin and more useful in France and on the Scottish borders. Richard Neville was heir to Salisbury.

We know little about Richard Neville's childhood. No documentary evidence remains. It can only be surmised from our understanding of how noble children were brought up in medieval times. The first seven years will have been spent in the care of his mother, Alice Montagu and nurses. It was most likely to have been at Middleham, a traditional Neville household renovated by Ralph and Joan, and leased to Salisbury.

At the age of seven, Richard would then have begun his education and training in military affairs in a more male dominated environment. This would involve learning how to ride and use arms, law and administration, and chivalry and faith. Richard would be taught about his ancestry and ancestors.

Grandfather Ralph who died shortly before he was born must have been a hero who shone brightly. Richard would have been told of his exploits, not least by his grandmother Joan. The switch of allegiance from Richard II to Henry IV perhaps stood out along with the territorial disputes with the Percy family and the *other* Neville family.

---

[54] *The House of Beaufort* by Nathan Amin. Amberley Publishing 2017. Pages 181-182.

Fortune lends a hand…

> *…his life was transformed by his unexpected succession to the earldom of Warwick in the summer of 1449, when he had not yet reached his twenty-first birthday…* [55]

Richard Neville was already well placed and positioned, due to the efforts of his grandfather Ralph, his grandmother Joan and his father Salisbury. At the tender age of seven years, Richard married the nine-year-old Anne Beauchamp, daughter of Richard Beauchamp. The wheel of fortune was already turning.

Salisbury, following in the footsteps of his father, set out to arrange advantageous marriages for his children. It was to be a marriage that would in due course transform Richard Neville's life and fortune although no-one knew or expected it at the time.

Richard Beauchamp, 13th Earl of Warwick, was a figure of great renown. Beauchamp led the English forces against the Owain Glyndwr rebellion in Wales, made a pilgrimage to the Holy Land but he made his name fighting in France. Henry V asked him to look after the education of his son, Henry VI.

Beauchamp came to an arrangement with Salisbury whereby his two children by his second wife, Isobel Dispenser, would marry Cecily and Richard Neville. The agreed marriage payment for Salisbury was large at £3,233. This showed how attractive to Salisbury were the matches. Warwick's annual income in 1436 of £3,116 was well above that for Salisbury at £1,238 and Joan at £667 according to tax records. Warwick presumably needed the money as he was still owed much for his service to the crown in France and he had debts. Salisbury's down payment was met by Parliament as part of the agreement in December 1435 whereby he would serve in France with Warwick. [56]

---

[55] *Warwick the Kingmaker* by Michael Hicks. Blackwell Publishers 1998. Premier Earl 1428-55. Page 16.
[56] *Warwick the Kingmaker* by Michael Hicks. Blackwell Publishers 1998. Premier Earl 1428-55. Pages 27-32.

Cecily who was ten years old married the eleven-year-old Beauchamp heir, Henry. Richard aged seven married ten-year-old Anne. The wedding took place around 4th May 1436 at Abergavenny in the castle chapel or the church of the Benedictine priory. [57] Richard probably joined Beauchamp's household. Betrothed children were usually looked after by the girl's parents. It was schooling fit for a King. Henry VI had been educated and trained there.

Richard would have grown up alongside his brother-in-law, Henry de Beauchamp. Both went on to serve the young King as part of his personal entourage. Richard was knighted by Henry VI, possibly at the coronation of Queen Margaret of Anjou in May 1445. In the same year, Salisbury was reappointed Lord of Pontefract and Master Forester of Blackburn and Bowland, jointly with Richard and his brother, Thomas. [58] It was probably at this time that the seventeen-year-old Richard gained valuable fighting experience with his father Salisbury in the marches near Scotland.

It was no real surprise that Earl Richard de Beauchamp died in 1439, aged fifty-seven years old. Countess Isobel who was eighteen years younger died soon after, albeit she was not in good health. Henry de Beauchamp succeeded his father. Henry was a close friend of the King and would be created Duke of Warwick by him in 1445. Anne de Beauchamp was born to Henry and Cecily on 14th February 1444. All was looking well when Henry suddenly and unexpectedly died on 11th June 1446.

Two-year-old Anne became Countess of Warwick. William de la Pole was granted her wardship and marriage rights by Henry VI. Suffolk saw her as the ideal spouse for his heir. Anne died three years later on 3rd June 1449 at Ewelme in Oxfordshire. Richard Neville's wife Anne moved from being the youngest Beauchamp

---

[57] *Warwick the Kingmaker* by Michael Hicks. Blackwell Publishers 1998. Premier Earl 1428-55. Pages 26-29.
[58] *Warwick the Kingmaker* by Michael Hicks. Blackwell Publishers 1998. Premier Earl 1428-55. Page 29.

daughter to being the *sole sister of the whole blood, the whole sister* of the late Duke Henry. She was Henry's heir under English law.

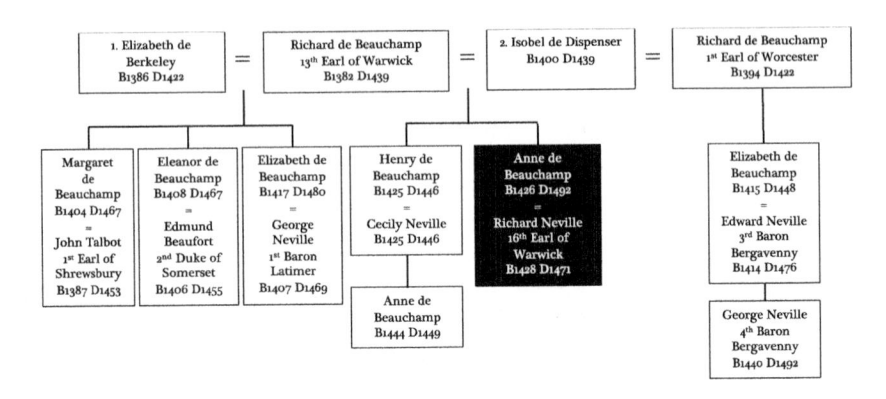

| 1. Elizabeth de Berkeley B1386 D1422 | = | Richard de Beauchamp 13th Earl of Warwick B1382 D1439 | = | 2. Isobel de Dispenser B1400 D1439 | = | Richard de Beauchamp 1st Earl of Worcester B1394 D1422 |

| Margaret de Beauchamp B1404 D1467 = John Talbot 1st Earl of Shrewsbury B1387 D1453 | Eleanor de Beauchamp B1408 D1467 = Edmund Beaufort 2nd Duke of Somerset B1406 D1455 | Elizabeth de Beauchamp B1417 D1480 = George Neville 1st Baron Latimer B1407 D1469 | Henry de Beauchamp B1425 D1446 = Cecily Neville B1425 D1446 | **Anne de Beauchamp B1426 D1492 = Richard Neville 16th Earl of Warwick B1428 D1471** | Elizabeth de Beauchamp B1415 D1448 = Edward Neville 3rd Baron Bergavenny B1414 D1476 |

Anne de Beauchamp B1444 D1449

George Neville 4th Baron Bergavenny B1440 D1492

Anne's three half-sisters Margaret, Eleanor and Elizabeth from their father's first marriage were not happy. Shrewsbury and Somerset, husbands to the eldest two Beauchamp daughters, were overseas in France, and could not help them. War had broken out once more. Parliament was recalled on 16th June. Richard Neville attended as Earl of Warwick. The letter of patent recognizing his title is dated 23rd July 1449. The letter refers to his kinship, his "intimate service" to the King, and his service in fighting the Scots at his own cost. [59]

Richard Neville became Warwick. Anne inherited the Beauchamp estates and the Lordship of Abergavenny from her brother, and the Dispenser estates jointly with her mother. The inheritance was Anne's by right, by English law. It did not stop her half-sisters and their husbands from contesting her rights. They continued to press for a quarter share each. Shrewsbury, the husband of the eldest daughter Margaret, in his will recorded his hope that he might "attain to the name and Lordship of Warwick." [60] Warwick had to expend considerable energy in subsequent years. Henry VI was a

---

[59] *Calendar of the Patent Rolls CPR 1446-1452*. Pages 235-236.
[60] *The Beauchamp Earls of Warwick in the Later Middle Ages* by A.F.J. Sinclair. London University PHD Thesis 1987. Page 387.

weak King with "little inclination or capacity to rule". [61] The ebbs and flows of influence at court were critical. It was not the end of the matter.

Richard would have been expecting not to inherit any title or lands until the death of his father, Salisbury. Now he was the Earl of Warwick and one of the wealthiest nobles in England. Richard's estates stretched across England and Wales but were concentrated around Worcestershire and Warwickshire and included the Lordship in the marches of South Wales and Gloucestershire. Richard Neville was far wealthier than his father and his grandfather, Ralph. It was some 21st birthday present.

Warwick, as he was now known, had gained so much, so quickly. Now he had so much to lose. The stakes were as high as they could be, for a non-royal noble. Warwick had arrived on the national political scene but continuing arguments over the inheritance would see the Neville family question their traditional Lancastrian loyalties.

---

[61] *Warwick the Kingmaker Politics, Power and Fame* by A.J. Pollard. Continuum Books 2007. Premier Earl. Page 22.

Troubled Times

> ...*Warwick was in retreat, striving to maintain his hold on those parts of his wife's inheritances to which he no longer had the right, playing for time and ignoring successive royal mandates. Fortunately, more pressing matters preoccupied his opponents until the early summer of 1453...* [62]

Warwick's coming of age and arrival at Westminster coincided with military defeat in France and a deepening political crisis. All was not well.

Humphrey of Gloucester, the King's uncle, was disgraced and dead. Cardinal Beaufort had died soon afterwards. Richard, Duke of York, the King's assumed heir, was exiled in Ireland. Edmund Beaufort had surrendered first Rouen and then Caen to the French King Charles VII. The French had retaken Normandy.

Suffolk was in power as the King's first and favoured counsellor. The cessation of Maine and Anjou had tarnished his reputation. The loss of Normandy resulted in his fall. Parliament was convened in November 1449. The commons sought blood.

Suffolk was accused of treason and was indicted in February 1450. The Commons declared that he "falsely and traitorously, hath imagined, compassed, purposed, forethought, done and committed diverse high, great, heinous and horrible treasons." [63] Warwick was present on 17th March when Henry VI exiled Suffolk from England for five years.

Suffolk's life had been saved by the King but not for long. His boat was intercepted near Dover by the *Nicholas of the Tower* and on 3rd May 1450 he was killed... "there was an axe, and a stock, and one of the lewdest of the Ship bade him lay down his head... and smote off his head within half a dozen strokes... and laid his body on the

---

[62] *Warwick the Kingmaker* by Michael Hicks. Blackwell Publishers 1998. Earl of Warwick. Page 76.
[63] *Parliamentary Rolls Henry VI* November 1449.

sands of Dover." [64] The *Brut Chronicler* wrote that the terrible act "began sorrow upon sorrow, and death for death." [65]

On 2nd March 1450 Warwick's title was confirmed anew. [66] Warwick was created the *Premier Earl*, and it was not without responsibility. It wasn't long before he was called upon to serve his King.

Warwick attended the Leicester Parliament on 5th May with "400 and more" men. [67] The Commons forced through an act of resumption. Resources were needed for the war in France and would be paid for by taking back grants made by the King previously to those in favour. Parliament was then adjourned on 6th June. There was a rebellion in Kent, led by a Jack Cade.

Local grievances in Kent against royal officials escalated. There was a rising which spread to neighbouring counties. A manifesto denounced those in power around the King who "hath had false counsel, for his lands and goods are lost, his commons destroyed, the sea is lost, France is lost, he himself is so poor that he may not pay for his meat and drink; he owes more than ever did any King of England, and daily his traitors that have been around him, waiting to ask of him anything that comes his way by law." [68] The rebels bolstered by bitter soldiers returning from Normandy marched on London. The King sought help from his nobles.

Warwick wrote to William Lord Ferrers of Chartley that the King "hath desired and charged me to be with him at St Albans next Saturday coming accompanied with such a fellowship as that I may and be content in case the commons of Kent well be rebel and be

---

[64] *Selections From the Paston Letters* transcribed by Sir John Fenn. Edited by Alice Greenwood. London 1920. Forgotten Books. Pages 61-62. Letter, from William Lomner to John Paston.
[65] *The Brut or the Chronicles of England* edited by F.W.D. Brie London 1906. Page 516.
[66] *Warwick the Kingmaker* by Michael Hicks. Blackwell Publishers 1998. Earl of Warwick. Page 44.
[67] *Selections From the Paston Letters* transcribed by Sir John Fenn. Edited by Alice Greenwood. London 1920. Forgotten Books. Page 63. Letter, from John Crane, Cousin, to John Paston.
[68] *Jack Cade's Rebellion* by I.M.W. Harvey. Oxford 1991. Page 189.

not to obey the laws, that then I with fellowship to be assisting band advancing upon his person that by the grace of our good lord ewe shall be of the power to withstand their malice and evil will, wherefore I pray you with all my heart with such persons as you now array and secure you will send to me at Warwick, to be on Wednesday next coming in semblable wise." The request was for armed men to be sent to him by 10th June. [69]

Lord Ferrers died the next day so was not able to comply with the request. Warwick accompanied the King to Blackheath. The rebels were successful in a skirmish near Tonbridge on 18th June. Warwick's retainer Stafford was killed. The King decided to withdraw to the safety of the Midlands and Kenilworth castle as the uprising widened. Warwick returned with him. Public order in the South deteriorated. On 29th June, the King's confessor, William Ayscough, Bishop of Salisbury was murdered in Wiltshire purportedly because he had married Henry to Margaret of Anjou.

Cade and his army arrived in Southwark on 2nd July. They sought to replace Henry's evil counsellors with Lords of royal blood such as the Dukes of York, Exeter, Buckingham and Norfolk. The rebels crossed London Bridge and caused mayhem. Baron Saye and Sele, the Lord Treasurer, was beheaded. Initial enthusiasm for the rebellion turned sour. Rioting and looting followed. London gathered itself together and forced the rebels out. Cade and his men dispersed. Cade was caught, executed and his head placed on a spike at London Bridge for all to see.

Warwick meanwhile remained in the Midlands tending to his new extensive estates and journeyed to South Wales in August. Valuable time was spent on consolidating his new interests and ensuring they were well looked after by people he could trust.

Henry appointed Cardinal Kemp Lord Chancellor, and Lord Beauchamp, Treasurer to replace Suffolk and Baron Saye and Sele. Cherbourg surrendered on 12th August. Charles VII of France was now free to focus on recovering Gascony. Somerset returned from

---

[69] *A Letter from a Kingmaker* by J.H. Bloom. 1919. Notes & Queries. Page 120.

France. Henry appointed him Constable on 11th September. All eyes though soon turned to York.

Richard Duke of York was in a strong position. The premier Duke in terms of royal blood and wealth, many saw him as the obvious person to head up the Government. He was not tarnished with the recent military defeats and political crises. York was isolated in Ireland. A letter to Salisbury confirms his fear of insurrection in Ireland, and the lack of money and men made available to him. It was time to return from Ireland, to come home, to take charge.

Not everyone saw it that way. Henry VI and those around him were suspicious of his motives. York's return was obstructed by royal officials. York left Dublin on 28th August but made slow progress. He arrived in London on 27th September at the head of a large armed retinue. York wanted to make peace with the King on his terms. The Brut chronicler wrote that he wanted "reformation of certain injuries and wrongs." [70] York offered and sought control. Henry reassured his "our true and faithful subject and as our well-beloved cousin" but would not oblige. York would be one member of a new "substantial council" but nothing more. Government would be undertaken through collective advice.

Parliament opened on 6th November 1450. It was the first one to which the new Earl of Warwick had been summoned. He rode "through the city with a mighty people arrayed for war". [71] These were troubled times. London was uneasy. Bale's Chronicle suggests that, around this time, there was fear of unrest in London "because of disputes between the lords." Chains had been put up across streets to keep order. Cade's revolt was still too fresh in the minds of those who had suffered hurt or losses. [72] The Commons were highly critical of foreign and domestic policy. Gregory's Chronicle speaks of "many strange and wonderful bills" put up in several

---

[70] *The Brut or the Chronicles of England* edited by F.W.D. Brie London 1906. Page 520.
[71] *Bale's Chronicle, Six Town Chronicles of England* edited by R. Flenley. Oxford 1911.
[72] *Bale's Chronicle, Six Town Chronicles of England* edited by R. Flenley. Oxford 1911.

locations, including the door of the King's own chamber at Westminster as well as St Paul's. [73] Henry VI was troubled. John Gresham advised John Paston by letter in October that the King has written to "all his men, to await on him at Parliament in their best array." [74]

Sir William Oldhall was elected speaker. A veteran of the wars in France, Oldhall had served as York's chamberlain. York did not arrive in London until 23rd November. All of the Lords had come to Parliament with large companies according to the chronicler Benet. [75] York was no different. The next day he was joined by Norfolk. The annals attributed to William Worcester comment "the Duke of Norfolk came to the parliament with a great company and favoured the Duke of York against the duke of Somerset." [76]

The Commons voiced concerns about law and order, the King's finances and the remaining English lands under threat in Gascony. They demanded resumption, reform and revenge in the form of the removal of those "misbehaving about your Royal person... by whose means your possessions have been greatly abused, your laws not executed, and the peace of your Realm not observed nor kept, to your great hurt, and trouble of the liege people of this, your Realm." [77] First amongst those named was Edmund Beaufort, Duke of Somerset.

Henry shrugged off the complaints saying that he was "not sufficiently learned of any cause why they should be removed" from his side. [78] This enraged those pressing for change. Benet's chronicle says that on 1st December some soldiers decided to take the law into their own hands. They attempted to seize Somerset who was lodging at the Blackfriars priory in Ludgate. Somerset escaped with Devon

---

[73] *William Gregory's Chronicle in the historical Collections of a Citizen of London in the Fifteenth Century* edited by J. Gairdner. London 1876.
[74] *The Paston Letters 1422-1509* edited by J. Gairdner. London 1872.
[75] *John Benet's Chronicle for the Years 1400-1462* edited by G.L. & M.A. Harriss. Camden 1972.
[76] *The Itineraries of William Worcester* edited by J.H. Harvey. Oxford 1969.
[77] *Parliamentary Rolls Henry VI* November 1450.
[78] *Parliamentary Rolls Henry VI* November 1450.

to the safety of the Tower of London. Further attacks were made on the houses of Thomas, Lord Hoo, and Sir Thomas Tuddingham.

Order was restored on 3rd December. The King rode through the city accompanied by his Lords. Warwick, Salisbury and York all were in attendance. Somerset was soon back out from the Tower. Benet informs us that he spent Christmas at Blackfriars Lodge. York left for his estates.

Warwick returned to the Midlands as a loyal supporter of Henry VI. On 6th December 1450 he was made Chamberlain of the Exchequer by the grateful King. Warwick had no reason at this time to change his allegiance, quite the contrary. He was not part of the inner circle of advisors but
Henry thought highly of him and had rewarded him accordingly.

Parliament reconvened on 20th January 1451. Not much was accomplished during this session. The King left for Kent on 28th January to oversee a commission of *oyer et terminer* in Kent. He was accompanied by Somerset and many other Lords. Warwick along with others sat in attendance to hear and determine offences committed against the crown. Thomas Hoo, late Treasurer of Normandy was tried but acquitted. [79]

Parliament though ended abruptly according to Benet, "quasi subito finitum est." [80] Thomas Young, a legal counsellor for York pushed for it to be made clear who was the King's heir for the security of the realm. Henry had no issue. Young was placed under arrest in the Tower. Henry did not want to answer the question. York's position as presumed heir was weakened. It did not help the already strained relationship between the royal cousins. The Commons achieved one aim by close. An Act of Resumption was passed.

Somerset improved his position and further increased his influence through 1451. On 11th September he was made Captain of Calais. Somerset was thanked by the King for having "rendered much

---

[79] *Calendar of Patent Rolls 1446-1456*. Pages 437-439.
[80] *John Benet's Chronicle for the Years 1400-1462* edited by G.L. & M.A. Harriss. Camden 1972.

fruitful service, especially in the rescue of the town of Calais against attack" and praised "for his merits and nearness of blood" and for his "exertions in war and wise counsel". [81] Soon thereafter, in December, he was made Lieutenant of the Marches of Picardy, Flanders and Artois. [82]

1451 was not such a good year for Warwick. Somerset, after all his problems in France, was keen to bolster his finances. The Warwick inheritance was a potential means of doing so. Somerset's wife was Eleanor Beauchamp. Somerset was buoyed in this endeavour by the return onto the political scene of John Talbot, Earl of Shrewsbury, returned from a pilgrimage to Rome following being held ransom in France. Shrewsbury was brother-in-law to Somerset. Margaret Beauchamp, the eldest sister, was his wife. His eyes were not just on a quarter share of the inheritance but on the title of the Earl of Warwick itself.

Lord Bergavenny challenged his Dispenser interests. Lord Cromwell took the opportunity to object to Warwick's new role alongside him as joint Chamberlain of the Exchequer as the position was declared the inheritance of all four Beauchamp sisters. Warwick would not forget.

Two grants made by Henry VI to Warwick's late brother-in-law Henry Beauchamp were annulled. Warwick lost the Channel Isles and the reversionary interest he held in Feckenham Forest gained by way of his wife's inheritance. Most importantly he lost custody of George Neville's half share of the Dispenser inheritance. Salisbury suffered too. He lost grants in Richmondshire and the West March. The act was not malicious. It was clearly not aimed at the Neville family alone. Henry VI had only conceded this Act with great reluctance. York's support for the Act and the damaging impact to their financial and business interests would not have endeared him to Warwick and Salisbury.

Warwick learned very quickly, if he did not know already, that he had a fight on his hands to retain his newly earned estates, income

---

[81] *Calendar of Close Rolls* Pages 292-294.
[82] *Proceedings and Ordinances of the Privy Council* Volume 6 xxxvii.

and titles. Everything and everybody seemed to be working against him. Parliament's 1451 Act of Resumption impacted him and his father, who had benefited from the King's patronage over the years. It was *backs to the wall*, Warwick and his father versus everyone else.

Warwick was cheered at least by a much happier event later in the year. A baby daughter Isabel was born at Warwick on 5th September 1451 to the Earl and Countess Anne. Warwick was twenty-two-years-old. Anne was three years older at twenty-five. It was not a son, but he now had an heiress.

Warwick experienced a number of setbacks through this period, but he hung on grimly to his holdings, where he could. He would not accept any local legal judgements. Possession, in this respect, was nine-tenths of the law. Warwick was young and without other responsibilities. He could focus on his retaining his estates and play the long game. At risk was three quarters of the inheritance.

Somerset was more intent on sustaining his improved influence with the King and his impact on national policy. Shrewsbury was appointed Keeper of the Seas in March 1451 and in September 1452 was sent back to France to rescue Aquitaine. Shrewsbury was more concerned in his personal affairs by his private feud or war with Lord Berkeley. The King had also asked him to intervene in the unrest in the West Country caused by way of the Courtenay and Bonville dispute. A quarter share of the Beauchamp inheritance was a much lower priority for Somerset and Shrewsbury.

Somerset soon was distracted by a renewed attack on his hold on power by York. It was inevitable but Somerset himself re-lit the fuse. Somerset arrested York's ally, Sir William Oldhall in January 1452 on grounds of treason. London was outraged that Oldhall was seized despite being in sanctuary in St Martin-le-Grand. Oldhall was released.

York was implicated in the charges made against Oldhall and felt himself the subject of a vicious whispering campaign against him. The Croyland chronicler explains… "In these recent times sprang up between our Lord, King Henry the Sixth and Richard, the most illustrious Duke of York, those dissensions, never sufficiently to be regretted, and never thenceforth to be allayed: dissensions indeed, which were only to be atoned for by the deaths of nearly all the nobles of the realm. For there were certain persons enjoying the royal intimacy, who were rivals of the said Duke, and who brought serious accusations against him of treason, and *made him to stink in the King's nostrils* even unto the death; as they insisted that he was endeavouring to gain the kingdom into his own hands and was planning how to secure the sceptre of the realm for himself and his successors." [83]

York felt the need to openly declare his allegiance to his King. In January 1452, he offered to swear an oath of loyalty. Shrewsbury and the Bishop of Hereford would be his witnesses. Any accusations of disloyalty were due to "his enemies, adversaries and evil willers". On 3rd February York published a letter to the citizens of many towns. The one to Shrewsbury remains. York was the King's "true liege man" Somerset had lost Normandy. Gascony and Guinee were next. Reform had been set aside through "envy, malice, and untruth". Somerset "whoever prevailed and ruled about the King's person" needed to be removed from power. [84]

York gathered together an army and arrived on 1st March at Dartford, just outside of London. Kent failed to mobilise in his favour. Other nobles including Warwick and Salisbury remained loyal to the King. Parliamentary opposition was one thing, but York had brought an army to London. It was seen to be a direct challenge to the authority of the King. Somerset presumably saw likewise. A Royal army was raised. Tensions were heightened. Civil war beckoned.

Sense prevailed. Negotiations led to a peaceful conclusion. York stood down his men. Reform had been promised. York had assumed that Somerset would be removed from his post on the

---

[83] *Ingulph's Chronicle of the Abbey of Croyland:* with the continuations by Peter of Blois and Anonymous writers. Translated by Henry Riley. Published by Nabu Press 2014. Originally published 1854. Written 1486. Page 418.
[84] *Original Letters Illustrative of English History Volume 1* edited by H. Ellis. London 1825. Pages 11-13.

Council. The London Chronicle reported that York entered the King's tent and was surprised to find Somerset "still waiting upon the King as chief about him." York was taken back to London "like a prisoner". There were unfounded rumours reported by the chroniclers that York's ten-year-old son, Edward, was riding to his father's rescue at the head of a large army. On 10th March York was made to swear his loyalty, to be "faithful and true" to the King at St Paul's. It was a very public humiliation, but it could have been so much worse. York retired to his estates. [85]

Warwick had responded to the King's urgent summons for help. Warwick's men were dressed in his colours. Financial records confirm the purchase of eighty-one yards of red and white cloth at a cost of £6 12s. 10d. Warwick needed to borrow £9 6s. 8d for this "right great necessity." [86] Warwick and Salisbury were two of the six ambassadors that secured an agreement. They were accepted by both York and the King.

Warwick received £300 for his "faithful and diligent service" and was appointed on two royal commissions set up to establish justice and peace in the wake of continuing unrest around the country.

Henry VI, together with his favoured lords, journeyed via the South-West, the Welsh marches and the Midlands. Commissions of oyer and terminer in York's heartlands around Ludlow were intended to show who was in charge. Salisbury and Warwick did not join the royal progress in the summer months.

Warwick had remained loyal to Henry despite the downturn in his fortunes and in the royal favour pointed in his direction. "It would take an escalation of his brother's feud with the Percy family, and his own with Somerset, a crisis of government in England and the strange illness of the King to threaten that loyalty." [87]

---

[85] *The Chronicles of London* edited by C.L. Kingsford. London 1905. Page 163.
[86] *Warwick the Kingmaker* by Michael Hicks. Blackwell Publishers 1998. The Polarization of Politics 1449-54. Page 81.
[87] *The Nevills of Middleham* by K.L. Clark. The History Press 2016. Death of a Grandchild and the Making of an Earl. Page 103.

From Lancaster to York

> *...The Nevilles, as close kinsmen to the King through their Beaufort blood, would, one might have predicted, taken the side of Edmund Beaufort... The deciding issue seems, therefore, to have been Richard Neville the younger's recent conflict with Somerset and the determination of the Nevilles, both father and son, to ensure that Warwick held on to all that he had secured in the last four years...* [88]

1453 did not begin well for Warwick and his father, Salisbury. The King decided to recognize formally his two Tudor half-brothers. They were made Earls in January. Jasper became Earl of Pembroke. Edmund became Earl of Richmond and was permitted to marry the young heiress, Margaret Beaufort. Salisbury lost whatever interest he believed he had in Richmond. Warwick saw the two new Earls move ahead of himself in terms of precedence, no longer the Premier Earl.

Henry VI replaced York as Lieutenant of Ireland with Wiltshire on 5th March. Somerset was gifted all the forest south of the Trent in thanks for his good service "on both sides of the sea" in place of York.

Warwick and Salisbury were clear on their position within the royal hierarchy, if they were not before, in terms of power and influence, recompense and reward. In this respect, it is interesting to note that Warwick, and his father Salisbury, were only present at two of fifty recorded gatherings of the royal council between 1450 and 1453. By comparison Somerset attended twenty. [89] Warwick and his father had drifted apart from their cousin, the King. Henry was not pushing them away nor isolating them like with York, but his actions were slowly damaging their interests, relative to other more favoured nobles.

---

[88] *Warwick the Kingmaker Politics, Power and Fame* by A.J. Pollard. Continuum Books 2007. Premier Earl. Page 26.
[89] *The Composition of the King's Council 1437-61* by R. Virgoe. Bulletin of the Institute of Historical research 1970 xliii

Parliament opened at Reading on 6th March 1453. Warwick was named as a trier of petitions for the first time. Parliament met "in circumstances uniquely favourable to Henry" and was "the most cooperative and generous one Henry ever met".[90] Henry VI had seemingly dealt with York and other errant Lords. Order had been restored. Royal progresses had helped re-establish his visible kingship. Queen Margaret was expectant with an heir at last. Generous taxation grants were granted based on the initial success of Shrewsbury's return to France and the regaining of Gascony. Sir William Oldhall forfeited his lands. Somerset and the Tudor brothers inevitably benefited.

Good news did not last. The position in France fast deteriorated. Shrewsbury was killed at the Battle of Castillon on 17th July 1453. England's historic lands were lost. Unrest broke out across the country as various local disputes intensified.

Troubles in the Midlands, arising from land disputes near Ampthill, led to those involved being imprisoned for a short time. Lord Cromwell, Lord Grey of Ruthin and the Duke of Exeter were unwilling examples that the escalation of private feuds would not be tolerated.

There were disturbances too in Yorkshire. Thomas Percy, Lord Egremont was behind a number of breaches of the peace. Egremont chose to ignore various summons by the Council. Sir John Neville took offence and attacked Egremont's castle at Topcliffe. A commission of oyer and terminer for the North Riding was ordered.

Warwick had already been concerned by licences granted in April to Lord Bergavenny to enter his lands at Abergavenny and Mereworth. Countess Anne was unwell. A papal licence was issued to allow Countess Anne to eat meat and eggs during Lent.[91]

On 15th June, Somerset was granted the custody of George Neville's half of the Dispenser inheritance. Somerset was intent on further

---

[90] *Henry VI* by Bertram Wolffe. Yale University Press 1981. Page 263
[91] *Calendar of Papal Letters 1447-55*. Page 151.

developing his interests in South Wales where he held the Lordships of Kidwelly and Monmouth. Warwick's man in Glamorgan, William Herbert, resisted entry by Somerset's men.

The dispute was escalated to the King's Council at Sheen on 27th July. They reviewed "diverse variances and controversies" regarding "unlawful gatherings and assemblies" and "the town of Cardiff… kept with great strength as it were in land of war". Henry VI and Somerset were present. Warwick was not. Warwick was ordered to desist and give up Glamorgan to Lord Dudley pending a decision on ownership. Somerset was flexing his influential muscles.

The Council, at the same time, took the opportunity to order Salisbury and Northumberland, as the senior nobles in the North, to end the feuding between them and their Neville and Percy families. A new commission led by Sir William Lucy would consider the situation and make recommendations accordingly. It appeared to do little good. The unrest continued.

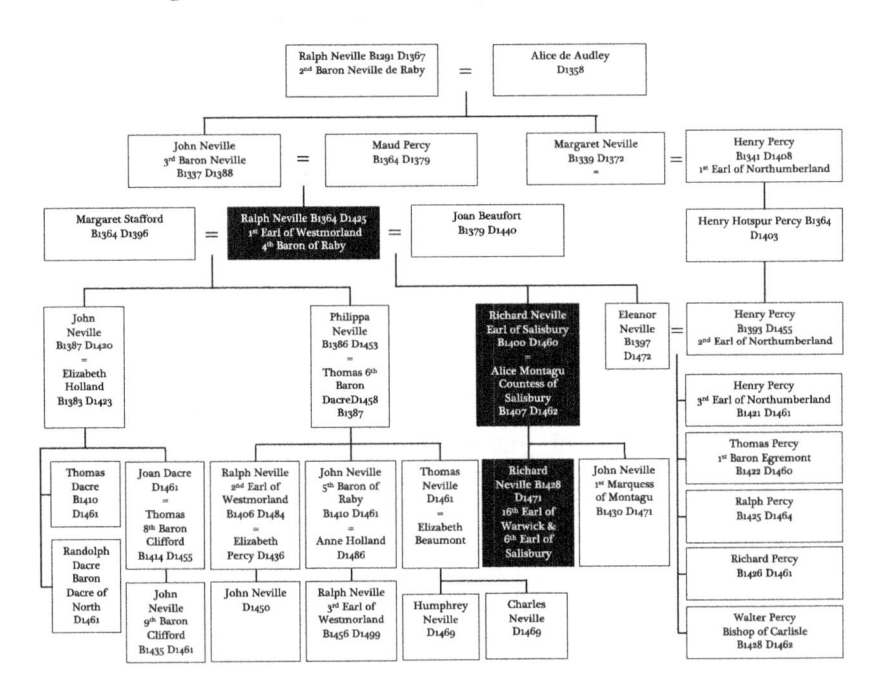

Page 53

On 24th August, Egremont attacked a Neville wedding party which included Salisbury and his sons, Thomas and John. The animosity in this specific instance was due to the bride being heiress to forfeited Percy lands now owned by Lord Cromwell.

Worcester reported the renewed outbreak of hostilities as follows… "In the month of August, Thomas Neville, the son of the Earl of Salisbury, married the niece of Lord Cromwell… and after the wedding, when returning home, there was great division between Thomas Percy, Lord Egremont, and the said Earl, near York. This was the beginning of the greatest sorrow in England." [92]

Soon there was sorrow in the land. Henry VI fell ill. Benet's chronicle says the date was 1st August 1453. Henry was at the King's Hunting Lodge at Clarendon, near Salisbury, in Wiltshire. Somerset was with him at the lodge according to Gregory's Chronicle. [93] Henry lapsed into a catatonic state and was "so incapable that he was neither able to walk upon his feet nor to lift up his head" according to Benet. [94] Others reported that he was "taken and smitten with a frenzy and his wit and reason withdrawn" and that he was "deprived of his senses and memory, unable to speak or use his limbs, incapable of even moving from the placed where he sat'. [95]

Henry's illness was kept quiet for a time, and he was moved to Windsor. Somerset sought to rule in his stead. The Queen trusted him. She granted an annuity of 100 marks to "her most dear cousin" who gave her "good counsel and worthy service" and showed her "affection and kindness". [96]

---

[92] *The Itineraries of William Worcester* edited by J.H. Harvey. Oxford 1969.
[93] *William Gregory's Chronicle in the historical Collections of a Citizen of London in the Fifteenth Century* edited by J. Gairdner. London 1876. Page 199.
[94] *John Benet's Chronicle for the Years 1400-1462* edited by G.L. & M.A. Harriss. Camden 1972.
[95] *The Nevills of Middleham* by K.L. Clark. The History Press 2016. A Crisis of Government. Page 105.
[96] *The Household of Queen Margaret of Anjou* by A.R. Myers. Bulletin of the John Rylands Library XL 1957-8. Page 418.

The King's health did not improve. Even the birth of his son and heir, Prince Edward, on 13th October 1453, did not awake him from his stupors. The situation could not last. Some form of government needed to be put in place. York was no longer the assumed heir and could be invited to attend Council.

Hostilities continued in the North. William Lucy, supported by the Council, appeared to favour with the Percy family. Warwick travelled north to help his father and brothers. On 20th October, the Neville and Percy forces met outside Topcliffe. No fighting ensued. The Archbishop of York managed to mediate, and both sides withdrew without battle. Northumberland stayed in the North.

Warwick and Salisbury made haste for London. Somerset had chosen to attack Warwick's interests in South Wales, after his initial challenges on Warwick's Beauchamp lands in the Midlands. The Somerset influenced Council had now shown bias against the Nevilles in the North. Warwick was heir to Salisbury's estates. Somerset had to be challenged. Warwick had already seen what Somerset was capable of and now he was unconstrained as the King was ill. Somerset had to be stopped.

Self-interest led them to side with York. It was not to support reform or for the common weal. It was for the good of the Nevilles. The timing was right. Somerset was the focus of their anger and opposition. They could attack him politically without being accused of treason against the King. ,

The assembly of the great Council met on 21st November 1453 supposedly to "set rest and union between the Lords of this land." York arrived in London on 12th November and used his time to mobilize fellow nobles against Somerset. York committed himself "to all that should or might be to the welfare of the King and his subjects". Somerset, Beaumont and Northumberland were notable absentees. Norfolk denounced Somerset's treasonable conduct of the war in France.

Somerset was arrested and imprisoned in the Tower on 23rd November. Devon was acquitted and released. York was appointed the King's lieutenant on 5th December. Chancellor Kemp was instructed to keep vital government business operations running. Salisbury and Warwick were appointed joint wardens of the west march for twenty years from 12th December 1453. The Lords retired to their estates for Christmas.

London was uneasy in January 1454. Parliament was due to resume. Benet wrote of unsuccessful attempts to raise the King and the growing anxiety. Exeter and Egremont had met near Doncaster to swear allegiance against the Nevilles and Cromwell. [97] Cardinal Kemp had an armed guard. Somerset had spies everywhere.

Paston's letters tell us "The Earl of Salisbury will be in London on Monday (25th January) or Tuesday next coming with seven score knights and squires besides other men. The Earls of Warwick, Richmond and Pembroke come with the Duke of York, as it is said, each of them with a goodly fellowship. And nonetheless, the Earl of Warwick will have 1,000 men awaiting on him besides the fellowship that comes with him." [98]

Queen Margaret presented a proposal that she should be "given the whole rule of this land" and made Regent for her husband and their son. It received short shrift from the Lords. This was not France. Parliament opened in February. York was pre-eminent. Not much was done. On 15th March the Lords recognized the infant Edward as Prince of Wales and Earl of Chester. Then on 22nd March Chancellor Kemp died. There was no-one to sign off with the great seal. Government could no longer function. Only the King could nominate a new Chancellor.

A group of Lords led by Warwick and the Bishop of Winchester were deputised to go before the King at Windsor and seek his guidance but with no success. On their return, on 27th March, York was appointed "Protector and Defender of the Kingdom of England, and Chief Councillor of the King". This had taken many

---

[97] *John Benet's Chronicle for the Years 1400-1462* edited by G.L. & M.A. Harriss. Camden 1972. Page 10.
[98] *The Paston Letters 1422-1509* Volume 2 edited by J. Gairdner. Chatto and Windus, London 1904. Page 297-298.

months. Salisbury was appointed Chancellor, Worcester became Treasurer. Buckingham was made Steward of England. Somerset was relieved of his position as Captain of Calais, which York took himself. York was reappointed Lieutenant of Ireland. Warwick regained his position as Chamberlain of the Exchequer.

There was still a great reluctance amongst many Lords to take responsibility, else they be blamed in future and punished for any actions taken. Most promised to do what they could subject to being able to attend Council. Some feigned sickness which would limit their attendance. Warwick claimed that he was "young of age and younger of discretion and wisdom… but he would, with right goodwill, do that which was in his power". [99]

Disturbances broke out once more in the North. Exeter and Egremont were behind the unrest which targeted the Nevilles. The new Protector decided he needed to take action against Egremont and Exeter, his son-in-law and former ward. York sped north to the city of York. Lord Stanley and Bonville were sent to put down the rebels. Exeter fled south, was taken and placed in custody at Pontefract. Warwick sat in judgement with others on those who had rebelled. Egremont was finally captured together with his younger brother, Richard Percy, by Thomas and John Neville. They were fined and imprisoned in London.

Warwick during this period was asked to serve on twelve commissions of oyer and terminer. These were for Worcestershire and Staffordshire in April, Gloucestershire, Nottinghamshire, Derbyshire, Leicestershire, Cumberland and Westmorland in May, the West Riding in June, North Riding in July, Northamptonshire in December and Herefordshire in February 1455.

Christmas 1454 saw a sudden and unexpected return to health by the King. Henry came to his senses. The King thanked God for his new son and heir and "he said he never knew till that time, nor knew what was said to him, nor knew not where he had been while he had

---

[99] *The Nevills of Middleham* by K.L. Clark. The History Press 2016. A Crisis of Government. Page 110.

been sick until now". Two visiting clergymen, Bishop Wayneflete and the Prior of St Johns "wept for joy". [100]

York was relieved of his Protectorate. Somerset and Exeter were released from prison. Somerset was reappointed Captain of Calais and resumed his former position of most favoured counsellor. Salisbury was replaced as Chancellor by Archbishop Bourchier. Wiltshire became Treasurer in place of Worcester. Somerset and York were bound over to keep the peace against bonds of 20,000 marks (£13,333). Henry was King once more, and not just in name.

Somerset was restored to grace and favour by Henry VI. Exeter was exonerated from his transgressions. Warwick and Salisbury had benefited from the Protectorate. They had operated closely with York. They would now once more be excluded from decision making. They knew from experience that they would be subject to fresh challenges and attacks on them. It was not a question of choice. York no doubt sought their help, but they were forced to join him to protect their interests. Somerset gave them no alternative. They sought respite or even resolution, not reform. It was though a very valuable and significant development for York and his cause as the Croyland chronicler made clear… "amongst the adherents of Richard, Duke of York were the Earls of Salisbury and Warwick, father and son, whose opposition was greatly dreaded. [101]

At Council in March, Somerset complained that he had been incarcerated for "a year, ten weeks and more… without any reasonable ground or lawful process". Somerset was embittered by his experience. He challenged anyone who still doubted his "truth and allegiance" to a trial by arms. The King declared Somerset to be

---

[100] *The Paston Letters 1422-1509* Volume 4 edited by J. Gairdner. Chatto and Windus, London 1904. Pages 13 & 30.
[101] *Ingulph's Chronicle of the Abbey of Croyland:* with the continuations by Peter of Blois and Anonymous writers. Translated by Henry Riley. Published by Nabu Press 2014. Originally published 1854. Written 1486. Page 454.

"his true and faithful liegeman and cousin, and had done unto him right true, good and pleasant service".

On 21st April 1455, a great Council was summoned to meet at Leicester on 21st May. The Lancastrian heartland seemed an ideal place for Somerset to take his revenge. York, Warwick and Salisbury saw it as such. There was precedent. Duke Humphrey had been arrested attending a special parliament at Bury St Edmunds in 1447. They returned to their estates and prepared accordingly. The "fire, rancour and envy' between Somerset and York was soon to erupt in "great band hot flames of open war and wrath" at St Albans. [102]

---

[102] *The New Chronicles of England and France* by R. Fabyan, edited by H. Ellis. London 1811. Page 629.

St Albans 22nd May 1455

...They ferociously broke in by the garden sides between the sign of The Key and the sign of The Chequer in Holywell Street, and immediately they were within the town, suddenly they blew up trumpets, and set a cry with a shout and a great voice... A Warwick! A Warwick ... [103]

Warwick and his father, Salisbury, went their respective ways to raise men under their colours. Warwick collected together dependable men from the Midlands. Salisbury called upon his trusted lieutenant in the North, Sir Robert Ogle, who brought 600 archers. Salisbury was probably accompanied by his younger sons, Thomas and John. York once more sought help from his retainers in the Welsh marches. Warwick had his estates in Wales but his men there were probably better deployed there should Somerset renew local hostilities.

The preparations were made in as much secrecy as possible. They did not wish to alert Somerset and others to their plans to intercept the King and persuade him of their wishes and wants. They were largely successful in this aim. News of their mobilisation did not reach Westminster until late.

This was not something new. York had raised troops previously in 1452. Henry VI sent a delegation to calm matters. Worcester, the Bishop of Coventry and the Prior of the Hospital of St John of Jerusalem were received by York but were detained in order that secrecy around their intentions and movements might be maintained.

Urgent letters were sent out on 18th May. Coventry received the call from the King for armed men to be sent "to be with us wheresoever we be in all haste possible". The Council resolved to send help to "our Sovereign Lord in St Albans" but unfortunately the battle was over before the men were assembled. [104] It was a similar case for

---

[103] *The Stow Relation: The Stonor Variant, in The Paston Letters 1422-1509* edited by J. Gairdner. Constable and Co 1895.
[104] *Coventry Leet Book*. Pages 247-248.

many Lords who received the call for arms but failed to arrive at St Albans on time.

On 19th May letters under seal were sent to York, Norfolk, Salisbury and Warwick that they should disband their troops otherwise they would be seen as committing treason against the King. York was limited to bringing 200 men. Norfolk, Salisbury and Warwick could only have 160 men.

This all disrupted the schedule. Henry left Westminster later than planned. They set off north on 21st May the date of the assembly. The King had with him many leading nobles. There were the Dukes of Somerset and Buckingham, and their sons, the Earls of Dorset and Stafford. There were four other Earls, Northumberland, Pembroke, Devon and Wiltshire, and five Barons, Roos, Sudeley, Clifford, Fauconberg and Dudley. Queen Margaret remained in London at Greenwich Palace with Prince Edward. At Kilburn, just four miles out, Lord Say delivered a letter from York and the Nevilles, dated the day before. It did not reach the King.

York, Salisbury and Warwick were at Royston, in Hertfordshire, on 20th May. The letter conveyed their response to the King's missives and the messages carried by his delegation. They complained of "the jealousy had against us" and their omission from a recent Council meeting. They took offence at the suggestion that the assembly at Leicester was purposed to address the King's safety implicating them as traitors. They demanded the King's advisors replaced and a truly representative council. On 21st they moved on to Ware, only fifteen miles from St Albans. York sent his confessor, William Willeflete, with another letter.

The King's party continued on their journey and stopped that night in Watford, some seven miles south of St Albans. Around 2:00 a.m. in the morning on 22nd May, Willeflete arrived and handed over the second letter. Once more the letter did not reach the King. Somerset and two of the King's servants, Thomas Thorpe and William Joseph, apparently prevented the letters from being read by the King. Yorkist accounts written after the battle are our only source in this respect. The communications were perhaps simply ignored.[105]

Somerset wanted to wait for expected reinforcements. Buckingham won the argument. He wanted to move on to St Albans and negotiate. Buckingham replaced Somerset as Constable. The Lancastrians reached St Albans around 7:00 a.m. and took control of the town. King Henry usually stayed at the Abbey. On this occasion he occupied a house in the town centre owned by a leading citizen, Edmund Westby. The Royal army was set up in defensive array. The Bars were lowered at all entrances. The town was not walled but it was surrounded by the *Tonman* ditch and fences.

The Yorkist army arrived in St Albans shortly afterwards and set up camp to the east in Keyfield which was "not more than a crossbow arrow" away from the town. The Yorkist army numbered around 3,000. The King's army present that morning was at 2,000 men, lower in quantity and quality. The scene was set for confrontation although it was far from certain in most minds that a battle would be fought. Negotiations ensued, led by heralds.

Somerset, it is said, sent Exeter's pursuivant, Lesparre, demanding that York "quit at once and withdraw, on pain of their allegiance and breach of honour". York did not respond to this insensitive gesture and harsh words.

The King sent Buckingham's herald as a more neutral mediator. Norfolk's Mowbray herald was chosen to meet with him. York's message was simple "Wherefore, gracious Lord, please it your high majesty to deliver such as we will accuse, and they to like as they have deserved and done." It was clear that this referred to Somerset. York said that he would not leave "until he will have them that deserve death, or else we to die". The not-so-distant memories of Dartford informed his reluctance to back down on mere promises of change.[106]

---

[105] *Politics and the Battle of St Albans 1455* by C.A.J. Armstrong. Bulletin of the Institute of Historical Research No 87 May 1960. Pages 1-72.
[106] *The Paston Letters 1422-1509* Volume 4 edited by J. Gairdner. Chatto and Windus, London 1904.

The King's answer was surprisingly aggressive, so much so, that it was probably written by the antagonistic Somerset. Henry commanded that York "void the field" and not to "make any resistance against me in my Realm". He declared that "I shall know what traitor dare be so bold to raise a people in my own land, where through I am in great disease and heaviness" and swore to "destroy them every mother's son, and they be hanged and drawn and quartered, that may be taken afterwards for them to have example to all such traitors." The Royal Standard was raised in the Market Square. It was treason to fight against the King.

Buckingham insisted he was there to support his King… "we have not come here to support any one person or for any other cause but only to be in the company with the King our said Lord as by right we are bound to do". Buckingham suggested York might withdraw to Hatfield or Barnet for that night pending further negotiations for he knew royal reinforcements were expected soon.

York did not delay, compromise or back down. A peaceful resolution had been sought. Letters had been sent. Lengthy negotiations had been conducted. It was perhaps intended that Norfolk's charges of treason against Somerset would be followed through to their natural and desired conclusion. The retinues they had brought with them were to help persuade people to see right and reason, and as protection against those who sought to do them harm. Negotiations had not worked. There was no alternative.

The Paston Letters record his impassioned speech. York told his men that "The King, our sovereign Lord, will not be reformed at our beseeching nor prayer, nor will understand the intent that we come hither and assembled for and gathered at this time… he will with all his power pursue us… to give us a shameful death, losing our livelihood and goods, and our heirs shamed for ever… better it is for us to die in the field than cowardly to be put to a great rebuke and a shameful death." [107]

---

[107] *The Paston Letters 1422-1509* Volume 4 edited by J. Gairdner. Chatto and Windus, London 1904.

York gave the fateful order just before midday to attack and thus began the battle of St Albans and the first of the many battles in the Wars of the Roses. [108] It was a battle to change those who governed in the name of the King, not to change the King himself. Yet everything changed within a few hours, in a small town in Hertfordshire. The battle unleashed civil war which lasted for more than thirty years. It ushered in a period when, as the Croyland Chronicler noted, "you might plainly perceive public and intestine broils fermenting among the princes and nobles of the realm, so much so, that in the words of the Gospel... brother was divided against brother, and father against father". [109]

We have the benefit of hindsight. The significance and importance of St Albans was, of course, not something that was understood at the time. It was an opportunity for Warwick, and his father Salisbury, to deal with troublemakers who challenged their livelihood and lands in Wales, the Midland and the North. They did not miss their chance to do so.

---

[108] *The Battles of St Albans* by Peter Burley. Michael Elliott and Harvey Watson. Pen & Sword 2007.

[109] *Ingulph's Chronicle of the Abbey of Croyland:* with the continuations by Peter of Blois and Anonymous writers. Translated by Henry Riley. Published by Nabu Press 2014. Originally published 1854. Written 1486. Page 419.

The 1st Battle of St Albans 22nd May 1455

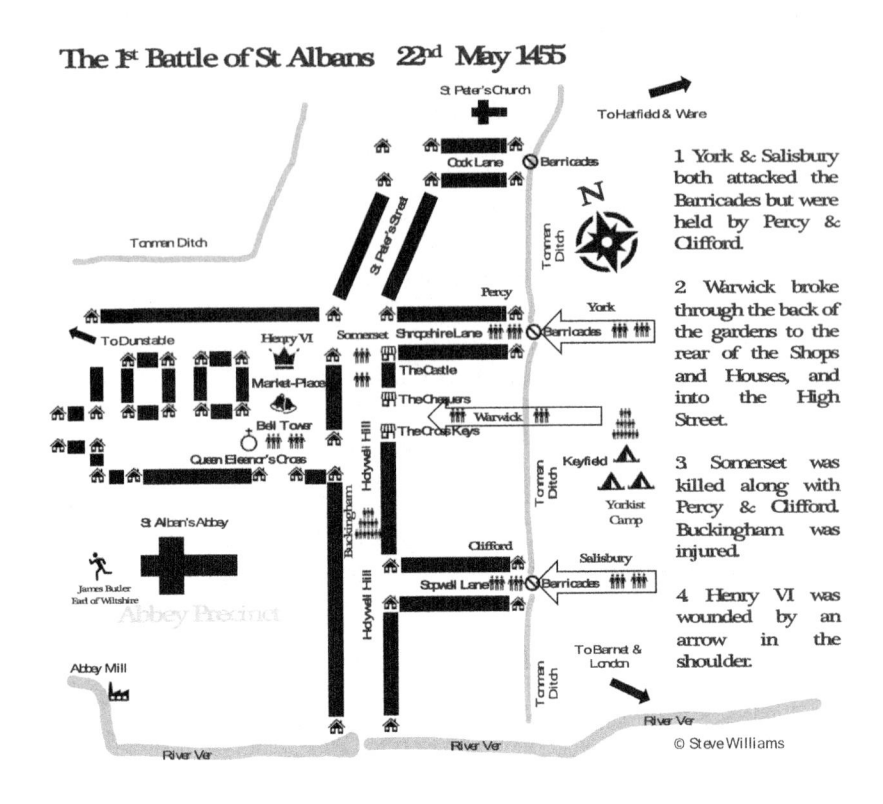

[Map of the battle showing St Peter's Church, Cock Lane, St Peter's Street, Tonman Ditch, To Hatfield & Ware, To Dunstable, Henry VI, Somerset, Shropshire Lane, Percy, York, The Castle, Market-Place, The Chequers, Bell Tower, The Cross Keys, Warwick, Queen Eleanor's Cross, St Alban's Abbey, James Butler Earl of Wiltshire, Abbey Precinct, Abbey Mill, Buckingham, Holywell Hill, Keyfield, Yorkist Camp, Clifford, Salisbury, Sopwell Lane, Barricades, To Barnet & London, River Ver]

1. York & Salisbury both attacked the Barricades but were held by Percy & Clifford.

2. Warwick broke through the back of the gardens to the rear of the Shops and Houses, and into the High Street.

3. Somerset was killed along with Percy & Clifford. Buckingham was injured.

4. Henry VI was wounded by an arrow in the shoulder.

© Steve Williams

York attacked via Shropshire Lane which was defended by Northumberland. Salisbury led his men through Sopwell Lane, held by Clifford. The fighting was fierce, but the defences held firm. They were able to repel the attackers. The narrow lanes, barricades and buildings provided a strong base.

Warwick together with Ogle and the 600 archers attacked over the ditch and through the fences gaining access to the gardens behind the high street shops, houses and inns. The English Chronicler wrote "they and their men violently broke down houses and fences on the East side of the town and entered St Peter's Street, slaying all that resisted them." [110]

---

[110] *An English Chronicle of the Reigns of Richard II, Henry IV, Henry V, and Henry VI* edited by J.S. Davies. Camden Society 1856.

Clifford and Northumberland died trying to defend the Bars against attacks from the front and rear. Their men faced with such opposition fled, any which way they might.

Somerset and his men fell back seeking defensible positions but to no avail. The Dijon Relation reported his valiant death, trying to escape from a building where he had taken refuge… "Somerset had no option but to come out with his men, as a result of which they were all surrounded by the Duke of York's men. After some were stricken down and the Duke of Somerset had killed four men with his own hand, so it is said, he was felled to the ground with an axe, and at once wounded in so many places that he died." [111]

Legend has it that a prophesy had forecast Somerset would die in the shadow of a castle. In the event he was trapped in the Castle Inn. The Tudor historian Hall told the story in his chronicle. Shakespeare included it within his writings.

York looks at the dead corpse of Somerset…

"So, lie thou there,
For underneath an alehouse's paltry sign,
The Castle in St Albans, Somerset,
Hath made the wizard famous in his death." [112]

The royal army was ill-prepared and unready. The sudden attack was unexpected. The curfew bell would be ringing loud but late. Knights were still in the marketplace putting on their armour. The royal standard was cast aside as arrows flew and those charged with its safe keeping sought safety. Many of those killed or wounded were of the King's household.

The Dijon Relation reported that "matters became so critical that four of the King's bodyguard were killed by arrows in his presence,

---

[111] *The Dijon Relation.* Archives de la Cote d'Or B. 11942. No. 258. In *Politics and the Battle of St Albans* 1455 by C.A.J. Armstrong Bulletin of the Institute of Historical Research Volume 33 1960.
[112] *Henry VI Part 2* Act 5 Scene II by William Shakespeare.

and the King himself was wounded in the shoulder by an arrow, although it only grazed the skin." [113] King Henry is said to have shouted "Forsooth, forsooth! You do foully to smite a King anointed so!" [114] Benet's Chronicle records that the King was found in the Tanner's shop. Both Benet and the Dijon Relation say the King was taken to the Abbey. [115]

Abbot John Whethamstede was horrified in the aftermath… "here you saw one fall with his brains dashed out, there another with a broken arm, a third with a cut-throat, and a fourth with a pierced chest, and the whole street was full of dead corpses." [116] The Abbot was also most unhappy at the looting and pillaging that took place subsequently, as were the towns folk of St Albans.

Somerset, Northumberland and Clifford were dead. The body of Edmund Beaufort, Duke of Somerset was interred in the Lady Chapel, in the Abbey of St Albans, not too far from the tomb of Duke Humphrey of Gloucester. Northumberland and Clifford's bodies were also buried in the Abbey.

Henry Beaufort, Earl of Dorset, Somerset's son and heir, was so badly wounded he was taken away in a cart and looked after by one of Warwick's men.

Buckingham was wounded in the face and neck, and taken to the Abbey, where he was later handed over to the victors. Humphrey, Earl of Stafford, his son, was wounded in the hand.

1st Baron Dudley and John Wenlock were wounded by arrows. Wenlock was taken in a cart back to Dunstable.

---

[113] *The Dijon Relation*. Archives de la Cote d'Or B. 11942. No. 258. In *Politics and the Battle of St Albans* 1455 by C.A.J. Armstrong Bulletin of the Institute of Historical Research Volume 33 1960.
[114] *Henry the Sixth, a Reprint of John Blacman's Memoir* by John Blacman. Cambridge University Press 1919.
[115] *John Benet's Chronicle for the Years 1400-1462* edited by G.L. & M.A. Harriss. Camden 1972.
[116] *Registrum Abbatiae Johannis Whethamstede* by Abbot J. Whethamstede. Edited by H.T. Riley. 1872.

Benet reports that "all who were on the side of Somerset were killed, wounded, or, at the least despoiled." [117]

John Crane wrote to his "worshipful and beloved" cousin, John Paston. "Tidings as we have here, these three Lords be dead, the Duke of Somerset, the Earl of Northumberland and the Lord Clifford; and as for any other men of name, I know none, save only Cotton of Cambridgeshire… there was at most slain six score, and as for the Lords that were with the King, they and their men were pilled and spoiled out of all their harness and horses." [118]

Wiltshire was nowhere to be found. Rumour has it he fled disguised as a monk. Wiltshire is much criticised in the chronicles. Benet has him fleeing in panic. Gregory's chronicle places him in charge of the Royal Standard which he abandoned as he was "fearful of losing his beauty, for he named the fairest knight of this land." [119]

York, Salisbury and Warwick went to the Abbey, knelt before the King and asked for forgiveness and grace. Their fight was with the traitors around him. There was never any intention of hurt to him. They were his true liegemen. The "victors showed the king ostentatious deference". [120]

Henry VI was led back to London the next day on 23rd May. York rode on his right, Salisbury on his left and Warwick up ahead bearing the King's sword. Henry was suitably paraded through the streets of London by his *loyal* subjects before being lodged at the Bishop's Palace. The next Sunday a service of thanksgiving ended with York placing the crown on the King's head. York became Constable. York's kinsman Thomas Bourchier, Archbishop of Canterbury, was already Chancellor, and his brother became Treasurer.

---

[117] *John Benet's Chronicle for the Years 1400-1462* edited by G.L. & M.A. Harriss. Camden 1972. Page 10.
[118] *Selections From the Paston Letters* transcribed by Sir John Fenn. Edited by Alice Greenwood. London 1920. Forgotten Books. Pages 79-80.
[119] *William Gregory's Chronicle in the historical Collections of a Citizen of London in the Fifteenth Century* edited by J. Gairdner. London 1876.
[120] *Parliamentary Rolls* Henry VI July 1455. Introduction.

Warwick and Salisbury had added their names to the letters sent by York. Others such as Norfolk declined to show such an overt form of support, fearful of possible subsequent accusations of treason. Their commitment to York was clear and evident. The relationship was fruitful. Somerset, Northumberland and Clifford were no more and could no longer threaten them or their lands. Henry VI was still their King and liege Lord.

Warwick was made Captain of Calais, his had been the decisive move at St Albans. York rewarded him for his efforts and contribution. Kendall wrote that "Warwick's dashing attack" won him a "military reputation and a sudden fame." [121] Warwick himself secured the position which gave him hopes of overseas military service like his father, and grandfather, before him and which had been so far denied to him by the loss of the other territories in France.

Warwick had come of age and York's eldest son, aged thirteen, Edward Earl of March, was there at St Albans, looking on with youthful interest. [122] St Alban's in 1455 was more a skirmish than a full-scale battle but blood was shed, noble blood. The heirs of those who died would not forget. It would cast a shadow over the years to come.

---

[121] *Warwick the Kingmaker* by Paul Kendall. George Allen & Unwin 1957. St Albans. Page 29.
[122] *The Life and Reign of Edward the Fourth King of England and of France and Lord of Ireland* by Cora L. Scofield. Volumes One and Two. Fonthill Media 2016. First Published 1923. Page 22. Note 5.

Captain of Calais

…No Lord of court took the jeopardy nor laboured for the honour of the land but only he, for the which manhood and his great policy and his… fortifying of Calais… all the commonality of this land had him in great laud and charity… and all other lands likewise: and so reputed and taken for as famous a knight as was living… [123]

Warwick was appointed Captain of Calais within days and although it took time for him to be accepted and take up his position, it was undoubtedly the making of him and his reputation in England and overseas.

Warwick was made steward and constable of Monmouth and the three castles of Grosmont, Skenfrith and White Castle. Further grants consolidated his hold on South Wales. Warwick's young brother was created Bishop of Exeter. Salisbury was made chief steward of the northern parts of the Duchy of Lancaster.

Soon after St Albans, writs dated 26th May were sent out to summon Parliament. York sought to bring the country back together. Olive branches were offered to recent opponents such as Buckingham, Wiltshire and the new Lords Northumberland and Clifford, and the new Duke of Somerset. All eyes were on him, in England and elsewhere.

The Milanese Ambassador on 31st May 1455 wrote from Bruges to advise the Archbishop of Ravenna that York "will now take up the government again, and some think that the affairs of the Kingdom will now take a turn for the better." A follow up letter a few days later added "peace reigns… the Duke of York has the Government, and the people are pleased at this." [124]

Peace may have reigned, but the new administration ruled uneasily. The King, Queen and Prince Edward were moved in June away

---

[123] *Warwick the Kingmaker* by Paul Kendall. George Allen & Unwin 1957. 'As Famous a Knight'. Page 46.
[124] *Calendar of State Papers* Milan 1, Pages 16-17.

from London to Hertford Castle. York resided nearby at Ware friary. Salisbury stayed at Sir Oliver Ogard's Rye House and Warwick at Sir William Oldhall's mansion at Hunsdon. [125]

Henry VI opened the session on 9th July 1455. The aim was to "set a perfect love and rest among the Lords of this land" and to draw them all together "in union and accord... to the honour, prosperity and welfare of the King our Sovereign Lord, and the politic and restful rule and governance of this land and people." Notable absentees were Exeter and Egremont who were otherwise detained. The new Earl of Northumberland and Beaumont attended.

There was no great enthusiasm by the Commons to be elected. "Some men hold it right strange to be in this Parliament and me thinketh they be wise men that so do" wrote John Jenny to John Paston on 24th June. The Duchess of Norfolk ensured that the county representatives were servants of her husband despite local resentment that one was not even from the shire. [126]

Thomas Bourchier, Archbishop of Canterbury, gave the opening address and set out the agenda. There were eight items; the finances of the royal household, wages for the Calais garrison, the defence of Calais and Berwick, the deployment of 13,000 archers, the achievement of "perfect love and rest" amongst the lords, the prevention of the export of bullion; the keeping of the sea; and unrest in Wales. Five committees of groups of Lords were established to deal with the most pressing matters. Warwick was to sit on the Calais, Berwick and Wales committees. Wenlock was appointed speaker for the commons.

An indemnity was agreed for acts committed at St Albans. The loyalty of York, Salisbury and Warwick was officially recognized and noted. Somerset was conveniently blamed for events along with two men of the King's household, Thorp and Joseph. St Albans was not an attack on the King but an attempt by Somerset on the lives of

---

[125] *Selections From the Paston Letters* transcribed by Sir John Fenn. Edited by Alice Greenwood. London 1920. Forgotten Books. Pages 80-81.
[126] *The Paston Letters 1422-1509* edited by J. Gairdner. Chatto and Windus, London 1904.

York and others due to "personal malice". Previous convictions of Yorkist supporters such as Oldhall, Devereux and Young were overturned.

It was reported that York, Salisbury and Warwick during Parliament took to travelling in armed groups and in armour using barges filled with weapons. They were fearful of reprisals and the atmosphere was tense. On 17th July Warwick quarrelled with Lord Cromwell. It was heated sufficiently for it to be noted in Paston's correspondence that Shrewsbury lodged Cromwell "at the hospital of Saint James, beside the Mews… for his safeguard." Cromwell was attempting to excuse himself of all blame for the events leading up to St Albans. Warwick accused him of being the one that began the troubles that led to the battle. [127]

Oaths of allegiance were sworn by all on 24th July. [128] On 31st July Parliament ended with a general pardon was issued which even included Exeter, Egremont and Sir Richard Percy. The late Duke of Gloucester was rehabilitated, his debts paid off, his reputation restored, and a declaration of his loyalty was publicly proclaimed.

Warwick was engaged with affairs of the Great Council and with his new responsibility as Captain of Calais was involved with negotiations with Duke Alencon of France. It was affairs much closer to home that needed attention.

The King fell ill once more and could not attend the reopening of Parliament on 12th November. Henry had not been well since St Albans and had been under the attention of his physician. He was not as incapacitated as previously and asked to be kept informed about any matters pertaining to his "honour, worship and safety of his most noble person". [129] York became once more the Protector and Defender of the Realm and King's chief councillor. Supreme power was granted to Council.

---

[127] *The Paston Letters 1422-1509* edited by J. Gairdner. Chatto and Windus, London 1904.
[128] *Parliamentary Rolls* Henry VI July 1455.
[129] *Parliamentary Rolls* Henry VI July 1455.

Troubles in the West Country were of concern. A simmering feud suddenly lit up. James Gresham wrote in detail to John Paston on 28th October 1455 "there is great variance between the Earl of Devonshire and the Lord Bonville, as hath been many days… the Earl's son and heir came, with sixty men of arms, to Radford's place, who was counsel with my Lord Bonville… and they on fire a house… to cause him to open the gates… and entreated Radford to come down… promising no bodily harm… in the meantime, his men robbed his chamber and rifled his coffers… and came nine men upon him and smote him on the head and felled him and cut his throat… The King is at Hertford, and some men are afraid he is sick again." [130]

York's second Protectorate did not last long. A proposal of a new Act of Resumption was opposed by many Lords and Queen Margaret. The King recovered his health sufficiently to return to Parliament and on 25th February 1456, York was relieved of his office. York was retained as a leading member of Council.

Warwick had yet to take up his position as Captain though it had been confirmed legally by Council on 4th August 1455. Negotiations had been ongoing with the garrison to settle outstanding arrears in wages. These at £65,444 were not insignificant. [131] This meant coming to terms with the Company of the Staple in Calais on the financial underpinning of any settlement based upon the wool industry customs and the proceeds of taxation. The garrison also wanted assurances about the new appointment of Warwick given their previous allegiances. Warwick's uncle, Lord Fauconberg, led the talks with both parties, assisted by York's man, Sir Edmund Mulso.

Warwick was concerned at the delay. On 13th December 1455 he gained Parliamentary protection should it be lost to France before he was able to take effective possession. Calais was under continual threat from France. Warwick did not wish to be held accountable

---

[130] *Selections From the Paston Letters* transcribed by Sir John Fenn. Edited by Alice Greenwood. London 1920. Forgotten Books. Pages 86-88.
[131] *Warwick the Kingmaker* by Michael Hicks. Blackwell Publishers 1998. Countdown to Civil War 1456-9. Page 140.

for its loss. Calais "had a symbolic importance quite out of proportion to its military value". [132]

A settlement was finally reached. Henry VI himself resolved the remaining issue by issuing full and individual pardons to the garrison. The agreement was concluded on 16th March 1456. Warwick's office would commence from 28th April. Fauconberg took over possession on his behalf.

York may have lost his pre-eminence as Protector, but Warwick was still held high in the esteem of the King and those advising him including Queen Margaret.

Warwick was at Council on 2nd March before returning home where he stayed until early June. Countess Anne was heavy with child. A second daughter Anne was born to them on 11th June 1456 and joined her five-year-old elder sister, Isabel. Warwick perhaps missed his second child's birth. He was in attendance at Council on 7th June, and then again on 3rd July and 8th July. Border troubles with James II of Scotland was on the agenda. James had declared war and even declared that York was rightfully King. York headed North and James soon backed down.

Everything seemed fine, at least for a short while. Tensions at Westminster had eased. Local regional rivalries had quietened. The King's finances were back on track. There was no expensive war in France to fund. All was soon to change.

Queen Margaret "persuaded her husband to remove himself, or carried him off, to her castle of Kenilworth" where the defences were strengthened with cannon, field guns and other armaments. [133] The court moved to the Midlands and changes were subsequently made to the top offices of the land. Archbishop Bourchier was replaced as Chancellor by Bishop Wayneflete, and his brother Viscount Bourchier was replaced as Treasurer by Shrewsbury.

---

[132] *Warwick the Kingmaker* by Michael Hicks. Blackwell Publishers 1998. Countdown to Civil War 1456-9. Page 139.
[133] *Henry VI* by Bertram Wolffe. Yale University Press 1981. Civil War. Pages 302-303.

Laurence Booth became Keeper of the Privy Seal and would become Bishop of Durham in July 1457 on the death of Warwick's uncle, Robert Neville.

Contemporaries such as the ecclesiastical Gascoigne saw it clearly as the Queen's work. Margaret's ire was aimed at York who she held responsible for her reduced household and income, and the death of her close friend. Somerset was perhaps too close. Yorkist rumours had it that he had fathered Prince Edward. [134]

Some have argued that the move and changes of government office were in direct response to new hostilities in Wales by those linked with York. Devereux and Herbert took the law into their own hands at Hereford. They then seized possession of Carmarthen and Aberystwyth castles. These had passed from Somerset to York, but Henry had granted them to his half-brother Jasper Tudor. Henry VI feared these incidents marked the start of renewed aggression by York to take back power. [135] Henry, Queen Margaret and Prince Edward moved to the Midlands.

Whatever the cause, the result was the same. The King was in charge, but he devoted himself more to religion. One third of his time was spent in monasteries and priories. Queen Margaret increased her influence, surrounded and supported by those who opposed York and, in particular, those who sought revenge for the blood of their fathers. It was a difficult time.

In September 1456 five dog's heads were impaled on the railings outside the London residence where York was staying with a clear message that as a traitor, and a son of a traitor, he should die not others.

"What planet compelled me, or what sign,
To serve that man that all men hate?
I would his head were here for mine,

---

[134] *Loci et Libro Veritatum* Thomas Gascoigne's theological dictionary edited by J.E. Thorold Rogers. Oxford 1881. Sub Regnum Angliae. Page 214.
[135] *The End of the House of Lancaster* by R.L. Storey. London 1966. Pages 178-82, 228-230.

For he hath caused all the debate." [136]

The members of the Great Council were summoned to Coventry for a meeting on 10th October. Somerset arrived with many men. A "great affray" with the city watchmen followed "to the great disturbance of all the Lords in the vicinity". Buckingham intervened to secure the peace and saved the young Duke from injury or worse. Somerset had to be restrained from attacking York at Council. [137]

Bale tells us that… "This year (1456) the Friday the 5th November came the Earl of Warwick unto London. And the same day after his coming rode against him to have distressed him the Dukes of Exeter and Somerset, the Duke's son of Somerset and the Earl of Shrewsbury, Treasurer and the Lords Roos and other with 400 people and more as was reported. But thanked be God the said Earl was thereof warned and purveyed a remedy against their malice and came in safety to the city of London and they durst not counter with him for he was named and taken in all places for the most courageous and manliest knight living." [138]

It was reported in December that there was "dissension and unkindness" between Somerset and Warwick's young brother, John Neville. There was a "great visaging" between them and they "bickered". London's Mayor stepped up the watch by those tasked with keeping the city safe and secure. [139]

Warwick had not spent much time in Calais. Sir Robert Chamberlain was sent there with additional troops in October to meet the renewed threat from France. On 20th January 1457 he appointed

---

[136] *Battle Royale; The Wars of Lancaster and York 1440-1462* by Hugh Bicheno. Head of Zeus 2015. Page 182.
[137] *The Paston Letters 1422-1509* edited by J. Gairdner. Chatto and Windus, London 1904.
[138] *Warwick the Kingmaker Politics, Power and Fame* by A.J. Pollard. Continuum Books 2007. Bale's Chronicle Page 144 in *Six Town Chronicles* edited by R. Flenley. Oxford 1911.
[139] *The New Chronicles of England and France* by R. Fabyan, edited by H. Ellis. London 1811. Page 629.

William Chamber, Rector of Olney, as receiver-general for all his estates, in England and Wales. This freed up his time to take a more active role as Captain. Once he had arranged and settled his affairs, he was ready to move his young family and take up residence, but not before another important family event.

John Neville married Isabel Ingoldisthorpe on 25th April 1457. Isabel was joint heiress to the earldom of Worcester, and the Queen's ward. Archbishop Bourchier presided over the ceremony at Canterbury. Warwick attended before setting off for Calais with Countess Anne, and his uncle, Lord Fauconberg. Warwick would spend most of the next three years in Calais. Financial records show that he received residency payments for 267 days, in the year to June 1458. [140]

---

[140] *Warwick the Kingmaker* by Michael Hicks. Blackwell Publishers 1998. Countdown to Civil War 1456-9. Page 142.

Calais in the mid 1450's consisted of the fortified port and around one hundred square miles of neighbouring territory. It was a military town of around 5,000 within the lands of the Duke of Burgundy. The Calais merchants of the staple held a monopoly over export of English wool. It was an important base for commanding the straits of Dover. There were low lying marshes to the East, and to the West, was more hilly and wooded country.

The forts of Hammes and Guines defended the town from the south. Rysbank fort protected the entrance to the harbour, which was dominated by Calais castle. Newenham bridge was the only road into Calais and was guarded by Nieulay fort. Sluice gates under the bridge allowed all the approaches to be flooded in the event of attack.

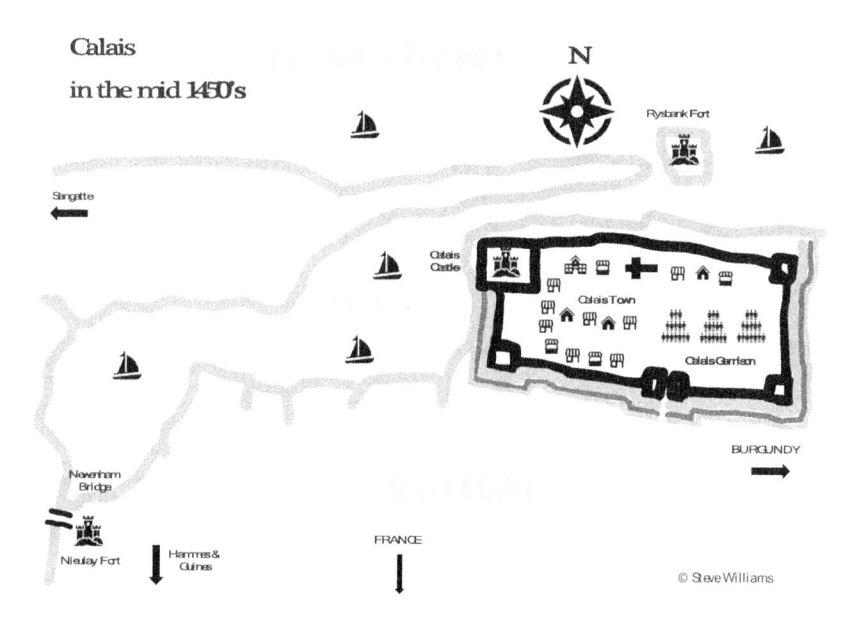

The Captaincy of Calais was usually treated as a sinecure. Warwick delegated authority initially before deciding to take a more "hands-on" approach than previous holders of the role. He would not be an absentee captain. Perhaps he had tired of his time in England spent between the administration of his estates and the politics of Council. Another reason might have been to escape from his new royal neighbours now in close proximity in the Midlands to his household at Warwick, or the aggressive young Dukes of Somerset and Exeter.

Warwick sought to ensure he had a good team around him. The Lancastrian Lords, Welles, Stourton and Rivers, and Sir Gervase Clifton, who had looked after Calais for Somerset, were sent home. Warwick kept the operational heads such as Sir Thomas Findern and Sir John Marny, who were respectively lieutenants of Guines and Hammes. Lord Fauconberg, Warwick's uncle, was his unappointed deputy. The Frenchman, Lord Duras, was a trusted naval officer. York's man, Sir Edmund Mulso, was appointed marshal. Mulso died in mid 1458. Warwick was an executor of his will and was left a suit of armour, given to him by the Dauphin. Warwick sought permission from York to appoint another of his men, Sir Walter Blount, in his place. [141]

Veterans of Calais such as Andrew Trollope were retained as promised by King Henry. Warwick though had gained agreement as part of his appointment to bring additional troops, 20 mounted men-at-arms, 20 mounted archers and 260 archers on foot. These were no doubt his own chosen men from his retinues at home.

Warwick's times with his father on the Scottish marches would have given him good experience of the volatile nature of life on the borders where the threat and danger of conflict was ever present. Calais was no different. The financial records show that while Calais itself was not under attack in 1457, its surrounding areas suffered. Revenue fell and the increased troops meant greater expenditure.

A priority for the new Captain of Calais was to build relationships with his neighbour, Philip the Good, Duke of Burgundy. Letters were exchanged. Warwick even sent a gift of a horse to his son, the

---

[141] *Warwick the Kingmaker* by Michael Hicks. Blackwell Publishers 1998. Countdown to Civil War 1456-9. Page 142.

future Charles the Bold. Face to face negotiations took place in July 1457. Warwick and others met Anthony, Grand Bastard of Burgundy and John of Burgundy, Count of Estampes. Further meetings took place and a truce on land was agreed tentatively later that year.

Warwick was mindful of those who did business with Calais and the English ports and people who supported the town. On 1st May 1457 it was reported that the "Earl of Warwick hath had the folk of Canterbury and Sandwich before him and thanked them of their good hearts and victualling of Calais and prayed for its continuance". [142] Warwick was adept at drawing upon public support and built a rapport with the people of Kent which was to benefit him in the years to come.

Warwick's learned much in Calais and it gave him exposure to new skills and knowledge including, diplomacy, artillery and the sea and ships. Warwick had received the traditional and customary training of an English Lord and knight. Calais gave him a much more rounded and extensive *career development* than the vast majority of his contemporaries. Warwick chose to do so and immersed himself in developing what we might today call competences. He would benefit greatly from so doing and his extensive operational capabilities would be admired not just by those he served but by those who served him.

The expected attack on Calais in 1457 did not materialise. France attacked English territory, but it was Sandwich. On 28th August 1457 Pierre de Breze, seneschal of Normandy led a raid at dawn. "They spoiled and robbed the good port… and slew many people". The looting and damage upset not just the locals. English opinion was outraged. France had struck at home. The English coast was vulnerable to further attacks.

Something had to be done. Council met to discuss. On 3rd October 1457, Warwick replaced Exeter as Keeper of the seas. He was appointed by the King "for the resistance of his enemies and

---

[142] *The Paston Letters 1422-1509* edited by J. Gairdner. Chatto and Windus, London 1904.

Page 80

repressing of their malice". The appointment was made legal on 26th November. Money was reallocated to give him ships and customs dues redirected to fund wages. Authority was given to him to issue safe conducts and keep the spoils of war. Warwick was in favour and for Hicks was "the regime's front line against France." [143]

It was not all good news. On 8th October 1457 Warwick's loss of the Channel Islands was reconfirmed with the appointment of John Nanfan as Governor. At least, Nanfan was Warwick's man and would prove loyal to him.

Piracy was not new. The Calais garrison supplemented their wages, or made up on their arrears, by profitable raids on merchants plying their trade through and along the Dover straits. Warwick himself suffered when in November 1455, two of his own fishing boats and presumably their catches were taken. On 4th March 1457 Warwick was commissioned on to arrest Andrew Trollope, a member of the Calais garrison, in connection with the seizure of Hanseatic cloth from an English ship owned by Lord Roos. No action was seemingly taken. Trollope was implicated soon after in the taking at Tilbury of three ships with wool. In April, Warwick was once more asked to look into piracy from Calais on Burgundian ships. [144]

Three larger ventures in the summer of 1458 received much publicity and attention in England. On 28th May he attacked a Spanish fleet of 22 ships. Six ships were taken and another six sunk. Warwick lost 80 men killed and 200 captured. A French commentator remarked "there was not so great a battle upon the sea this winter." Later that summer, seventeen Hanseatic ships were attacked returning from La Rochelle. The Hanse complained to King Henry who appointed a commission to look into the matter. This did not stop Warwick. His men set upon a small group of vessels from Genoa and Spain. All but one ship was taken. [145]

---

[143] *Warwick the Kingmaker* by Michael Hicks. Blackwell Publishers 1998. Countdown to Civil War 1456-9. Page 131.
[144] *Warwick the Kingmaker* by Michael Hicks. Blackwell Publishers 1998. Countdown to Civil War 1456-9. Page 146.
[145] *Warwick the Kingmaker* by Michael Hicks. Blackwell Publishers 1998. Countdown to Civil War 1456-9. Page 147.

Warwick was treading a fine but profitable and popular line. Warwick's commission as keeper
of the seas authorized him to 'arrest sufficient vessels and ships to serve at the usual wages and masters and mariners ... and the victuals necessary' in order to fulfil the role and meet his responsibilities. [146] Evidence is mixed on the actual level of concern for his activities at sea.

Chroniclers and others spread word of his exploits. Attacks on those with special privileges and foreign ships found favour with many, aside from his opponents and those on the receiving end. England was still at war with France and Spain (Castile) was its ally. Success on the seas helped build his reputation.

Bale was just one chronicler who marvelled at his exploits... "The Earl of Warwick being in Kent had gathered a great fellowship and a navy of ships intending to keep the sea and to meet with the fleet of Spain and do some enterprise upon the sea in resisting the malice of the King and the Lord's adversaries wherein that no Lord of the land took the jeopardy nor laboured for the honour and profit of the King and the land but only he, for the which manhood and his great policy and deeds doing of worship in fortifying of Calais and other feats of arms that all the commonality of this land had him in great laud and charity... and so reputed and taken for as famous a knight as was living." [147]

Not everyone in government agreed with attacks on the ships of friendly or neutral nations. Exeter wanted his job back. Somerset had very strong personal and business reasons for seeking Warwick's downfall. Warwick undoubtedly by many of his actions fuelled the arguments of those who opposed him and wanted revenge. However, for the merchants of London and the Commons, Warwick was becoming a true Englishman of great

---

[146] *Calendar of Patent Rolls 1452–61* Page 413.
[147] *Warwick the Kingmaker Politics, Power and Fame* by A.J. Pollard. Continuum Books 2007. Pages 5-6. Bale's Chronicle Page 147 in *Six Town Chronicles* edited by R. Flenley. Oxford 1911.

renown. Henry VI wanted a peaceful life but at least Warwick was successful.

Penny Tucker in a well-argued article on Warwick's use of sea power concluded… "Objectionable though Warwick and his actions may have been to his political enemies, there is no good reason to believe that he was disobeying his orders or engaging in piracy, let alone, that his maritime misconduct in 1458 and 1459 caused the arrangements agreed as part of the reconciliation to collapse. [148]

---

[148] *The Earl of Warwick's Use of Sea-Power in the Late 1450s* by Penny Tucker. Southern History Review. June 2022.

Love Day

…This cloaked pageant and dissimulating procession… For their bodies were joined by hand in hand, whose hearts were far asunder: their mouths lovingly smiled, whose minds were inflamed with malice: their tongues spoke like sugar, and their thoughts were all hostile… [149]

Henry VI chose in the Spring of 1457 to sit in judgement over Devereux and Herbert at Hereford on a commission of oyer and terminer. Imprisonment followed though they were perhaps fortunate to escape worse punishment. The King's half-brother, Edmund Tudor, had died of the plague subsequent to being held prisoner by Herbert.

York did however receive compensation for the loss of his Welsh castles which "at the King's desire he has granted to the King's brother, Jasper, Earl of Pembroke". The Calendar of Patent Rolls on 21st April 1457 notes a grant of £40 a year. [150]

York, Salisbury and Warwick were not officially excluded from Government, but they withdrew from court and Council. Warwick remained in Calais. York and Salisbury tended their estates and business affairs. The normal arguments and agreements of political life ground to a halt. Not much happened of note through the summer. On 1st September 1457, Warwick's brother, Sir Thomas Neville, was recognised and recompensed for his role as acting as lieutenant for Warwick and Salisbury in the West Marches where they held the joint role.

In the autumn, they were summoned to Council. but there appears to have been little progress. No real mention is made of the discussions therein in the chronicles. The only report is of yet more intended trouble. Exeter and Somerset tried to ambush Warwick on his way to London on 5th November but "thanked be God, the said

---

[149] *Hall's Chronicle: Containing the History of England*, by Edward Hall. Published by Forgotten Books 2018. Originally published by Richard Grafton 1548. Page 238.
[150] *The End of the House of Lancaster* by R.L. Storey. London 1966. Page 181.

Earl was thereof aware and purveyed a remedy against their malice and came in safety to the city". The chronicler was clearly pro Warwick and continued "for they dare not counter him for he was named and taken in all places as the most courageous and manliest knight living". [151]

Henry VI was unhappy with the state of affairs. The King wanted peace in his Kingdom and summoned his Lords in January 1458 to a Great Council at Westminster "to set apart such variances as be between various Lords of this our realm". We know there was much unease and fear of strife in London at this gathering of the dissenting nobles. A chronicler reported that the mayor, Geoffrey Boleyn, "had daily in harness 5,000 citizens and rode daily about the city and suburbs to see the King's peace were kept; and nightly he provided for 3,000 men in harness to give attendance upon three aldermen, and they kept the night-watch until seven o clock in the morning, until the day-watch were assembled". [152] All the protagonists brought their own retinues. Accounts vary but significant numbers of armed men descended on London in their various colours.

York lodged at his residence at Baynard's castle. Salisbury made use of the Neville's London home, the Erber. Warwick stayed with his father but arrived later around mid-February. He needed to await favourable winds in order to cross from Calais. Warwick was reported as bringing 600 men. They would have been dressed in red jackets with the *bear and ragged staff* badge of Warwick on their front and back.

Somerset, Exeter, Northumberland, Egremont and Clifford and their men were refused entrance to the city "because they came against the peace... to destroy utterly the said Duke of York and the Earls of Salisbury and Warwick... the city was every day armed for

---

[151] *Bale's Chronicle, Six Town Chronicles of England* edited by R. Flenley. Clarendon Press Oxford 1911. Page 144.
[152] *The New Chronicle of England and France in two parts by Robert Fabyan* edited by Henry Ellis. London 1811.

to withstand the malice of those young Lords if needed." [153] The young Lords had to find accommodation outside the city walls.

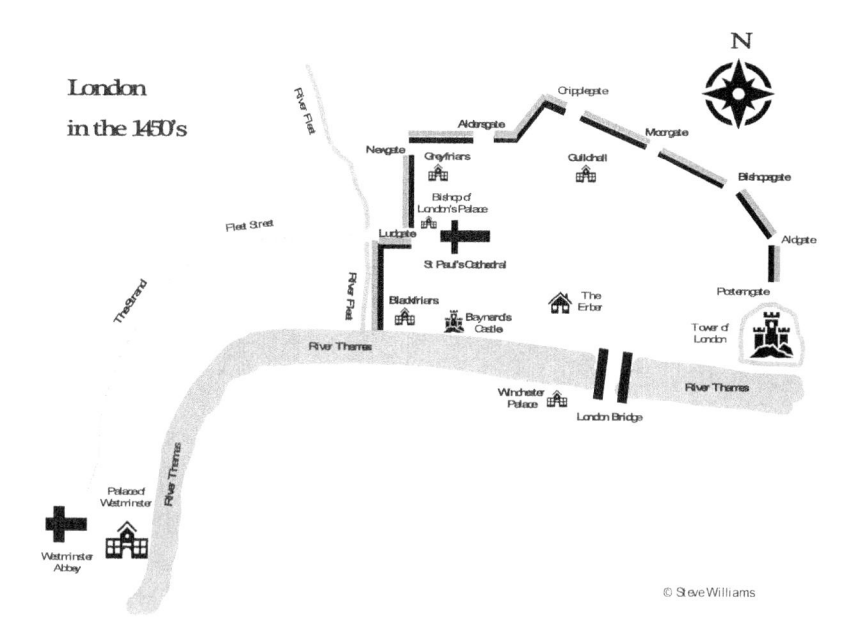

London in the 1450's

(Map showing London in the 1450's with landmarks including Cripplegate, Aldersgate, Moorgate, Newgate, Greyfriars, Guildhall, Bishopsgate, Bishop of London's Palace, Fleet Street, Ludgate, St Paul's Cathedral, Aldgate, The Strand, River Fleet, Blackfriars, Baynard's Castle, The Erber, Postengate, Tower of London, River Thames, Winchester Palace, London Bridge, Palace of Westminster, Westminster Abbey. © Steve Williams)

William Botener wrote to update Sir John Falstolf on events in a letter dated 1st February 1458, "The King came last week to Westminster, and The Duke of York came to London with his own household only to the number of 140 horses, the Earl of Salisbury with 400 horses in his company, four score Knights and Squires. The Duke of Somerset came to London the last day of January with 200 horses and lodges without Temple Bar. And the Duke of Exeter shall be here this week with a great fellowship and strong, it is said. The Earl of Warwick is not yet come, because the wind is not for him; and the Duke of Exeter taketh a great displeasure that my Lord

---

[153] *An English Chronicle of the Reigns of Richard II, Henry IV, Henry V, and Henry VI* edited by J.S. Davies. Camden Society 1856.

Page 86

Warwick occupieth his office and taketh charge of the keeping of the sea upon him." [154]

York and Salisbury learnt of a plot by Northumberland, Egremont and Clifford to ambush them on route to Westminster but changed their plans and were more cautious in their travel arrangements.

The King opened Council with a personal plea for peace and an end to dissension amongst the Lords. The troubles between them would be settled by arbitration. Compromises would be needed for the sake of the realm. The King himself would sit in final judgement. The process would be assisted by Bishops and the King's Judges. Henry removed himself to Berkhamsted Castle to stay distant but remain close enough.

Consultations took place. York, Salisbury and Warwick attended morning sessions at Blackfriars. Somerset, Northumberland, Egremont and Clifford had afternoon sessions at Whitefriars in Fleet Street. [155] Compensation and atonement arrangements between the Lords were negotiated, documented and agreed.

The King required a settlement of the variances between them "for the tranquillity and conservation of his realm and territories and against external threats". Such divisions bad for "sane direction and rule at home" and were very much welcomed by foreign enemies such as France. The moderations were to resolve "controversies and differences… caused principally by a certain siege and attack before this time at the town of St Albans".

---

[154] *Selections From the Paston Letters* by Sir John Fenn. Ed. A. Greenwood. London 1920. Forgotten Books. Pages 88-9.
[155] *The Chronicles of The White Rose of York:* Edited by James Bohn. Published London 1845. Introduction Page lxiv. Letter to Sir John Fastolf from John Bocking 15th March 1458. Fenn's Paston Letters Volume 1 Page 155.

An agreement was reached. A chantry would be endowed by the Yorkists with income of £45 a year to pray for the souls of the dead. York was to pay the Dowager Duchess of Somerset and the new Duke 2,500 marks (£1,666) each. Warwick was to pay Clifford 1,000 marks. Salisbury would forgo fines due from Egremont. The payments were offset against royal debts. York even agreed profitable new licences to export wool. Penalties were set for non-compliance. Egremont's conviction and escape were set aside but he needed to post a bond for 4,000 marks to keep the peace. [156]

The financial arrangements were not onerous. Henry seemed to understand that peace required no-one to remain aggrieved due to the terms of settlement and was not averse to encouraging reconciliation through monetary sleights of hand. Henry is a much-criticised King. In the eyes of many since, subsequent events belittled the agreement and accord reached. Contemporary chronicles were more hopeful and optimistic that this might be a turning point. It is what the Commons, the Merchants and the King wanted, whatever was in the hearts and minds of the participating Lords. Exeter remained unhappy, "…my Lord of Exeter is displeased that the Earl of Warwick shall keep the Sea…" [157]

Henry did insist on a very public demonstration of peace and unity and a religious celebration, blessing and thanks. On 25th March 1458, on the feast of the Annunciation of the Blessed Virgin Mary (Lady Day) there was a great procession of Lords temporal and spiritual to St Pauls. Salisbury walked alongside Somerset and Warwick by Exeter. The King followed, his crown on show and behind, Queen Margaret walked alongside York "with great familiarity". The Tudor historian Grafton captures the scene thus,

---

[156] *Registrum Abbatiae Johannis Whethamstede* by Abbot J. Whethamstede. Edited by H.T. Riley. 1872. Page 298.
[157] *The Chronicles of The White Rose of York:* Edited by James Bohn. Published London 1845. Introduction Page lxv. Letter to Sir John Fastolf from John Bocking 15th March 1458. Fenn's Paston Letters Volume 1 Page 155.

"their bodies were joined hand in hand, whose hearts were far asunder". [158]

A contemporary ballad written by a John Lydgate commemorated what became known as 'Love Day'.

"Rejoice, and thank God for evermore,
For now, shall increase this consolation;
Our enemies quake and dread full sore,
That peace is made, there was division,
Which to them is great confusion,
And to us joy and felicity;
God hold them long in every season,
That England may rejoice, the concord and unite.

Now is sorrow with shame fled into France,
As a felon that hath forsworn this land;
Love hath put out malicious governance,
In every place both free and bonded
In York, in Somerset, as I understand,
In Warwick also is love and charity,
In Salisbury, in Northumberland,
That every man may rejoice in concord and unite.

At St Paul's in London, with great renown,
On our Lady Day the peace was wrought;
The King, the Queen, with Lords many one,
To worship that virgin as they ought,
Went a procession. And spared right nought,
In sight of all the commonality,
In token that love was in heart and thought;

---

[158] *Richard, Duke of York, King by Right* by Matthew Lewis. Amberley Publishing 2017. Page 274.

Rejoice England the concord and unite." [159]

Another ballad of the time, *On the Ship or Poop*, had Henry as "the noble ship of good tree" and his son, Prince Edward as the mast. All the King's nobles made up the rest of the ship in wholesome unity. St George was the figurehead leading the way. [160]

---

[159] *Historical Poems of the Fourteenth and Fifteenth Centuries* edited by R.H. Robbins. New York 1959. Page 194.
[160] *Historical Poems of the Fourteenth and Fifteenth Centuries* edited by R.H. Robbins. New York 1959. Pages 191-193.

The Road to Ludford

> ...*The King's part, however, waxed stronger and stronger every day in consequence of endless multitudes of the nobles and common people, who now flocked together to his support; and the more especially after Andrew Trollope and his paid followers, from Calais, who had been summoned by the Earl of Warwick, their captain, from the parts beyond the sea, as though to aid the King, had deserted the Duke of York* ... [161]

Things seemed to improve for a while but there was unrest in London in the Spring... "a great fray between the city of London and the men of court, who were driven with archers of the city from standard in Fleet Street to their Inns the 13th day of April, and some were slain, and some were taken". Warwick rode through the city on 9th May at the King's command to make a strong display "in embassy with a goodly fellowship" of Warwick's brothers and Bishop Richard Beauchamp of Salisbury. [162]

Warwick stayed at Canterbury on 11th May and sailed to Calais the next day. Formal letters of instruction were issued on 14th May for negotiations with Burgundy on breaches of the agreement between the two countries. Warwick as Captain of Calais led discussions.

Peace at home meant attention could be focused through the summer on securing peace on, and over, the seas. Diplomatic initiatives with the envoys of both France and Burgundy took place. There were discussions with both countries on securing marriage treaties involving Prince Edward, Somerset and a son of York, presumably Edward, but nothing came from them.

---

[161] *Ingulph's Chronicle of the Abbey of Croyland:* with the continuations by Peter of Blois and Anonymous writers. Translated by Henry Riley. Published by Nabu Press 2014. Originally published 1854. Written 1486. Page 454.
[162] *Bale's Chronicle, The Chronicle of John Stone* edited by W.G. Searle. Cambridge Antiquarian Society 1902. Page 73.

Henry spent Easter at St Alban's Abbey, before moving on to Greenwich Palace and then his hunting lodge at Woodstock. Autumn saw him back at the abbey at St Albans. The King's interest in affairs of the state was not high.

Warwick's seafaring activities, some might say piracy, were causing consternation and by the Autumn of 1458, there were worries that Warwick's raids on shipping were putting at risk England's safety, security and prosperity. Trade was being prejudiced. Relations with other countries were being damaged increasing the possibility of revenge attacks on English coasts. Chancellor Wayneflete wrote to Southampton on 7th September expressing such sentiments. [163]

Warwick was summoned to Westminster to account for his actions at Council on 11th October. Warwick delayed his attendance until pressed by the King. At Westminster he became caught up in a fracas between his men and some of the King's household.

Fabyan wrote that Warwick was attacked unexpectedly by the King's servants… "An affray happened between a servant of the King and a servant of the Earl of Warwick, who hurt the King's servant and after escaped. Wherefore the King's other menial servants seeing they might not be avenged upon the party that thus had hurt their fellow, as the said Earl of Warwick was coming from the Council, and was going toward his barge, the King's servants came unwarily upon him so aggressively, that the cooks with their spit forks and other officers with their weapons came running as mad men, intending to have slain him, so that he escaped with great danger and took to his barge and in all haste rowed to London, not without great hurt received by many of his servants… in so much as the Queen's Council would have the said Earl arrested and

---

[163] *Letters of the Fifteenth and Sixteenth Centuries from the Archive of Southampton* edited by R.C. Anderson. Southampton Record Society xxii 1921. Pages 12-13.

committed into the Tower… he shortly after departed… and so sallied to Calais…" [164]

Contemporary reports are confused. Some report that Warwick was removed from office. The English Chronicle says he was replaced by Somerset, but Warwick refused to give up his position. [165] Bale reports that the altercation started by accident and tempers flared, and weapons were drawn. Warwick fled the scene by barge to avoid being blamed for the brawl with the King's men and being arrested. [166]

Warwick reportedly saw it as an attempt on his life and swiftly made his way back to Calais. [167] "The Duke of York and the Earl of Salisbury, somewhat stirred, and moved with this double dealing, began to grudge and murmur". [168]

Gregory's Chronicle notes that after this time, the Lords never came together, in council or Parliament, except "in field with spear and shield". [169] Fabyan reported that "the old rancour and malice, which never was cleanly cured, anon began to break out". [170] It does seem like a turning point. "By this unhappy fray, and sudden chance of

---

[164] *The New Chronicles of England and France* by Robert Fabyan. Edited by Henry Ellis London 1811. Forgotten Books 2018. Originally edition by Pynson 1516. Page 634.
[165] *Warwick the Kingmaker Politics, Power and Fame* by A.J. Pollard. Continuum Books 2007. York's Lieutenant. Page 38.
[166] *Bale's Chronicle, Six Town Chronicles of England* edited by R. Flenley. Clarendon Press Oxford 1911. Page 113.
[167] *Recueil des Croniques et Anciennes Istories de la Grant Bretaigne* by J. de Waurin, edited by W. Hardy 1864-91.
[168] *The Chronicles of The White Rose of York:* Edited by James Bohn. Published London 1845. Paperback Version Reprint 2012. Introduction Page lxvii.
[169] *William Gregory's Chronicle of a Citizen of London in the Fifteenth Century* edited by J. Gairdner. London 1876.
[170] *New Chronicles of England and France* by Robert Fabyan. London 1811. Page 634.

malice, there arose such daily and terrible war, that every man was in trouble and no person was in quiet". [171]

500 pikes and 500 leaden clubs were ordered on 2nd December for the royal household in order to protect the King from "certain misruled and seditious persons", Three large guns were also acquired. [172]

There is a lack of clarity and record as to what occurred exactly over the next six months or so and why. It is inviting to the historian to link events knowing what happened next.

The omens were not good. The English Chronicle reported that "in a little town in Bedfordshire, there fell a bloody rain, whereof the red drops appeared in sheets, which a woman had hanged out to dry... The realm of England was out of all good governance... the King was simple and led by a covetous council and owes more than he is worth". The Queen "ruled the realm as she liked" and sought the King's resignation in favour of Prince Edward.[173] Much was blamed upon the Queen, that in her "rested nothing but fraud and feminine malice, who ruling the King at her pleasure and will, studied nothing so much, as the destruction of the nobility, and peers of the realm". [174] And she was French by birth…

A Council was held in January 1459. Exeter was arrested for assaulting a lawyer. Another Council sat in April. Attendance was poor. Relations with France deteriorated. There was talk of further raids on the English coast by their ships. The Scots attacked Roxburgh. Warwick remained in Calais. Salisbury left London and was at Middleham by 10th May when he made his will.

---

[171] *The Chronicles of The White Rose of York:* Edited by James Bohn. Published London 1845. Paperback Version Reprint 2012. Introduction Page lxvii.
[172] *Public Records Office* E.404/71/3/43.
[173] *An English Chronicle* edited by J.S. Davies. Camden Society 1856. Page 79.
[174] *The Chronicles of The White Rose of York:* Edited by James Bohn. Published London 1845. Paperback Version Reprint 2012. Introduction Page lxvii.

Margaret Paston wrote to her brother John on 29th April 1459 telling him that "on Thursday last was there brought into this town many privy seals" signed "with the King's own hand" including one for him, and another for his son. It was a call from the King for them to bring "as many persons defensibly arrayed as they might according to their degree" to him at Leicester, by the tenth day of May, with expenses for two months. The Queen raised armed men in Cheshire who dressed in the livery of her son, the Prince of Wales.

Queen Margaret was reportedly behind the move back to the Midlands for the royal family and the court at the end of May. Kenilworth castle was fortified in preparation. 3,000 bowstaves and sheaves of arrows were ordered on 7th May 1459 "considering the enemies on every side approaching us, as well upon the sea as upon the land". [175] Jasper Tudor, the Earl of Pembroke and the King's half-brother, was left in charge to protect and defend the Palace at Westminster in the absence of the King. The phrase "enemies on every side" probably refers to Scotland and France but it may also have referred to the Yorkists as well.

A Council was called to meet in Coventry at the end of June. It seems that despite Henry's hopes and prayers, dissension had arisen once more amongst his nobles. In later Yorkist accounts, Queen Margaret is implicated as leading the move against York and his Neville allies. The council was not well attended nor unfortunately do records survive. We are reliant on deducing what happened through brief mentions by chroniclers, and what happened next. Chancellor Wayneflete set out the charges against York. Buckingham argued vehemently for justice. Henry though would not agree with the judgement of the Lords present that York had committed treasonable activities, time and again.

Buckingham begged the King that York and others "so often charged" should be shown no more mercy and should receive their just "desserts and have as they deserved" and this was required "seeing the great jeopardy for your most noble person" for "the

---

[175] *Public Records Office* E.28/88/49.

security of you, sovereign Lord, and the general security of all your Lords and people". [176] Buckingham did leave Coventry with something. On 20th July his second son Henry and his new wife, Margaret Beaufort, were granted an annuity of £600 a year.

York, Salisbury and Warwick felt as outcasts in their own country despite being of royal blood. "The Duke of York, the Earls of Warwick and Salisbury, saw that the government of the realm stood most by the Queen and her council, and how the great princes of the land were not called to council but set apart; and not only so but that it was said through the realm that the said Lords shall be destroyed utterly". [177] They made preparations to visit themselves upon the King at Kenilworth in order to press upon him their loyalty, once more. Salisbury gathered together the men of Middleham and the surrounding areas. York was at Ludlow raising his men of the Welsh Marches. Warwick called upon the men of Calais for help against the evil counsellors who only sought to "enrich themselves, peeled the poor people and disinherited rightful heirs and did many wrongs".

Warwick issued a manifesto on behalf of his father Salisbury and uncle York. They expected help from "Lords of like disposition" and complained of the "utter malice against them as the very lovers of the common weal". An audience with the King was sought to open his eyes to the "parlous" state of the country and the action he needed to take for the benefit of all. Good government had been overturned. Crown property had been taken over such the royal finances were in disorder. Unfair taxes had impoverished merchants and the people. All sorts of crimes had been allowed, encouraged rather than punished. Those close to the King had hidden these things from him. They sought the help of the King to redress all

---

[176] *The Nevills of Middleham* by K.L. Clark. The History Press 2016. The Gathering Storm. Page 171.
[177] *The Brut*. Friedrich W.D. Brie. Early English Text Society London 1905. Pages 526-527.

these evils. They wanted to replace those around the throne, not the King himself. [178]

Salisbury set off from Middleham mid-September with his sons, Thomas and John, and a sizeable army of retainers to join York at Ludlow. The King initially conducted a short circuit through the Midlands from Coventry to Nuneaton, Burton upon Trent, Lichfield, Coleshill and back to raise troops. On 20th September, Henry marched his forces from Coventry to Market Harborough and on to Nottingham so blocking the path south to the Midlands down the Great North Road.

Salisbury's army marched around Clifford's stronghold at Skipton to Halifax and turned west, before turning south once more. They stayed overnight outside the towns of Hyde, Macclesfield and Newcastle under Lyme. Salisbury passes close to his son-in-law Baron Thomas Stanley who is married to his daughter Eleanor. Stanley has only recently inherited the title and lands after the death of his father. Thomas's younger brother William rode with Salisbury along with the Cheshire knights, Robert Bold and Henry Radford who acted as guides.

---

[178] *The Chronicles of The White Rose of York:* Edited by James Bohn. Published London 1845. Paperback Version Reprint 2012. Introduction Page lxviii. Based upon Harleian MSS 543 Page 164.

Salisbury's March to Ludlow September 1459

Salisbury neared Market Drayton on 23rd September. The King moved west from Nottingham. The Queen with another army advanced north and had reached Eccleshall only nine miles distant. Stanley followed behind with his men, but his loyalties were unknown. Another army under the command of James Tuchet, 5th Baron Audley and John Sutton, 1st Baron Dudley marched south from Cheshire. Audley clashed with Salisbury at Blore Heath where "both companies ran together and had a strong bickering". [179]

---

[179] *The New Chronicles of England and France* by Robert Fabyan. Edited by Henry Ellis London 1811. Forgotten Books 2018. Originally edition by Pynson 1516. Page 634.

The Battle of Blore Heath 23rd September 1459

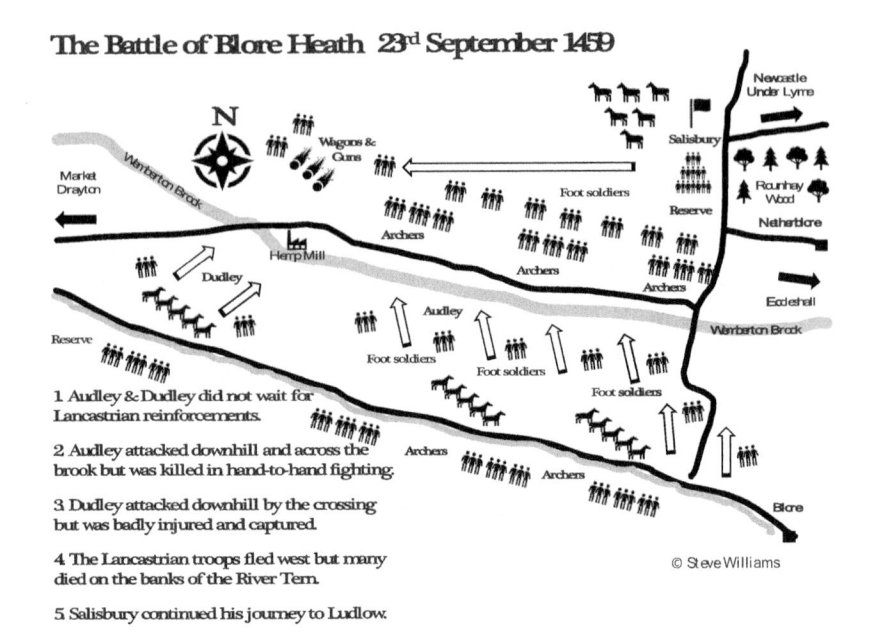

Map labels:
- N (compass)
- Newcastle Under Lyme
- Market Drayton
- Wemberton Brook
- Wagons & Guns
- Salisbury
- Hemp Mill
- Dudley
- Archers
- Foot soldiers
- Reserve
- Rounhay Wood
- Netherlore
- Audley
- Eccleshall
- Wemberton Brook
- Blore

1. Audley & Dudley did not wait for Lancastrian reinforcements.
2. Audley attacked downhill and across the brook but was killed in hand-to-hand fighting.
3. Dudley attacked downhill by the crossing but was badly injured and captured.
4. The Lancastrian troops fled west but many died on the banks of the River Tern.
5. Salisbury continued his journey to Ludlow.

© Steve Williams

Salisbury's men approached through Rounhay wood. The banners of the Lancastrian army fluttered in the distance across the valley on the high ground near Blore village. A sizeable contingent of archers from Cheshire were deployed behind the hedgerow along the ridge.

Salisbury did not want or need a battle against the royal army. A messenger was sent to negotiate safe passage. It was refused. Audley demanded surrender. Salisbury refused and sent his wagons and guns down to the lower crossing of Wemberton brook. They were positioned to cover the crossing. The main forces of his men were lined up in formation within arrow shot of the brook.

Audley and Dudley were well placed. Time was on their side, yet they chose to attack. They perhaps did not want to share the glory of victory with the other royal armies moving to join them. Salisbury possibly feigned retreat. Whatever the reason, Audley's mounted soldiers charged downhill to cross the brook east of the mill pond. The foot soldiers followed on. The attack foundered in the face of an arrow storm and strong defensive action.

Page 99

The "fight was sore and dreadful". Audley was killed in fierce hand to hand fighting by Roger Kynaston, York's constable of Denbigh castle. Dudley was badly injured and captured. The Cheshire knights and squires fled leaving the foot soldiers to be trapped and slaughtered in 'Deadman's Den' on the banks of the river Tern. The baggage wagons at Market Drayton were looted. The wounded men left behind by Salisbury included Thomas and John Neville. They were captured at Acton Bridge whilst trying to make their way home but are quickly released on the orders of Lord Stanley.

Salisbury pressed on as quickly as he could to avoid the other nearby royal armies. Gregory's chronicle tells the tale of an Augustine friar left to fire captured royalist guns through the night to discourage any advances by the Queen's army at Eccleshall.[180] Men had been lost, arms and munitions expended. Most importantly it was never the plan to engage with royal forces. Fighting "was not their intent but happened casually and against their will".

Warwick was in London on 20th September before heading north. On the 21st he passed through Midlands and narrowly avoided a confrontation with Somerset and his men before meeting up with Salisbury and York at Ludlow.

York and the Nevilles marched their army south alongside the river Teme towards Worcester. Word was sent to the King that they wished to talk. The King sent his emissary, Richard Beauchamp, Bishop of Salisbury. They swore loyalty and documented the same before having it consecrated before God in the cathedral.

Henry offered a pardon to York and Warwick and grace to their men. The offer was rejected. Previous pardons had done them no good. Their loyalty had been called into question and they had been excluded from government. Somerset and Exeter, the King's relatives, did as they pleased. Warwick had been attacked at

---

[180] *William Gregory's Chronicle of a Citizen of London in the Fifteenth Century* edited by J. Gairdner. London 1876.

Westminster.[181] Salisbury and others were excluded from the offer of pardon. Salisbury and all who fought with him at Blore's Heath, including Warwick's two brothers, had been declared traitors for it was treason to fight against, and kill, the King's men.

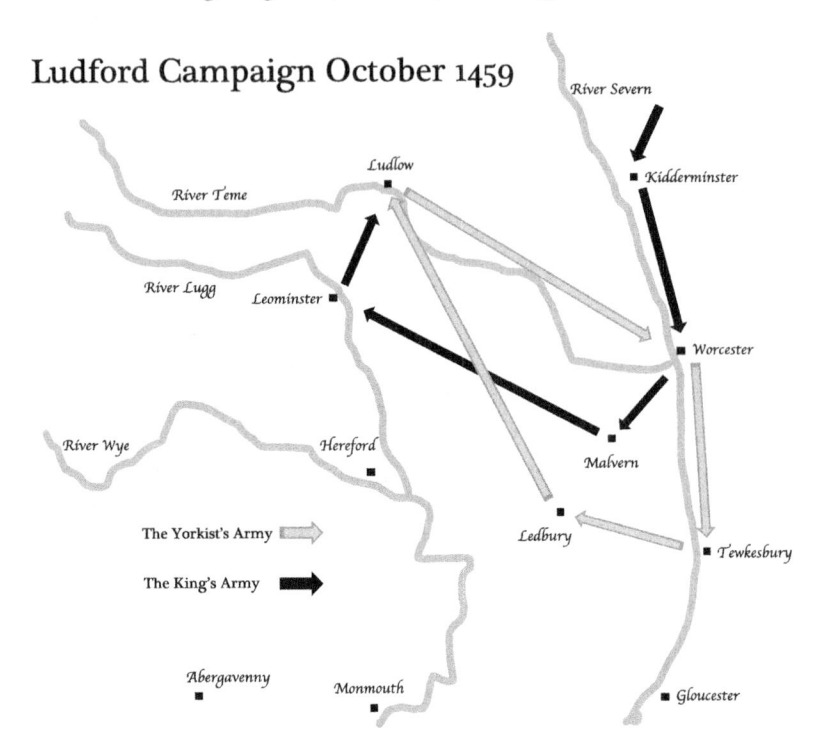

Ludford Campaign October 1459

Henry's army moved south towards them and had reached Kidderminster. York and the Nevilles withdrew to Tewkesbury. The royal army moved to Malvern threatening to cut off their retreat, so they hurriedly made their way back to Ludlow, via Ledbury, where they took up defensive positions nearby at Ludford. They were shadowed by the King's men who camped just ten miles distant outside Leominster before moving up closer to Ludlow.

---

[181] *The Chronicles of The White Rose of York:* Edited by James Bohn. Published London 1845. Paperback Version Reprint 2012. Introduction Page lxix. Whethempstede Page 457.

The King's camp increased daily as more Lords joined him with their retinues. Salisbury's numbers were much reduced after the battle at Blore Heath. Warwick had brought men from Calais but his retinues in the Midlands and South Wales were required there for defensive duties. York had raised some men from the Welsh Marches, but Herbert and the Vaughans had cautiously remained at home having been reprimanded and bound over by the King two years previously.

On 9th October, a summons was sent out by the King from Leominster for Parliament to meet in the Autumn on 20th November. York, Salisbury and Warwick were not included. The message was clear. The rebellious Lords were to be punished.

The following day on 10th October, York and the two Earls sought the King's forbearance asking him to "receive our truth and intent" and not to give his weight or blessing to those "of extreme malice" who wish "under shadow of your high might and presence" to destroy them being "covetousness of our lands". They promised not to use their forces unless needed for their own defence. [182] The letter to the "most Christian King" sought a peaceful resolution to avoid "the loss of Christian blood". But it was to no avail.

Henry was in no mood to concede. Life and liberty were still selectively on offer but no more. Reports of a rousing speech such as that his father gave at Agincourt are probably well wide of the mark. The King's standard was raised, Henry was dressed in armour and crown and paraded on horseback. Rumours of his ill-health, even death, spread by the Yorkists were demonstrably untrue. Pardon was offered to those who gave up their arms.

---

[182] *The Chronicles of The White Rose of York:* Edited by James Bohn. Published London 1845. Paperback Version Reprint 2012. Introduction Page lxix. Stowe's Chronicle Page 405.

The Battle of Ludford Bridge 12th October 1459

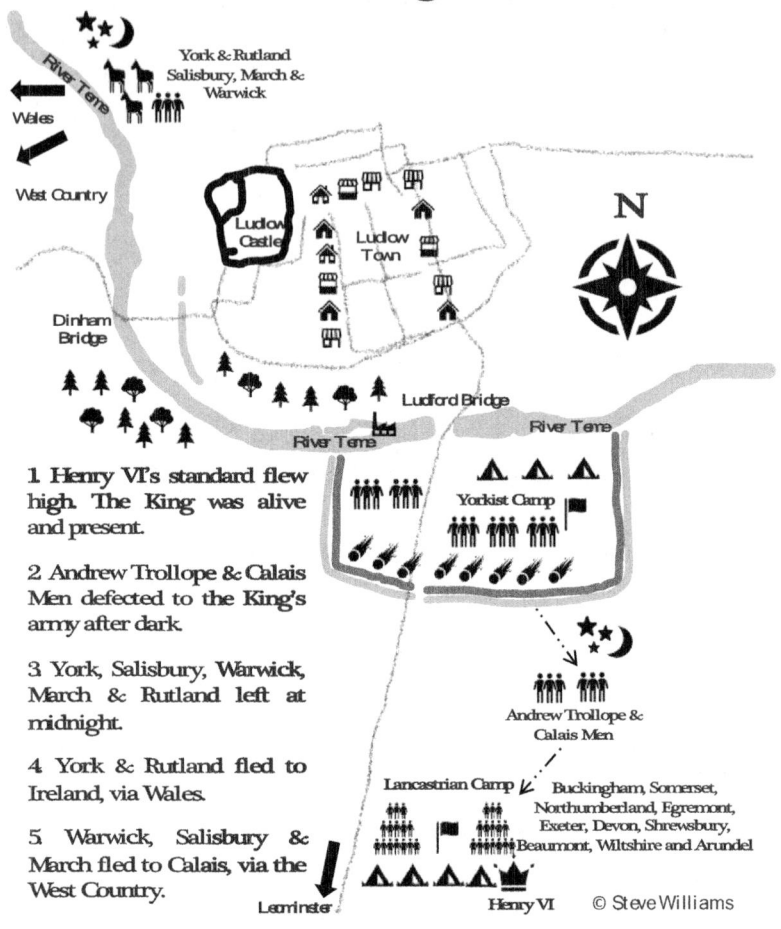

Map showing positions at the Battle of Ludford Bridge, including Ludlow Castle, Ludlow Town, Dinham Bridge, Ludford Bridge, River Teme, the Yorkist Camp and Lancastrian Camp. © Steve Williams

Key locations and forces:
- York & Rutland, Salisbury, March & Warwick (north of River Teme)
- Wales (west)
- West Country (southwest)
- Yorkist Camp
- Andrew Trollope & Calais Men
- Lancastrian Camp: Buckingham, Somerset, Northumberland, Egremont, Exeter, Devon, Shrewsbury, Beaumont, Wiltshire and Arundel
- Henry VI
- Leominster (south)

1. Henry VI's standard flew high. The King was alive and present.

2. Andrew Trollope & Calais Men defected to the King's army after dark.

3. York, Salisbury, Warwick, March & Rutland left at midnight.

4. York & Rutland fled to Ireland, via Wales.

5. Warwick, Salisbury & March fled to Calais, via the West Country.

Andrew Trollope and the men of Calais climbed over the earthworks and made their way to the King's camp under cover of darkness on 12th October "…for finding that contrary to their expectations they had really been brought over to act against the King, they left the Duke of York, and sided with the King, whose

Page 103

provisions and pay they had been in the habit of receiving". [183] "They were received joyously, for they knew the intent of the other Lords and also the manner of their field" [184] It was a grievous loss and a bad example to others. The Yorkists had not just seen their most professional and experienced soldiers abscond, but their enemies would now know all their plans and the layout of their defences.

Late night discussions ensued in Ludlow castle when news of Trollope's defection reached the Yorkist Lords. They were unwilling to compromise and throw themselves on the mercy of Henry. Salisbury in any case was excluded from the King's offer of grace. York, Salisbury and Warwick could not stay and fight. The King's army was too large. More men might defect. They wisely decided to flee and fight another day. They left the castle around midnight through a back gate, making their way north along the river Teme before turning west and making good their escape.

York and his younger son, Edmund, Earl of Rutland, headed west through Wales for the coast and a boat to Ireland.

Warwick, Salisbury and Edward, Earl of March, headed south to Warwick's estates in South Wales, and then the West Country before crossing the Channel to Calais.

The Croyland chronicler remarked that it was "...not so much a battle as a semblance of a battle… at the town of Ludlow, in the Marches of Wales, in the month of October". [185]

---

[183] *Ingulph's Chronicle of the Abbey of Croyland:* with the continuations by Peter of Blois and Anonymous writers. Translated by Henry Riley. Published by Nabu Press 2014. Originally published 1854. Written 1486. Page 454.
[184] *The Brut or the Chronicles of England* edited by F.W.D. Brie London 1906. Page 520.
[185] *Ingulph's Chronicle of the Abbey of Croyland:* with the continuations by Peter of Blois and Anonymous writers. Translated by Henry Riley. Published by Nabu Press 2014. Originally published 1854. Written 1486. Page 455.

The Parliament of Devils

> *...They ferociously broke in by the garden sides between the sign of The Key and the sign of The Chequer in Holywell Street, and immediately they were within the town, suddenly they blew up trumpets, and set a cry with a shout and a great voice... A Warwick! A Warwick ...* [186]

Ludlow awoke the next morning to find the Duke of York and his fellow rebel Lords had gone. Those who remained quickly gave themselves up to the King and his followers, laying down their arms and being granted pardon. Few lives were lost. Heads may not have rolled but significant monetary penalties were levied. One John Russell was fined £40 on 13th October 1459 for his indiscretions "in the fields of Ludford, beside Ludlow". [187]

Search parties were sent out in all directions. "Upon the morrow, when all this coven was known to the King and the Lords in his party, there was sending and running with all speed toward every coast to take these Lords, but none might be found. And forthwith, the King rode into Ludlow and despoiled the town and castle and sent the Duchess of York with her children to her sister the Duchess of Buckingham where she rested long after." [188]

The royal army sacked and looted York's town of Ludlow. Gregory's chronicle reported that "when they had drunken enough of wine that was in taverns and other places, they full ungodly smote out the heads of the pipes and hogsheads of wine, that men went

---

[186] *The Stow Relation: The Stonor Variant, in The Paston Letters 1422-1509* edited by J. Gairdner. Constable and Co 1895.
[187] *The Life and Reign of Edward the Fourth King of England and of France and Lord of Ireland* by Cora L. Scofield. Volumes One and Two. Fonthill Media 2016. First Published 1923. Page 37. Note 1.
[188] *The New Chronicles of England and France* by Robert Fabyan. Edited by Henry Ellis London 1811. Forgotten Books 2018. Originally edition by Pynson 1516. Page 635.

wetshod in wine, and then they robbed the town and bare away bedding, cloth and other stuff, and defouled many women". [189]

The English Chronicle recounted that "the town of Ludlow, belonging then to the Duke of York, was robbed to the bare walls, and the noble duchess of York unmanly and cruelly treated and spoiled". [190] Another story was told that the brave Duchess of York stood by the market cross with her two young sons by her side. It is more likely that she and other wives and their children were moved elsewhere to safety in advance.

There were reports of further indiscipline as the royal soldiers looted places on the route back to Worcester despite the estates not belonging to either York or the Nevilles. It did not endear the King to his subjects in that area.

Warwick was replaced as captain of Calais by Henry Beaufort, Duke of Somerset. The Treasurer was ordered to pay Somerset, Rivers, Clifton and Thorpe £450 to meet the cost of soldiers, supplies and a ship.

Parliament opened on 20th November 1459 in the chapter house of St Mary at Coventry with a sermon from the Chancellor and Bishop of Winchester, William Wayneflete on the text *'Grace to you and peace be multiplied'*. Thomas Tresham was elected Speaker.

York and those who supported him were portrayed as traitors, driven by personal ambition, who persisted in wrongdoing in spite of the king's generous forgiveness. Cade's insurrection planned to place York on the throne. York had sworn loyalty to the King but had allied himself with Warwick and Salisbury. They had waged war at St Albans, wounding the King and killing various Lords of royal

---

[189] *William Gregory's Chronicle of a Citizen of London in the Fifteenth Century* edited by J. Gairdner. London 1876.
[190] *An English Chronicle* edited by J.S. Davies. Camden Society 1856. Page 79.

blood. The King preferring mercy before justice brought them together in accord with those whose fathers had been slain. They had sworn oaths of loyalty once more.

"And after these things had been done, your highness, trusting that tranquillity and due obedience on the part of the same duke of York and earls of Warwick and Salisbury would follow, sent for them at various times to come to your councils, which they disobeyed, and they made up false excuses of trivial business, which were, however, accepted by your highness, whereby they enriched themselves by your gifts and grants while continuing in their premeditated malice and damnable opinions and in their false and traitorous desires, and yet again falsely and traitorously conspired, seeking the time and means to accomplish their insatiable will and desire and to destroy you, sovereign lord, the queen our sovereign lady, and your descendants, and such lords of your land as they considered would, unlike them, risk their lives for you." [191]

The Yorkist Lords had planned to surprise the King and fulfil their traitorous intentions at Kenilworth. Salisbury had raised war against the King and slew Lord Audley. The King still found it within his mercy to offer pardons to York and Warwick if they and their men submitted to his grace within six days. This had been rejected. They said mass as if the King was dead and waged war against him. A follower of York named Robert Radford confessed that they wanted to take the very throne of England! In cowardice, they fled, and some went to Calais.

Warwick had been given much by the King and had been graciously granted "precedence over all the earls of your land, with other great graces, allowing him to hold various offices jointly with his father… so that your subjects should think that you were prepared to forget what had passed, your high grace made the said earl of Warwick

---

[191] *Parliamentary Rolls Henry VI* November 1459. Persistence of the duke of York in wrongdoing. Item 13.

captain of your town and castle of Calais and of the marches there, as fully as any of your uncles or any other prince or lord that was ever captain there. And moreover, you granted the same earl the governance and rule of the sea and appointed him your great captain of the sea; and to support this charge you granted him all the tonnage and poundage belonging to you in any way, together with £1,000 a year, to be taken by the hands of your receiver from the enfeoffed lands and tenements of your said duchy of Lancaster."

St Albans was an "execrable and most detestable dead". The rebel Lords had exhibited the "most diabolical unkindness and wretched envy" and "persistent treachery and ingratitude". Such "unnatural behaviour" warranted an attainder whereby all their goods and possessions were forfeited, and their heirs disinherited.

"And that they and each of them forfeit from themselves and their heirs, by the same authority, all their estates, honours and dignities, which they or any of them have within your realm of England, and within Wales and Ireland. And that the said duke of York, the earls of March, Warwick, Salisbury and Rutland, John Clinton, Lord Clinton, Thomas Neville, John Neville, Thomas Harrington, John Wenlock, James Pickering, John Conyers, Thomas Parre, John Bourchier, Edward Bourchier, William Stanley, Thomas Meryng, Thomas Colt, John Clay, Roger Eyton, Robert Boulde, Alice, William Oldhall and Thomas Vaughan, forfeit to your highness, from themselves and their heirs forever, all honours, castles, lordships, manors, lands, tenements, rents, reversions, annuities, offices, fees, advowsons, fee-farms, hereditaments and other possessions that they or any of them, or anyone else to their use, or to the use of any of them jointly or individually, have or had in fee-simple or fee-tail, within this your realm of England, and within Wales and Ireland, or in your town of Calais, and in the marches there, and in the isles of Jersey and Guernsey, on the said Friday or at any time since, from them, their heirs and assigns forever: and all the goods and chattels that they or any of them, or anyone else to their use, or to the use of any of them, have: and that they and each of them be rendered unable forever to have or enjoy any inheritance in any way hereafter within this your said realm of England, and within Wales and Ireland, and in your town of Calais, and likewise their heirs, and the heirs of each of them, are to be rendered unable forever to have or enjoy any inheritance, by them or any of them." [192]

The interests of their wives were protected aside from Countess Salisbury who "falsely and traitorously schemed and plotted the death and final destruction of you, sovereign lord". It was probably more to do because she was wealthy in her own right as the Montagu heiress and better her assets were sequestrated than left to fund the rebellious Lords.

Henry VI was praised for being "so witty, so knightly, so manly, in so comfortable wise, with so princely carrying and assured manner" that all his faithful subjects "desire was only to haste to fulfil your courageous knightly desire". Henry still showed mercy despite many shouts from those around him for what they saw as justice. The King insisted that he had the authority to grant "full pardon and restoration to those who humbly sought his grace". Lord Powys and Walter Devereux had submitted to the King after Ludford and been pardoned. The bill of attainder called for their inclusion, but Henry removed their names from the final list.

Thomas Lord Stanley was still under suspicion by many, following his non-intervention at Blore Heath. The commons judged him guilty and wanted retribution. The King declined their request.

The assembly later became known as the "Parliament of Devils" by those who wrote up events under the later Yorkist rule. Yet it seems that there was a real debate and discussion around what action might be taken. This is characterised in a text written it is thought by the

---

[192] *Parliamentary Rolls Henry VI* November 1459. Their Estates forfeited. Item 22.

Queen's man, Lawrence Booth, Bishop of Durham and Lord Privy Seal. The work is entitled *Somnium Vigilantis* or 'Dream of the Vigilant' and puts forward the arguments for and against the attainder of the Yorkist Lords. The punish or pardon debate is carried forward by two advocates, Mercy and Justice. In the absence of Parliamentary records detailing the arguments therein, it is the next best thing. The work was written up by Abbot Whethamstede of St Albans. [193]

The Yorkist spokesman argues for mercy and "labours for grace". The Yorkists are not "Lords of time passed... the latent truth is otherwise". They acted for the common good. This is no time, given England's foreign enemies, for them to be destroyed. Neither is it wise, for they are powerful and have many friends. Mercy makes sense.

The Lancastrian arguments for justice centre around the innate wickedness and malice of the rebels who have broken their oaths on many occasions. A pardon is no good. It will not stop them reoffending once more. They have caused death at St Albans and Blore Heath and "done their utmost to undo" the King. Justice is right.

The French speaking arbitrator finds in favour of justice. Pardons will leave the rebel lords strong. Exemplary punishment will weaken the King's enemies and strengthen his allies. In the event, the Yorkist Lords receive justice, but Henry reserves his right to grant mercy. The final decision to take away the lands and offices of York and the Nevilles stored up trouble which inevitably occurred. There was no attempt to bring them back into the fold. They had no incentive to do anything but prepare to take back what had been seized from them and to enforce the wider changes they wanted in government.

---

[193] *Registrum Abbatiae Johannis Whethamstede* by Abbot J. Whethamstede. Edited by H.T. Riley. 1872. Pages 346-356.

The attainder, once passed, was eagerly jumped upon by those seeking a share of lands owned or occupied by Warwick. The Beauchamp half-sisters gained parliamentary approval for a review of their inheritance claims which saw them be granted their quarter shares on 8th May 1460. Lawrence Booth, Bishop of Durham, laid claim to Barnard Castle.

Not much other business was conducted. Payments to the mayor and Staple of Calais were authorised. The Earl of Northumberland sought and received payment for keeping the Scottish border.

The last business of the Parliament was for "all the lords temporal and spiritual" to swear an oath of loyalty to Henry, his Queen and his heir, Prince Edward. Such oaths had been sworn by the Yorkist Lords but to no avail as per the subject matter of the Parliament. No matter, everyone present took the knee before their sovereign Lord on 11th December 1459 and declared their loyalty in more than a few words, signed, sealed and documented…

"I acknowledge you, most high and mighty and most Christian prince, King Henry VI, to be my most dread sovereign lord, and rightfully by succession born to reign over me and all your liege people. Whereupon I voluntarily, without coercion, promise and bind myself, by the faith and truth I owe to God, and by the faith, truth and allegiance that I owe to you, my most dread sovereign lord, that I shall be unwaveringly a true, faithful, humble and obedient subject and liegeman to you, my most dread sovereign lord; and that I shall until my life's end, at all times and places, be ready and attendant upon your calling, in my most wholehearted way and manner, as any true liegeman ought to be to his sovereign lord, promptly doing my best to do everything necessary for the weal and security of your most royal person, of your most noble estate, and the true preservation and continuance of your most high authority, pre-eminence and prerogative; for the weal, security and preservation of the person of the most high and gracious Princess Margaret the queen, my sovereign lady, and of her most high and noble estate, she being your wife; and also for the weal, security and honour of the person of the most high and mighty Prince Edward, my most dread lord the prince your first-born son, and of his most high and noble estate; and faithfully, truly and obediently, in my most humble way and manner, honour, serve, obey and hold my allegiance to you, my most dread sovereign lord, during your life, which God, the father of mercy, preserve, long to remain in prosperity, to my particular comfort: and if God in his infinite power takes you from this transitory life while I am still living, then I shall take and accept my said dread lord Prince Edward, your said first-born son, for my sovereign lord, and hold my truth, faith and allegiance to him, as my natural born sovereign lord; and after him, to his descendants lawfully begotten of his body; and in default of his descendants, which God forbid, to any other descendants lawfully begotten of your body. And that I shall never at any time, for any reason, pretext, relationship or cause, consent, lend aid, assistance or support, or agree to anything which I perceive or discover by any means to be prejudicial or contrary to the foregoing; but that I shall as soon as I have such knowledge, promptly do my best, in my most wholehearted and effective way and manner, without pretence or fraud, with my body, goods, might, power, counsel and by giving warning, to resist, withstand and subdue all those who would in any way presume to do the contrary, or any of them… so help me God and these holy gospels. In witness of which I set my seal and my signature to this document." [194]

The oath was taken by the three Dukes (Exeter, Norfolk and Buckingham) all kinsmen of York by marriage, five Earls (Pembroke, Arundel, Northumberland, Shrewsbury and Wiltshire), two viscounts (Beaumont and Bourchier) and twenty-two lords, two

---

[194] *Parliamentary Rolls Henry VI* November 1459. Oath made by the Lords below… Item 26.

archbishops (Thomas Bourchier and William Booth), sixteen bishops including Warwick's brother, George Neville, Bishop of Exeter, fourteen abbots and two Priors (Coventry and the Prior of St John's). [195]

Somerset was not present. He was busy elsewhere, trying to take possession of Calais for the King. Devon, Oxford and Westmoreland were also absent, perhaps on the King's business, perhaps not. Parliament was dissolved on 20th December. Everyone went back to their estates to celebrate Christmas. Henry and the royal family did so at Leicester.

On 20th December Henry granted Duchess Cecily 1,000 marks a year from her husband's former estates "for the relief and sustenance of her and her infants, who have not offended against us". [196]

On 21st December Exeter and Wiltshire and others were given a commission of array to raise men to "resist the rebellion of Richard, Duke of York" and those who support him.

Lord Clifford was made Warden of the West Marches replacing Salisbury and Warwick.

The King's carver, Sir William Catesby was granted the stewardship of all York's former land in the shires of Northampton and Buckingham. Catesby was also made constable of Wigmore Castle and steward of York's properties in Herefordshire. [197]

The Yorkists were proclaimed attainted traitors in London on 21st January 1460.

---

[195] *Parliamentary Rolls Henry VI* November 1459. Introduction and Item 26.
[196] *Calendar of Patent Rolls 1422-1477*. 8 Volumes. 1897-1910.
[197] *Calendar of Patent Rolls 1422-1477*. 8 Volumes. 1897-1910.

The Lords of Calais

… Lord Rivers was brought to Calais, and before the Lords, with eight score torches, and there my Lord Salisbury rated him, calling him 'Knave's son, that he should be so rude to call him, and these other Lords traitors; for they should be found the King's true liege men, when he would be found a traitor'. And my Lord Warwick rated him, and said, 'that his father was but a squire, and since made himself by marriage, and that it was not his part to hold such language of Lords, being of the King's blood… [198]

Warwick and his father, Salisbury, together with Edward, Earl of March, made their way speedily to South Wales. They were accompanied by Wenlock, Sir Walter Blount, Sir James Pickering and the loyal remnant of the Calais contingent. They may well have swapped horses and taken supplies at one of Warwick's strongholds before heading on towards the coast.

The only account of their journey across the seas we have is that by the chronicler Waurin… "When the Earl of Warwick saw his father and all the others were afraid, to comfort them he told them that with God's pleasure and St George's, he would get them to a safe harbour, he stripped to his doublet so he could take the tiller, he set the sail, so the wind pressed against them hard until they arrived at the island of Jersey". [199] Waurin probably merged two journeys into one in his account.

Warwick requisitioned a boat to take them across the Bristol channel. The master of the ship was reluctant to do so, not knowing the waters well, so Warwick took the tiller and steered the ship himself. In North Devon they met with John Dynham who helped them travel south to his mother's house at Nutwell on the Exe

---

[198] *The Chronicles of The White Rose of York:* Edited by James Bohn. Published London 1845. Paperback Version Reprint 2012. Introduction Page lxxii. Paston Letters Volume 1 Page 187.
[199] *Recueil des Croniques et Anciennes Istories de la Grant Bretaigne* by J. de Waurin, edited by W. Hardy 1864-91. Page 277.

estuary, near Newton Abbot, where they purchased a ship to onwards to Calais.

The Tudor writer Hall in his chronicle wrote that York, Salisbury and Wenlock "came into Devon, whereby the means of John Dynham they bought a ship which cost CX marks at Exmouth, and sailed to Guernsey, and after came to Calais". [200] Edward IV would later refund Dynham's mother £84 for the costs involved and grant her a valuable wardship and marriage for her help and good services "which at our last departing out of this our realm towards our town of Calais they did for the safeguard of our person, conduct and guiding thither in safety". [201]

They sailed first to Guernsey where Warwick's friend, John Nanfan, was Governor. They waited some eight days for favourable winds to take them forward and possibly for news that Calais was not held against them. They arrived on 2nd November where they were let in through a postern gate by Lord Fauconberg and were "enthusiastically received by the troops". [202]

Warwick would have been pleased and relieved to meet up with his wife, Countess Anne, and his two daughters, Isabel aged nine and Anne aged three. Waurin wrote that "after the joyful reunions they all went on pilgrimage to Notre Dame de St Pierre (in the Pale of Calais) and when they returned to Calais those of the staple came to meet them, the mayor of the town and all the soldiers who were on their side, so they had that night very good cheer as for a long time they were expecting to find their enemies facing them in Calais". [203]

---

[200] *Hall's Chronicle: Containing the History of England*, by Edward Hall. Published by Forgotten Books 2018. Originally published by Richard Grafton 1548. Page 242.
[201] *Calendar Patent Rolls 1452-1461* Page 435
[202] *The Chronicles of The White Rose of York:* Edited by James Bohn. Published London 1845. Paperback Version Reprint 2012. Introduction Page lxxi.
[203] *Recueil des Croniques et Anciennes Istories de la Grant Bretaigne* by J. de Waurin, edited by W. Hardy 1864-91. Page 278.

It was not before time. Somerset had been delayed by contrary winds and sent his herald in advance to the town with notice of his appointment by the King. The men of the Calais watch responded that Warwick was their captain. Access was denied.

Somerset and Trollope landed further up the coast at Scales Cliff. Others in his fleet of ships were not so fortunate. Waurin tells us that a tempest arose causing some boats to be blown into Calais harbour where they were taken over by Warwick's men. Warwick seized the ships, supplies and anything of value. On board the ships there were some men returning to Calais who had sworn loyalty to Warwick yet defected at Ludford.

Fabyan wrote that "some of the shipmen… for good will that they owed the Earl of Warwick, conveyed their ships straight into Calais haven and brought with them certain persons named Genyn Fenbyll, John Fellow, Kaylis and Purser, which were enemies unto the said Earl… and soon after… they were beheaded." [204]

Somerset took possession of Guines castle and Hammes fort promising to pay long overdue wages. He launched almost daily attempts to gain Calais as "he and his people began to make strong war against those of Calais" but without success. The duke's men "made out and skirmished with them of Calais many and sundry times. In which assaults many men were slain and hurt on both parties, but it most weakened the duke's party; for albeit the Lords lost many men, yet they daily came so thick to them out of diverse

---

[204] *The New Chronicles of England and France* by Robert Fabyan. Edited by Henry Ellis London 1811. Forgotten Books 2018. Originally edition by Pynson 1516. Page 635.

parts of England". Their only loss, according to Fabyan, was the money with which they had to pay the replacements. [205]

Lord Rivers and the Sheriff of Kent were commissioned to raise men and to seize all ships belonging to Warwick. [206] Lord Rivers, his son Anthony Woodville and Gervase Clifton made ready a fleet at Sandwich to take back Calais. Crews were hired and supplies sourced for a sufficient force of men for the purpose. Orders were more generally given "that no victuals, men, arms, horses, fuel or any other thing be taken in such ships for maintenance, victualing, fortification or the relief of Calais". [207] The King pronounced an embargo on trade with Calais. The move proved counterproductive. The Staple firmly backed Warwick and even loaned him money.

Warwick met with representatives of Philip, Duke of Burgundy at Gravelines. Marshall Charolais spent most of November in Calais in discussions. A temporary truce was agreed for three months between those in Calais and Burgundy. A wider commercial treaty between England and Burgundy had lapsed. Commissioners were appointed in London, but no formal diplomatic activity ensued between the two countries.

Warwick was kept informed of progress with preparations at Sandwich and made his own plans. Early on the morning of 15th January 1460, he sent a small fleet of ships under John Dynham to raid the port and take what they could. The ships sailed into the harbour and attacked from the landward side catching by surprise those supposedly defending the town. Lord Rivers, his wife and son were seized in their beds and carried back to Calais. Ships and

---

[205] *The New Chronicles of England and France* by Robert Fabyan. Edited by Henry Ellis London 1811. Forgotten Books 2018. Originally edition by Pynson 1516. Page 635.
[206] *Calendar Patent Rolls 1452-1461* Page 555.
[207] *The Brut or the Chronicles of England* edited by F.W.D. Brie London 1906. Page 529.

supplies were taken. Only the Grace Dieu was left behind as she was not seaworthy. William of Worcester wrote that Sandwich had been attacked "with a number of eight hundred men on Tuesday between four and five o'clock in the morning". [208]

William Paston, in a letter dated January 1460, writes that Lord Rivers "was brought to Calais, and before the Lords, with eight score torches, and there my Lord Salisbury rated him, calling him 'Knave's son, that he should be so rude to call him, and these other Lords traitors; for they should be found the King's true liege men, when he would be found a traitor'. And my Lord Warwick rated him, and said, 'that his father was but a squire, and since made himself by marriage, and that it was not his part to hold such language of Lords, being of the King's blood. And my Lord of March rated him in likewise". [209]

The raid on Sandwich caused great consternation in England. It was feared that this was just the start and that an invasion was imminent. Commissions of array were sent to the counties to prepare accordingly and to defend Canterbury. [210] Sir Baldwin Fulford of Devon promised that "on pain of losing his head, he would destroy the Earl of Warwick and his navy, if the King would grant him his expenses". On 1st February he was authorised by the King to press ships and sailors. Fulford was promised a share of any valuables recovered and payment for named prisoners such as Wenlock, Pickering or Colt. [211]

---

[208] *The Life and Reign of Edward the Fourth King of England and of France and Lord of Ireland* by Cora L. Scofield. Volumes One and Two. Fonthill Media 2016. First Published 1923. Pages 51-52.
[209] *The Chronicles of The White Rose of York:* Edited by James Bohn. Published London 1845. Paperback Version Reprint 2012. Introduction Page lxxii. Paston Letters Volume 1 Page 187.
[210] *Calendar Patent Rolls 1452-1461* Pages 563-564.
[211] *The Life and Reign of Edward the Fourth King of England and of France and Lord of Ireland* by Cora L. Scofield. Volumes One and Two. Fonthill Media 2016. First Published 1923. Pages 53-54.

Henry remained in the Midlands moving from the monastery of Leicester to that of Northampton. He did not return to London until March. Exeter, Wiltshire and Sir John Fortescue were appointed to a special commission in the meanwhile to deal with "treasons, rebellions and the giving of liveries" in London and Middlesex.

York "passed into Ireland, where he was with all joy and honour gladly received". [212] York was "hailed as another Messiah". [213] York was accompanied by Edmund, Earl of Rutland, Lord Clinton and Thomas Colt. He had the support of the Earls of Kildare and Desmond. York was reaffirmed as Lord Lieutenant of Ireland by the Parliament in Dublin and he was to be shown "such reverence, obedience, and fear... as our sovereign Lord". York was authorised to set up a mint in his castle at Trim and Rutland was appointed Chancellor. Parliament even enacted a bill stating that though Ireland was subject to English rule, any law had to be passed and agreed by them.

The Earl of Wiltshire was appointed Lieutenant of Ireland in York's place by Henry VI. Wiltshire was Earl of Ormond and not without influence in Ireland. William Overy was sent to arrest York but Overy himself was arrested, tried and found guilty of having "imagined, compassed and incited rebellion and disobedience". Overy was hung, drawn and quartered. No further attempt was made to remove York from his position.

---

[212] *Hall's Chronicle: Containing the History of England,* by Edward Hall. Published by Forgotten Books 2018. Originally published by Richard Grafton 1548. Page 242.
[213] *The Chronicles of The White Rose of York:* Edited by James Bohn. Published London 1845. Paperback Version Reprint 2012. Introduction Page lxxii. Whethempstede Page 474.

Warwick and York maintained communications through this period, but it was difficult and dangerous. There is the tale of Thomas Desseforde, the London wine merchant, who agreed to carry letters from Dublin to Calais but was captured and held in Ostend "in great duress of imprisonment" until Warwick learned of his fate and secured his release. [214]

Warwick determined to travel himself to Ireland presumably once he and his fellow Lords of Calais were satisfied that Calais itself was safe from attacks by Somerset and others. He took a small fleet with him. The Gascon Lord Duras was his "captain and admiral". In mid-March Warwick met up with York. Warwick and Lord Duras sailed into Waterford on 16th March with a larger fleet of twenty-six ships to a great welcome by the mayor and leading townsfolk… "the reception they gave and those with him was very grand, according to the ways of that savage country". [215]

News reached London that Warwick was in Ireland with York. Finance was made available to both Exeter and Fulford to ready their ships and men to ensure Warwick did not make it home should he try to return to Calais. Ships were seized in London, but three Venetian vessels slipped anchor and made their escape. Venetian merchants in London were imprisoned as a result. Foreign merchants turned against Henry's government and ministers as a result.

Somerset too heard of Warwick's absence and resolved to take Calais, but he was short of money and men. Some money was sent but not enough. Lords Audley and Stafford were sent with further aid but storms forced them to seek shelter in Calais and they were

---

[214] *The Life and Reign of Edward the Fourth King of England and of France and Lord of Ireland* by Cora L. Scofield. Volumes One and Two. Fonthill Media 2016. First Published 1923. Page 59.
[215] *Recueil des Croniques et Anciennes Istories de la Grant Bretaigne* by J. de Waurin, edited by W. Hardy 1864-91. Page 286.

imprisoned. Somerset determined to make one last big attempt and marched all his available men along the causeway to Newenham Bridge. They were met there and defeated decisively by the Yorkists on 23rd April. Somerset retreated with barely sufficient men to hold Guines.

On 23rd May a fresh relief force was pulled together. Osbert Mountfort and John Baker were sent to Sandwich with two hundred armed men and archers to ready themselves to cross the channel to assist Somerset.

Warwick returned from Ireland at the end of May taking with him his mother, the Countess of Salisbury. The return journey proved more challenging. Both Exeter and Fulford were supposedly awaiting his passage through the waters off the south coast of Devon and Cornwall. Warwick was ready if necessary. Fulford was a "no show" and, although he had spent the King's money, was nowhere to be seen. Exeter however took his ships out from Dartmouth to meet his foe for "he had vowed to God and the King that the Earl would never see Calais".

Waurin tells us that Warwick was "very wise and imaginative" and used a small ship *La Toucque* to scout ahead. The carvel sighted Exeter's fleet of the *Grace Dieu* and fourteen other ships and returned with the news… "the Earl of Warwick called his admiral and all the ship's masters, asking what would be the best way forward, to which with one voice they responded that they wanted to fight because they were strong enough… he was very joyful… he had faith in God that he would give them the victory". [216]

Fabyan reported that Warwick "kept his course till he came unto the West country where at the time was the Duke of Exeter, as Admiral of the sea, with a competent number of ships well

---

[216] *Recueil des Croniques et Anciennes Istories de la Grant Bretaigne* by J. de Waurin, edited W. Hardy 1864-91. Pages 288-9.

manned... but the duke heard such murmer and speech amongst his own company, which sounded in the Earl of Warwick's favour, he thought it was more into his profit to suffer him to pass rather than to fight with him". [217] Exeter took his boats back to Port. Warwick passed by keeping a safe distance and reached Calais without any mishap. Waurin tells us that Warwick's mother had "great joy... for her husband, who she had not seen in a long time".

Somerset was expecting the relief force at any time. On 5th June he was given permission to grant a King's pardon to all in Calais should they surrender with the exception of a few of the rebel Yorkist commanders. It was expected by all that Exeter and Fulford would destroy Warwick and his fleet. Warwick's return was a surprise, and it allowed the Yorkists to conduct a pre-emptory strike against the force being readied to support Somerset. Fauconberg, Dynham and Wenlock attacked and successfully took Sandwich on 24th June. The relief force was no more. Dynham sustained a severe leg injury which caused him to limp ever after. Dynham captured Mountfort, took him back to Rysbank Tower at Calais "and there smote off his head". Fauconberg remained in Sandwich to hold the town for the Yorkists.

Henry's government were concerned. Exeter and Fulford had failed to stop Warwick's return to Calais. Sandwich was in Yorkist control. They reacted by declaring that anyone who helped the Yorkists would be considered a fellow rebel and face the consequences.

"A gentleman of the Temple called Neville and a wine merchant called John Goode, and other persons were going to Calais to the

---

[217] *The New Chronicles of England and France* by Robert Fabyan. Edited by Henry Ellis London 1811. Forgotten Books 2018. Originally edition by Pynson 1516. Page 636.

Earl of Warwick with bowstrings and arrows" were "damned of treason, and their heads set on London Bridge". [218]

Wiltshire, Scales and Hungerford presided over a commission of justice at York's town of Newbury. Property was confiscated. Men were imprisoned and executed. It was not justice so much as vengeance and seen as such by many. It made the task of the Yorkists seeking a change of government easier not more difficult.

---

[218] *Three Fifteenth Century Chronicles with Historical Memoranda* by John Stowe. Edited by J Gairdner for the Camden Society. Published by Nabu Press 2012. Originally published 1881. A Short English Chronicle Page 73.

Northampton 10ᵗʰ July 1460

...so forth to Northampton. And there they met with the King and fought manly with the King's Lords and many, but there was much favour in that field unto the Earl of Warwick... And in that field was slain the Duke of Buckingham, standing still in his tent, the Earl of Shrewsbury, the Lord Beaumont, and the Lord Egremont, with many other men... [219]

Francesco Coppini, Bishop of Terni was sent to England in January 1459 by Pope Pius II to raise support for a universal crusade against the Turks. It was not a good time to do so. Henry VI met with him respectfully and raised the issue at Council but there were other things on everyone's minds. Coppini spent time visiting London, Canterbury, Coventry and St Albans.

The Abbot of St Albans tells us that Coppini was short and small of stature but very spirited and eloquent such that "his words dropped from his lips like dew".[220] Coppini preached for peace but his dew like words fell on deaf Lancastrian ears. Coppini was made a Papal legate in December 1459 to give him more authority and make him more influential. The Yorkists sought his help to intercede on their behalf with King Henry who was asked to receive them "with a tranquil and open mind".

Coppini wrote to the Duke of Milan on 22ⁿᵈ March 1460... "Some days ago, I wrote to your Lordship in haste a brief abstract of English affairs... Although we have no actual certitude, it is believed, nevertheless, that the one newly chosen (Edward IV) together with Warwick will perform marvels... I am leaving for a while because it is necessary and also by Warwick's advice. I expect to return any day according to the encouragement received from thence, and we have

---

[219] *Historical Collections of a Citizen of London* in Gregory's Chronicle, edited by J. Gairdner. Camden Society 1876.
[220] *Registrum Abbatiae Johannis Whethamstede* by Abbot J. Whethamstede. Edited by H.T. Riley. 1872. Pages 331-332.

no doubt of success if we have help thence. Bruges, 22nd March 1460." [221]

Coppini travelled from Bruges to Calais and joined the Yorkists in their preparations to return to England. Warwick, Salisbury and March were determined to take back what they had lost. They crossed by boat to Sandwich on 26th June 1460 "having wind and weather at their pleasure". Coppini travelled with them as did the young Lord Audley who had been let out of prison after converting to the Yorkist cause.

The Yorkist's ground had been prepared in advance by Warwick and others. Letters were sent. A manifesto was published and signed off by York, Salisbury, Warwick and March. It was shared widely by many as if their own.

Henry VI's government was unpopular and ready to support those who declared the need for change. London and the South-East were left estranged by the move of the government and court to the Midlands. Kent had seen no real progress since rebelling ten years before. It was not surprising therefore, that the men of Kent were amongst those who published the manifesto in their own name.

"These be the Points and Causes of the gathering and assembling of us, the King's true liegemen of Kent, the which we trust to remedy, with help of him, the King, our Sovereign Lord, and all the Commons of England.

1. The King, by the insatiable covetousness, malicious purpose, and false-brought-of-nought persons, daily and nightly about his highness, is daily informed that good is evil and evil is good.
2. They say, that our Sovereign Lord is above law, and that the law was but to his pleasure; and that he may make and break

---

[221] *Calendar of State Papers* Milan 1460 22nd March 1460 Francesco Copino, Bishop of Terni, Papal Legate to Francesco Sforza, Duke of Milan.

it as often as him likes, without distinction. The contrary is true. And also, that he should not have been sworn, in his coronation to keep it, which we conceive for the highest point of treason that the subject may do against his Prince, to make him reign in perjury.
3. They say, how that the King should live upon his commons, so that all their bodies and goods be his. The contrary is true; for then he need never to set parliament to assess any goods of them.
4. Item, they inform the King, how that the commons would first destroy the King's friends, and after himself and then bring in the Duke of York to be their King; so that by these false men's lies they made him to hate and to destroy his friends, and love his false traitors, that call themselves his friends.
5. They say, it is a great reproach to the King to re-assume what he has given away for livelihood.
6. The false traitors will suffer no man to come into the King's presence, for no cause without he will give a bribe.
7. That the good Duke of Gloucester was impeached of treason by one false traitor alone. How soon was he murdered! And never might come to an answer. And that false traitor Pole, impeached by all the commonality of England might not be suffered to die as the law would, but rather these said traitors, at the said Pole's assent, that was as false as *Fortiger* would that the King should hold battle in his own realm, in the destruction of all his people, and of himself both.
8. They, whom the King will, shall be traitors, and whom he will not, shall be none.
9. The law seems only to do wrong.
10. That our Sovereign Lord may well understand that he hath had false counsel; for his law is lost, his merchandise is lost; his commerce been destroyed; the sea is lost; France is lost; himself is made so poor, so that he may not pay for his meat nor drink; he owes more, and is greater in debt, than ever was King of England. This notwithstanding, yet daily these said traitors that have been about him, awaiting when

anything should fall, and come to him, and profit by his law, they have been ready enough to ask it from him.
11. They ask gentleman's lands and goods in Kent, and call us risers and traitors, and the King's enemies; but we shall be found his true liegemen.
12. We will that all men know, that we neither rob nor steal; but the defaults amended, we will go home. Wherefore we exhort all the King's true liegemen to help and support us.
13. We blame not all the Lords about the King's person, nor all the gentlemen, nor all men of law, nor all bishops, nor all priests; but only such as may be found guilty, by a just and true inquiry by the law.

God be our Guide
And then we shall speed,
Whoever says, nay!" [222]

The Yorkists were in tune with what people thought. The government was failing. It was corrupt. Taxation enriched the few and even the King was poor. France had been lost. They specifically named Wiltshire, Shrewsbury and Beaumont "our mortal and extreme enemies" as the evil and false councillors, before later adding Buckingham, almost as an afterthought, for he was "high and fat of grease".

Warwick, Salisbury and March made their way to Canterbury. Men flocked to their fold as they progressed. Their numbers grew. At Canterbury the captains asked to bar their way, went over to their side. John Fogge, John Scott and Robert Horne joined the Yorkists as did the local Lord Cobham. They visited the cathedral and gave thanks to God.

A popular ballad was pinned on the city gates.

---
[222] *The Chronicles of The White Rose of York: A series of Historical Fragments, Proclamations, Letters and Other Contemporary Documents relating to the Reign of Edward IV* Edited by James Bohn. Published London 1845. Paperback Version Reprint 2012. Introduction Pages lxxiv-lxxvi. Harleian MSS 543.

"Send home, most gracious Lord Jesu most benign,
Send home thy true blood unto his proper vein
Richard, Duke of York, Job thy servant assign,
Whom Satan not ceases to set at care and disdain,
But by the preserved he may not be slain;
Set him that he may sit amongst the princes, as he did before,
And so, to our new song, Lord, thine ears incline,
Glory, praise and honour be to you that is Christ the Redeemer King!

Edward, Earl of March, whose fame the earth shall spread,
Richard, Earl of Salisbury named prudence,
With that noble knight and flower of manhood,
Richard, Earl of Warwick shield of our defence,
Also, little Fauconberg, a knight of great reverence;
Jesu is restored to their honour as they had before,
And ever shall we sing to thine high excellence,
Glory, praise and honour be to you that is Christ the Redeemer King!" [223]

The Yorkist Lords moved on from Canterbury to London. Lords Hungerford and Scales, and Sir Edmund Hampden, had been sent there to hold London against them. The Mayor of London and the Council debated at length but at last they decided to receive the Yorkist Lords mindful of the gathering support in their favour. The Lancastrians made themselves secure in the Tower.

Warwick and his fellow Yorkist Lords arrived in Southwark on 2nd July and were met by the Bishop of Ely and Warwick's brother George, Bishop of Exeter. They crossed London bridge not without incident. Some of the Bishops' men were crushed in the crowds. Once in the city, they rode to St Pauls and gave thanks once more to God. They stayed in the house of the Grey Friars and next day together with Coppini, the Papal Legate, they met with Thomas Bourchier, Archbishop of Canterbury and other members of his

---

[223] *An English Chronicle* edited by J.S. Davies. Camden Society 1856. Pages 91-94.

convocation of Bishops in the cathedral. They set out their case for reform and swore to uphold their allegiance to their sovereign Lord, King Henry.

They remained in London for a couple of days preparing their army and receiving visiting deputations from towns such as Lydd and Rye who sought instructions and favour with the Lords. A request for food and drink for those who had taken refuge in the Tower was refused. The Council loaned the Yorkists £1,000 to be repaid in two instalments within the year.

Coppini wrote two letters to Henry VI and the Pope on 4th July 1460. The letter to Henry VI was an open one, shared with the convocation of clergy and placed for all to see at St Paul's cross. The legate, seeking to fulfil his duties as a "faithful shepherd, nuncio and mediator", beseeched Henry to make peace and not be responsible for the blood which otherwise would be shed. Henry must ignore those around him who are "clerks and ministers of the devil". Henry is warned "Do not listen if anyone says that you have just cause to fight against your subjects".

Coppini made his case for the Yorkist Lords… "Nevertheless, after I had conferred with them and exhorted them to peace and obedience, they gave me a written pledge that they were disposed to devotion and obedience to your Majesty, and to do all in their power for the conservation and augmentation of your honour and the good of your realm. But they desired to come to your Majesty and to be received into their former state and favour, from which they declare they have been ousted by the craft of their opponents, and begged me to cross the sea with them to interpose my efforts and prevent bloodshed, assuring me that they would do anything honourable and just that I should approve for the honour and estate of your Highness and the welfare of your realm." [224]

---

[224] *Calendar of State Papers* Milan 1460 I Pages 23-26.

The letter to the Pope from Coppini enclosed a copy of the Yorkist conditions for peace (manifesto) and told the Pontiff of his "good work" including his journey and welcome as "an angel of peace" and a mediator. Coppini had preached on the Pope's behalf to a crowd of "perhaps one hundred thousand Christians"!

That same day on July 4th the advance guard of the Yorkist army under Lord Fauconberg started north and marched towards St Albans on Watling Street. Warwick set off the following day on 5th July towards Ware with the main guard of the army as it was rumoured that the King had fled to Ely. [225] News soon arrived that the King was at Northampton. The two sections of the army joined together once more at Dunstable.

"The Earl of Salisbury, the Lord Cobham, and Sir John Wenlock, were left in London with the mayor" to hold the city and to take the Tower. Cobham led the attack from the town side, Wenlock from St Katherine's side and "much harm was done on both sides". [226]

Henry VI left Queen Margaret and Prince Edward in Coventry and travelled to Northampton where he awaited his rushed plea for men to join him on a promise of booty and plunder from those counties who had risen up against him. It was not the best act of a King seeking to show himself wise and merciful. It simply raised up those counties more against his government. They clearly had nothing to lose, and memories are long. Henry was accompanied by many of his Lords and notably many from the North hostile to Warwick and his Neville kinfolk.

One Lancastrian Lord decided not to stay and fight on hearing that the Yorkist Lords were coming. Wiltshire travelled to Southampton,

---

[225] *Bale's Chronicle, Six Town Chronicles of England* edited by R. Flenley. Clarendon Press Oxford 1911.
[226] *Three Fifteenth Century Chronicles with Historical Memoranda* by John Stowe. Edited by J Gairdner for the Camden Society. Published by Nabu Press 2012. Originally published 1881. Page 74.

supposedly to put to sea and stop Warwick, "but specially to steal privately out of the realm". Wiltshire took possession of five large carracks from Genoa and fled to Holland with money and men for he feared retribution.

The King was encamped with his troops outside the walls of Northampton, to the south, in a meadow known as Hardingstone field, close to the nunnery of St Mary de Pratis, and to Sandyford mill and bridge. We know this because William Wayneflete, Bishop of Winchester, resigned his position as Chancellor on Monday 7th July and left the great seal in a chest in the King's own tent. The record of his resignation says it took place in the King's tent "tunc situate in quodam campo vocato Hardyngstonefelde juxta abbatiam de pratis".

The Short English Chronicle confirmed that the battle took place "beside Northampton in the new field between Harsyngton and Sandyfforde." [227] The English Chronicle tells us that "The King was at Northampton at the Friars and had ordered a strong and mighty field, in the meadows beside the Nene, armed and arrayed with guns, having a river at his back." [228]

The Chronicle of John Stone tells us that the battle was fought in "Cow Meadow and Nuns Field... near Sandyfforde Bridge, next to the Town. On the east side there is a water mill called Sandford Mill." [229] The chronicler John Benet wrote that the King's camp was between Hardingstone and the Abbey. [230]

---

[227] *Three Fifteenth Century Chronicles with Historical Memoranda* by John Stowe. Edited by J Gairdner for the Camden Society. Published by Nabu Press 2012. Originally published 1881. Page 74.
[228] *An English Chronicle* edited by J.S. Davies. Camden Society 1856. Page 96.
[229] *The Chronicles of John Stone* edited by W.G. Searle. Cambridge 1902. Page 80.
[230] *Benet's Chronicle for the years 1400 to 1462* Edited by G.L. and M.A. Harriss. Camden Miscellany Volume XXIV London 1972. Page 226.

It seems from the records and from the peace loving Wayneflete's resignation that there was a serious disagreement amongst those who advised the King. The King himself would have favoured peace but was persuaded otherwise by the hawks such as Buckingham. This was not the time or place to show mercy to the returning rebel Lords.

Warwick and March and their army approached Northampton and made camp on Hardingstone Hill, and possibly also on Hunsbury Hill, on the southern approaches overlooking the town. They had a goodly collection of Lords temporal and spiritual which included the Archbishop of Canterbury, the Bishops of London, Exeter, Lincoln, Shrewsbury, Ely and Rochester, the Prior of St Johns, Viscount Bourchier and Lords Fauconberg, Audley, Abergavenny, Say and Scrope of Bolton, and the Papal Legate Coppini. [231]

The Bishop of Rochester, according to Jean de Waurin, was sent with others to seek peaceful discussions but to no avail. Rochester returned with information about the King's camp… "a great preparation of men at arms and artillery and the great ditches they had made around the camp, in which the water of the river flowed, which encircled the whole army". [232] The Abbot of St Alban's writings says it was the Bishop of Salisbury that led the delegation of Bishops.

The English Chronicle tells that Bishop Stanberry of Hereford was sent to mediate with Henry as his confessor. Stanberry "exhorted and encouraged the king's party to fight" rather than negotiate for peace and did not return "but privily departed away". In

---

[231] *The Life and Reign of Edward the Fourth King of England and of France and Lord of Ireland* by Cora L. Scofield. Volumes One and Two. Fonthill Media 2016. First Published 1923. Pages 86-87.
[232] *Recueil des Croniques et Anciennes Istories de la Grant Bretaigne* by J. de Waurin, edited by W. Hardy 1864-91.

consequence 'after the battle he was committed to the castle of Warwick, where he was long in prison". [233]

Waurin in his original text uses the word *riviere* as opposed to *fleuve*, a small river or stream rather than a larger river that flows into the sea. There is a natural spring running down from Hardingstone Hill past the Abbey. This is probably the *riviere* to which Waurin refers. Michael Drayton wrote of the battle in 1613…

"The King from out of the town, who drew his foot and horse,
As willingly to give full field room to his force
Does pass the river Nene near where it down does run
From its fountain's head, is near to Hardingstone,
Advised of a place, by nature strongly wrought." [234]

The Ordnance Survey Leisure map shows two springs starting on the high ground near Hardingstone which join to together to flow towards the Abbey. A 1756 map of the area shows a 'battle dyke' on the west side and an adjacent 'battle furlong' on the east side of a stream known as Fulbrook. The Eleanor Cross is referred to by Waurin as "a cross on a hill above the said camp". John Stone in his chronicle wrote that the cross was "headless" and was from where the Archbishop of Canterbury watched the battle.

The English Chronicle recounts what happened leading up to the battle and beyond… "The Earls came to Northampton and sent certain Bishops to the King beseeching him to eschew the effusion of Christian blood by admitting and suffering the Earls to come unto his presence to declare them self as they were. The Duke of Buckingham that stood beside the King said unto them 'you come not as Bishops for to treat for peace but as men of arms' because

---

[233] *Battle Royale; The Wars of Lancaster and York 1440-1462* by Hugh Bicheno. Head of Zeus 2015. Page 236.
[234] *The Battle of Northampton 1460* by Mike Ingram. Northamptonshire Battlefields Society 2015. Pages 78-79.

they brought with them a notable company of men of arms. They answered and said 'we come thus for the safety of our persons, for they that be about the King be not our friends'. 'Forsooth' said the Duke of Buckingham, 'the Earl of Warwick shall not come unto the King's presence, and yet if he comes, he shall die'."

"Then the Earl of Warwick sent a herald to the King, beseeching that he might have hostages of safe going and coming, and he would come naked to his presence, but he might not be heard. And he sent to the King and said that at two o'clock, he would speak with him, or else die in the field".

"Then on the Thursday the 10th day of July, the year of our Lord 1460, at two o'clock in the afternoon, the said Earls of March and Warwick let cry through the field that no man should lay a hand upon the King nor on the common people, but only on the Lords, knights and squires, then the trumpets blew, and both hosts countered and fought together for half an hour. The Lord Grey that was the King's vanguard broke the field and came to the Earl's party, which caused many a man's life; many were slain, and many fled, and were drowned in the river."

"The Duke of Buckingham, the Earl of Shrewsbury, the Lord Beaumont, the Lord Egremont were slain by the Kentishmen beside the King's tent, and many other knights and squires. The ordinance of the King's guns availed not, for that day was so great with rain, that the guns lay deep in water, and so were quiet and might not be shot". [235]

The Short English Chronicle records that "the King was taken in his tent. And there was slain the Duke of Buckingham, the Earl of Shrewsbury, the Viscount Beaumont, the Lord Egremont, and Sir William Lucy, and many other knights and squires, and many commoners were drowned". And then the Earl of March, and the

---

[235] *An English Chronicle* edited by J.S. Davies. Camden Society 1856. Page 96.

Earl of Warwick, with other Lords, brought the King to Northampton with much royalty". [236]

Gregory's Chronicle gives us a more human and personal background on the death of Sir William Lucy... "And that good knight Sir William Lucy that dwelt beside Northampton heard gun shots, and came to the field to help the King, but the field was done, and one of the Staffords was aware of his coming, and loved that knight's wife and hated him, and anon caused his death". [237]

Warwick and March, pressed by the many religious Lords in their presence, sought to meet with the King to discuss their grievances subject to promise of "safe passage" but those who had the ear of Henry would not let them do so. They readied for battle and split into three. Fauconberg took the van guard. Warwick and March took the other two guards. Waurin writes that Warwick told his men before the battle not to kill those with the black ragged staff badge of Lord Grey of Ruthyn. [238]

It was at this point, if true, that Coppini gave plenary remission of sins to all whilst declaring an anathema on their opponents. Pope Pius in his *Commentaries* writes that Coppini "raised the standard of the Church of Rome, and on the ground that they were to do battle against the enemies of the Faith, he granted plenary remission of sins to those who were to fight on the side of the Earl of Warwick...

---

[236] *Three Fifteenth Century Chronicles with Historical Memoranda* by John Stowe. Edited by J Gairdner for the Camden Society. Published by Nabu Press 2012. Originally published 1881. Page 74.
[237] *Historical Collections of a Citizen of London* in Gregory's Chronicle, edited by J. Gairdner. Camden Society 1876.
[238] *Recueil des Croniques et Anciennes Istories de la Grant Bretaigne* J. de Waurin, ed. by W. Hardy 1864-91. Pages 299-300.

and pronounced anathema on their enemies". [239] Coppini later denied that he had done so. [240]

Le Seigneur de Griffin led a sizeable Lancastrian force on horseback out of their camp. They mustered around the south gate of the town before being attacked and repulsed by the forward horsemen of the Yorkist vanguard led by Scrope and Stafford. [241] The skirmish lasted around one hour. The Yorkists entered the town perhaps chasing down Lancastrian soldiers. They caused considerable damage and set homes on fire based on local evidence as well as royal remission of rent payable soon thereafter. [242]

---

[239] *Pius II Commentaries* Volume II edited by M. Meserve and M. Simonetta. Cambridge Mass 2007. Page 270.
[240] *Calendar of State Papers* Milan 1461 9th January 1461
[241] *Recueil des Croniques et Anciennes Istories de la Grant Bretaigne* by J. de Waurin, edited by W. Hardy 1864-91. Pages 322-324. *The Battle of Northampton 1460* by Mike Ingram. Northamptonshire Battlefields Society 2015. Page 85.
[242] *The Battle of Northampton 1460* by Mike Ingram. Northamptonshire Battlefields Society 2015. Page 86.

The Battle of Northampton 10th July 1460

Northampton — South Gate

- St Thomas Hospital
- River Nene
- St Leonards Hospital
- Sandyngford bridge
- Le Seigneur de Griffin
- William Neville Lord Fauconberg
- Richard Neville Earl of Warwick
- Edward Earl of March
- Yorkist Guns
- Queen Eleanor's Cross
- Yorkist Camp — Hardingstone Hill
- London Road
- Nunns or Sandford Mill
- Church
- Abbey of St Mary de la Pre
- Fleeing Lancastrian Troops
- Lancastrian Camp
- Baron Egremont
- Earl of Shrewsbury
- Henry VI
- Duke of Buckingham
- Viscount Beaumont
- Lord Grey of Ruthyn
- Delapre Wood

1. The Lancastrian Camp was in a strong defensive position but guns underwater due to floods.

2. Fauconberg's cavalry forced retreat of Lancastrian horsemen under Le Seigneur de Griffin.

3. Fauconberg, Warwick & March attacked the Lancastrian Camp. March helped into camp by Lord Grey of Ruthyn.

5. Buckingham, Beaumont, Shrewsbury & Egremont were killed. Henry VI was captured.

6. Lancastrians fled north-east. Many drowned in the floods and died or were killed.

© Steve Williams

The Yorkists fired their guns downhill towards the camp. There was little if any response. We know from the accounts that the Lancastrian guns lay mostly under water due to flooding from unseasonal rains. The not inconsiderable numbers of archers were at the ready.

The Yorkist order was given to advance and attack. Trumpets sounded. Men shouted. Once the archers had shot their arrows, the Lancastrian ranks closed up to defend the fortified camp. The attackers faced a stream, a bank and men waving swords, billhooks and axes, literally fighting for their lives. Then fate, or rather treachery, intervened.

Lord Grey and his one hundred or so men defected to the Yorkists. Perhaps it was the common enemies Warwick and Grey had in relation to their business and landed interests, or perhaps it was money or the promise of influence. We do not know. There are no records of Grey receiving grants of land or titles in the near term although subsequently his tenure over Ampthill was confirmed. It was three years before he was appointed Treasurer and five years before being made Earl of Kent. Warwick, just like at St Albans, had his break and "the battle was decided by a distraction followed by an abrupt dislocation of expectations". [243]

Lord Grey of Ruthyn's men gave way and helped their opponents over the ditches. They were situated on the left-hand side of the camp. March's men on the right of the Yorkists advance were able enter the camp with relative ease to turn the defence. The Lancastrian defenders found themselves being attacked from in front, and from behind. What might have been expected to be a long hard fight turned quickly. Men started to break away and flee. Some made it. Many did not. They either drowned in the flooded marshland around the swollen river Nene or were caught and killed in flight.

Buckingham was killed by the King's tent. Shrewsbury, Beaumont and Egremont died nearby. Waurin tells us that an archer called Henry Montfort captured and stood guard over King Henry. Warwick and March finally caught up with Henry once the area had been made safe. They praised God for their triumph "over their mortal enemies, who by their venomous malice have untruly steered and moved your highness to exile us out of your land and would have put us to final shame and confusion". They were there for his

---

[243] *Battle Royale; The Wars of Lancaster and York 1440-1462* by Hugh Bicheno. Head of Zeus 2015. Page 238.

"welfare and prosperity" as his "true liegemen, while our lives shall endure". [244]

Henry was taken to the Abbey where a mass was conducted in thanks to God for his gift of victory. The king was then led into Northampton where the victors stayed some three days before the journey back to London.

The dead were buried near St John's hospital close to the city walls and outside the Abbey Church which was destroyed at the time of the dissolution of the monasteries. Most of the nobles who lost their lives were taken back to their manors, but Buckingham was buried at Greyfriars in the town itself. Leland wrote that "there was a great battle fought in Henry VI's time at Northampton on the hill outside the South Gate, where is a right goodly cross, as I remember, the Queen's cross, and many Welsh men were drowned in the river at this conflict. Many of them that were slain were buried at de la Pray and some at St John's Hospital." [245]

Waurin provides contradictory accounts as to who was there at the battle for the Lancastrians. In his second and shorter account, both Somerset and Exeter are at Northampton. Neither feature in his first and longer account nor in other sources. Somerset probably remained safe in Guines where we know he is in early August. Exeter may have been awaiting his allies, Northumberland and Clifford mustering their men in the north.

There are doubts as to whether Queen Margaret and Prince Edward remained at Coventry or Kenilworth, or whether they had travelled to be close to King Henry. Hall writes that the Queen visited Northampton where she "encouraged her friends and promised

---

[244] *An English Chronicle* edited by J.S. Davies. Camden Society 1856. Pages 97-98.
[245] *The Itinerary of John Leland in or about the years 1535-1543* Edited by L. Toulmin Smith. 1907-10, I, Page 8.

great rewards to her helpers". [246] It is on record that the royal treasure was stolen after the battle at nearby Gayton. On 15th July 1460 Thomas Mascy of Podynton, William Stanley and three other men were commissioned to arrest Thomas Gless, John Glegg and two others for the theft of 20,000 marks worth of money and jewels from the King at Gayton. [247]

Gregory's chronicle tells us, however, that before leaving, Henry VI bade farewell to his wife and pressed her to stay safe until he sent her "a special token". The chronicler added that the Yorkists "knew well that all the workings that were done grew by her, for she was wittier (cleverer) than the King". [248]

More interesting are the words attributed to Warwick in the writings of Pope Pius II in his *Commentaries* which appear to confirm the Yorkist aim to rule in the king's name.

"Our King is a dolt and a fool who is ruled instead of ruling. The royal power is in the hands of his wife and those who defile the king's chamber... many feel as I do, among them the Duke of York, who would now be on the throne if there were any regard for justice... If God gives us victory, we shall drive our foes from the king's side and ourselves govern the Kingdom. The King will retain only the bare name of sovereign... before long, when the Kingdom is again at peace, we will equip a fleet in defence of religion". [249]

Warwick's victory was well publicised far and wide particularly by those whose opinion he had courted whilst at Calais. The Milanese

---

[246] *Hall's Chronicle: Containing the History of England* - Published by Forgotten Books 2018. Originally published by Richard Grafton 1548. Page 244.
[247] *Report of the Deputy Keeper of Public Records* Volume 37 Part II London 1876. Page 677.
[248] *Historical Collections of a Citizen of London* in Gregory's Chronicle, edited by J. Gairdner. Camden Society 1876.
[249] *Pius II Commentaries* Volume II edited by M. Meserve and M. Simonetta. Cambridge Mass 2007.

Ambassador at the Papal court wrote to Duke Sforza of Milan… "The ambassador of the Duke of Burgundy hears that a certain English lord (Warwick), enemy of the King of England, who had gone to Calais with a great following of other Englishmen, has returned to England and taken a great part of it, and it is hoped that he will deprive the king of that lordship and that the said lord is a very great friend of the aforesaid duke. Siena, the 6th May, 1460."
[250] The letter appears to have been written prior to Warwick's actual return but the sentiment remains valid.

The Duke of Sforza received news in July from Bruges and London of Warwick's success… "When the king heard of Warwick's arrival, he betook himself to a valley between two mountains, a strong place. But Fortune, who throughout showed herself favourable to Warwick, willed that it should rain so heavily that they were forced to come out of that place and encounter Warwick. Without a serious fight or much slaughter, Warwick very soon had the king in his power. He forthwith put to death the Duke of Buckingham, one of the great lords of that country, and the Lords of Beaumont, Egremont and Shrewsbury, all great lords…

…In that place are several other lords, and thither also the Duke of York will go soon and all their friends, and they will gather for mutual support and appoint new offices and arrange the government of the country. This will remain in the hands of Warwick. It is not thought that he will stay his hand but will put to death all those who have acted against him. It is also thought that they will make a son of the Duke of York king, and that they will pass over the king's son, as they are beginning already to say that he is not the king's son… Thus, one may say that to-day everything is in Warwick's power and the war at an end, and that he has done

---

[250] *Calendar of State Papers* Milan 1460. Letter from Otto de Carreto, Milanese Ambassador at the Papal Court, to Francesco Sforza, Duke of Milan dated 6th May 1460.

marvellous things. God grant him grace to keep the country in peace and union!" [251]

Warwick was being talked about not just in England, and the inns of London and Kent, but in the courts of Europe. Warwick had arrived on the political stage in no uncertain manner.

---

[251] *Calendar of State Papers* Milan 1460. Various Newsletters from Bruges and London.

Wakefield 30th December 1460

> *...The Duke of York, having in company with him his son, the Earl of Rutland, and Richard, Earl of Salisbury, set out for the purpose of offering resistance to their movements; but he was defeated at Wakefield, and there slain...* [252]

Queen Margaret fled north through Yorkshire to Durham according to Hall and Vergil. The English Chronicle, however, records that she sped to Harlech and then Denbigh Castle in Wales. Her path north was not without danger. Gregory's chronicle tells us that "one of her own servants, whom she had created an officer of her son the prince, plundered and robbed her, and put her in doubt of her life and her son's also". [253] William of Worcester shares the same story and names the wrongdoer as John Cleger, a servant of Lord Stanley. [254]

Warwick stayed three days in Northampton before leaving for London. The Crowland Chronicle records that "a great battle was fought near Northampton... the Earls having thus gained the victory, paid all the honours of royalty to King Henry, and conducted him with a most august escort to London; Richard Neville, the before-named Earl of Warwick, on this occasion, carrying a sword before the King, bare-headed, and with every mark of humility and respect." [255]

---

[252] *Ingulph's Chronicle of the Abbey of Croyland:* with the continuations by Peter of Blois and Anonymous writers. Translated by Henry Riley. Published by Nabu Press 2014. Originally published 1854. Written 1486. Page 456.

[253] *Historical Collections of a Citizen of London* in Gregory's Chronicle, edited by J. Gairdner. Camden Society 1876.

[254] *The Itineraries of William Worcester* edited by J.H. Harvey. Oxford 1969. Page 774.

[255] *Ingulph's Chronicle of the Abbey of Croyland:* with the continuations by Peter of Blois and Anonymous writers. Translated by Henry Riley. Published by Nabu Press 2014. Originally published 1854. Written 1486. Page 454.

The procession through London showed all who was in charge. Henry was lodged at the Bishop's Palace. Warwick resided at the Black Friars and March at his father's London house, Baynard's Castle. On their return the Tower was quickly taken. "Hunger and discouragement" accomplished more than any guns in this respect although the walls had been breached in many places by the bombards placed across the river. Wenlock and a merchant called Harow took control of the Tower on 19th July.

Lord Scales though was caught attempting to escape from the Tower to sanctuary in Westminster and paid the price with his life. Scales was recognised by a woman who gave him up to a group of boatmen according to the chronicles. The boatmen "followed him and fell upon him and killed him and cast him on the land beside St Mary Overy". The chronicler Worcester saw the body himself "despoiled naked as a worm". [256] Warwick and March arranged for his lifeless corpse to be recovered from the wasteland and gave him an honourable burial.

Warwick still had to ride to the Tower to disperse a group of Londoners angry with those in the Tower who had fired guns and sent wildfire upon the city killing many citizens. Warwick promised justice and told them to return to their homes.

---

[256] *The Itineraries of William Worcester* edited by J.H. Harvey. Oxford 1969. Pages 773-774.

The Tower of London in the 1450's

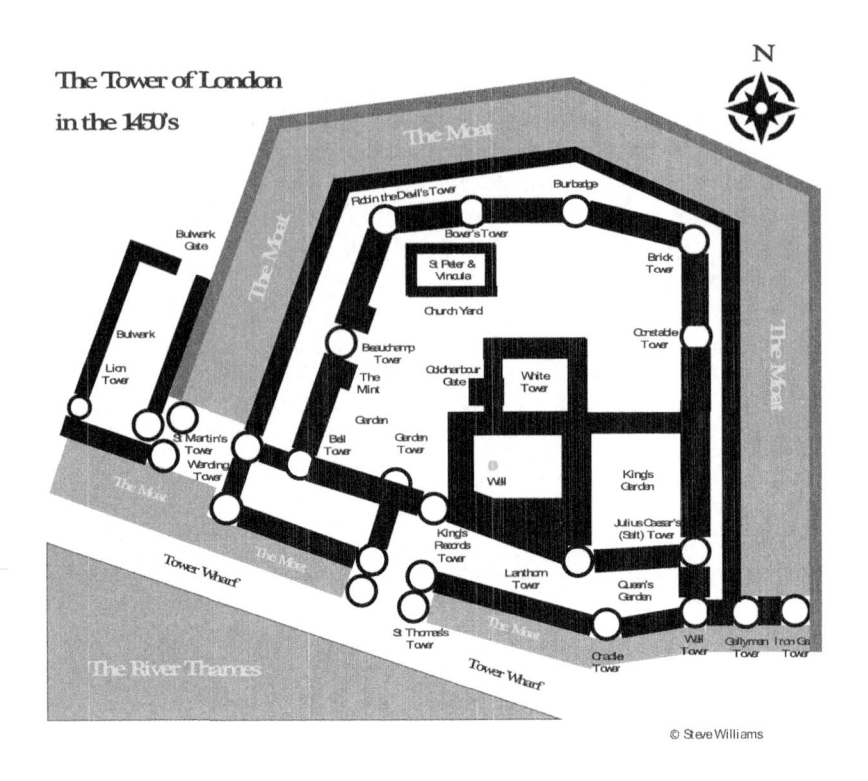

© Steve Williams

Warwick's brother, George Neville, was made Lord Chancellor on 25th July 1460. Viscount Bourchier became Treasurer and Robert Stillington was given the Privy Seal. A proclamation was made in every county that the Duke of York and the Earls of Warwick, Salisbury and March were the King's true subjects and friends. [257]

Henry visited Canterbury in early August accompanied by Warwick. On 5th August Henry issued an order to Somerset to give up possession of Guines castle before returning to London where he stayed at Greenwich. Somerset was not pleased to receive the orders to give up Guines to Warwick. A very disappointed and frustrated Duke left the castle with his close group of men and travelled to France having been granted safe passage and accommodation in Montivilliers by King Charles VII. It was at this time that Somerset

---

[257] *Calendar of Patent Rolls 1452-1461* Page 647.

developed a friendship with Charles, Count of Charolais, heir to the dukedom of Burgundy.

Parliament was summoned at the end of July. All were invited, but Somerset and Exeter, Northumberland and Devon, and others from the north did not attend. Parliament opened on Tuesday 7th October. The new Chancellor, George Neville, gave the opening sermon which set out the many wrongs that needed to be righted. A relative unknown Essex knight, John Green, was elected speaker for the commons. The newly returned Duke of York arrived late and made an appearance on Friday 10th October [258] which was commented upon in all the main accounts of that time.

The Croyland Chronicle tells the story. "In the month of October, the Duke of York came over from Ireland; and repairing to Westminster, while the Parliament was there assembled, entered the upper chamber of the royal palace, where the lords spiritual and temporal were sitting; after which, going up to the royal throne, he claimed the right of sitting there as belonging solely to himself by way of his lineal descent from Lionel, Duke of Clarence". York could "no longer put up with the injustice which had been done to his line for so many years by the three Henrys, who were only usurpers... making his way into the inner rooms of the royal palace, he compelled the King to remove to the Queen's apartments, while he himself took possession of the whole of the King's abode." [259]

Abbot Whethamstede wrote of "varied and contrary rumours amongst the people" about York's return. "Some said that his arrival was peaceful and that he intended nothing else but the restoration of harmony among the quarrelling Lords of the realm, bringing peace to the kingdom, and reforming it, by his authority. Yet others, including those who were older and wiser, suspected that he meant

---

[258] *Benet's Chronicle for the years 1400 to 1462* Edited by G.L. and M.A. Harriss. Camden Miscellany Volume XXIV London 1972.
[259] *Ingulph's Chronicle of the Abbey of Croyland:* with the continuations by Peter of Blois and Anonymous writers. Translated by Henry Riley. Published by Nabu Press 2014. Originally published 1854. Written 1486. Page 454.

to act litigiously against the King for the royal crown and claim it for himself by title of hereditary right." York arrived with "great pomp and splendour and in no small exaltation of mood, for he came with trumpets and horns, men-at-arms and a very large retinue... he marched straight through the great hall until he came to the solemn chamber... made directly for the King's throne, where he laid his hand on the drape or cushion as if about to take possession of what was his by right." [260]

Waurin gives his account which includes a falling out between York and Warwick. "The Duke of York rode straight to the palace, at which the people were greatly taken aback. When he had dismounted, he went to the lodge in the royal chamber and the King was placed in the custody of six of the duke's men." Salisbury who observed the proceedings told Warwick who "became very angry" and went straight to the duke's chamber... "there were angry words between the two of them, for the Earl disclosed to the duke how the lords and people were unhappy at his desire to strip the King of his crown". [261]

Warwick had travelled to Ireland from Calais and met with York. Future plans must have been on their agenda. It seems that York decided to make his own play for the throne rather than ruling through a lame duck Henry. It was a bad move. Not only did York surprise the Lords that were present in Westminster but he it appears that he had not informed Salisbury or Warwick of his intentions. Westminster was thrown into disarray.

Parliament spent the rest of the session discussing York's claim to the throne. This is very clear from the Parliamentary Rolls. [262] The Brut chronicle even relates how the crown hung in the House fell down suddenly whilst the subject was under discussion "which was take for a sign or token that the reign of King Henry was ended".

---

[260] *Registrum Abbatiae Johannis Whethamstede* by Abbot J. Whethamstede. Edited by H.T. Riley. 1872.
[261] *Recueil des Croniques et Anciennes Istories de la Grant Bretaigne* J. de Waurin, ed. by W. Hardy 1864-91.
[262] *Parliamentary Rolls Henry VI* October 1460.

[263] York's petition setting out his right to the throne was presented first to the Lords on 16th October, and then to Henry who asked for advice. The justices argued that it was not a matter upon which they could judge. Others declined to opine, saying it was beyond their competence.

The Lords discussed the matter at length and produced their critique of the petition with five objections to York's claim. Firstly, the Lords had sworn oaths to King Henry. Secondly, Acts of Parliament had given authority to Henry's title. Thirdly, the crown had been passed to Henry by diverse chronicles and parliaments. Fourthly, York had typically born the arms of Edmund Langley not Lionel of Clarence. Fifthly, Henry IV took the crown not as conqueror but as the inheritor of Henry III. York answered these five points in writing. Man must answer to the higher authority of God and justice was his main point. Henry IV had taken the crown by force, not by inheritance. and hence had needed parliament's agreement. At last, after much discussion, a compromise was thrashed out and agreed by all including the King. This agreement recognised York's undeniable right and yet would respect the honour of the King.

Parliament passed the Act of Accord on 24th October 1460 by which it was "accorded, appointed and agreed that Richard Duke of York be entitled, called and reputed from henceforth, very and rightful heir to the crowns and, after the death of Henry, the duke and his heirs shall immediately succeed to these crowns." York and his two sons, March and Rutland were granted land and estates giving them considerable income. The Coventry Parliament was declared null and void… "all acts, statutes, and ordinances made by its authority be reversed, annulled, repealed, revoked, and of no force or effect." [264] The accord was duly enrolled, and on Friday 31st October, York and his two eldest sons took an oath to observe its terms, on the condition that Henry did likewise. The agreement was publicly proclaimed in London and elsewhere on 9th November.

---

[263] *The Brut or the Chronicles of England* edited by F.W.D. Brie London 1906.
[264] *Parliamentary Rolls* October 1460.

The Croyland chronicler summarised the position. Parliament was "occupied with the discussion of the genealogical question, and the rights of the before-mentioned duke" for three weeks. "The differences were brought to a conclusion… The duke and his sons… were to swear fealty to the King, and to recognize him as King as long as he should live… as soon as the King should have departed this life, it should be lawful for the said duke and his heirs to lay claim to, and take possession of the crown." [265]

Henry vacated the palace of Westminster for York and returned to the Bishop of London's palace. York took over the reins of power. Salisbury was made Lord Chamberlain on 29th October. John Dynham became Chancellor of Ireland on 5th November. Sir John Wenlock became chief butler on 24th November. [266] Warwick was rewarded with the positions of Warden of the Cinque Ports and constable of Dover Castle. [267] Lord Fauconberg became Warwick's official number two at Calais. [268]

Queen Margaret met up with her brother-in-law, Jasper Tudor, Earl of Pembroke, in Wales. She sought help from Charles VII of France but then sailed to Scotland to seek help from the young James III or rather his mother, Mary of Gueldres. Tudor remained in Wales to drum up support for the Lancastrian cause. News of the Act of Accord and the disinheriting of her son, Prince Edward, would have given further stimulus to the Queen's /efforts to raise arms to take back what had been lost.

Margaret promised everything she could and more to Mary to gain Scottish help. Scotland would be given the border castle and town of Berwick. Prince Edward would marry one of Mary's daughters. Scottish soldiers would not be paid. Margaret had little money. They

---

[265] *Ingulph's Chronicle of the Abbey of Croyland:* with the continuations by Peter of Blois and Anonymous writers. Translated by Henry Riley. Published by Nabu Press 2014. Originally published 1854. Written 1486. Page 455.
[266] *Calendar of Patent Rolls 1452-1461* Pages 627, 640 & 644.
[267] *Calendar of Patent Rolls 1452-1461* Pages 642 & 652.
[268] *Calendar of Milanese Papers I*, Page 47.

could take what they want by way of plunder on route. Margaret had nothing much more to lose. Desperate times require desperate measures.

The Croyland chronicler explains… "As the decree of Parliament appeared to the northern partisans of the Queen most odious and execrable, a commotion took place there, among the nobles and common people, their object being, to have that enactment altered". [269]

Letters were sent to Lancastrian Lords to muster at Kingston-upon-Hull. Somerset had returned to England in September and was residing in Corfe Castle. Somerset joined with Devon and with around eight hundred men travelled north to join with Exeter, Northumberland, Clifford, Dacre and Neville who had been causing mischief and targeting the estates of York and Salisbury.

York determined to march north to meet the Queen and her supporters. Orders were sent out to call for armed men. Monies were raised by loan from the Council of London. On 9th December York left London with Salisbury and his second son, Rutland. March was sent west to Wales to raise more men from the marches.

Warwick and the Duke of Norfolk remained in London to hold the city and look after the King. Letters from the Queen, Prince Edward, Pembroke and even Northumberland asked the Council for their support and although these were ignored, Warwick felt it necessary to call the mayor and his aldermen together with the leading merchants and citizens to give their reassurance of support. The Council strengthened the watch and the city's defences. Henry was given wine as a Christmas present, and he hosted the mayor and aldermen to a festive feast after processing to St Pauls and celebrating mass.

Warwick also needed to look after Calais and ensure the seas and coasts around England were secure against possible French

---

[269] *Ingulph's Chronicle of the Abbey of Croyland:* with the continuations by Peter of Blois and Anonymous writers. Translated by Henry Riley. Published by Nabu Press 2014. Originally published 1854. Written 1486. Page 455.

incursions. On 16th December Warwick appointed Geoffrey Gate as Governor of the Isle of Wight with all relevant authorities [270] to take control from Somerset's brother Edmund Beaufort and make good the defences.

York and Salisbury travelled north gathering troops on the way. Their journey was slow. The poor summer weather had damaged roads, bridges and the harvest. The advance guard skirmished near Worksop with Somerset's men. They pressed on for the safety and security of Sandal Castle near Wakefield. Defences were repaired but provisions were light. York underestimated the strength of Lancastrian forces and sallied forth to forage under an agreed truce or to fight. [271] Contemporary chronicles are brief on the exact details aside from York, Salisbury and Rutland were killed.

The Croyland chronicler writes... "It being the week of our Lord's Nativity, the said Richard, Duke of York, incautiously engaged the northern army at Wakefield, which was fighting for the King, without waiting to bring up the whole of his forces: upon which. A charge was made by the enemy on his men, and he was without any mercy or respect relentlessly slain. There fell with him at the same place many noble and illustrious men; and countless numbers of the common people, who had followed him, met their deaths there, and all to no purpose." [272]

The *Annales Rerum Anglicarum* suggests that York was out looking for food and drink when he was attacked by the Lancastrians... "On 29th December 1460 at Wakefield, while the Duke of York's

---

[270] *Calendar of Patent Rolls 1452-1461*, Pages 391, 488, 637 & 638.
[271] *The Life and Reign of Edward the Fourth King of England and of France and Lord of Ireland* by Cora L. Scofield. Volumes One and Two. Fonthill Media 2016. First Published 1923. Pages 120-121.
[272] *Ingulph's Chronicle of the Abbey of Croyland:* with the continuations by Peter of Blois and Anonymous writers. Translated by Henry Riley. Published by Nabu Press 2014. Originally published 1854. Written 1486. Page 421.

men were roaming about the countryside in search of victuals, a fierce battle was fought… [273]

The English Chronicle reports that "The Duke of York, the Earl of Rutland his son, and the Earl of Salisbury, a little before Christmas, with a few people, went to the north, intending to repress the malice of the northern men who loved not the Duke of York nor the Earl of Salisbury… when they (Northumberland, Clifford, Somerset & Neville) saw a convenient time to fulfil their cruel intentions, on the last day of December, they fell upon Duke Richard, and killed him." [274]

The Tudor writer Hall says York was caught "like a fish in a net or a deer in a buckstall" on the plain between the castle and the town. [275]

Waurin and the English Chronicle talk of treachery, that Salisbury's half-brother, John Neville, "went to the said Duke of York, desiring a commission of him to raise an army for to chastise the rebels of our country". Andrew Trollope also falsely pretended to be an ally. York rode out in confidence but then Neville and Trollope turned on him. The Tudor historian Grafton wrote that York "manfully fighting, was within half-an-hour slain and dead". York is likely to have been killed swiftly. The later story of him being captured, sat on an ant hill with a crown of weeds, and taunted, is just a tale.

Worcester writes that York and Salisbury "hastened from London with a large force towards York but coming unexpectedly upon the troops of the Duke of Somerset at Worksop, their vanguard was

---

[273] *Annales Rerum Anglicarum in Letters and Papers illustrative of the Wars of the English in France*. Edited by J. Stevenson. Rolls Series. Volume 2. Pages 774-775.
[274] *An English Chronicle* edited by J.S. Davies. Camden Society 1856. Pages 106-107.
[275] *Hall's Chronicle: Containing the History of England*, by Edward Hall. Published by Forgotten Books 2018. Originally published by Richard Grafton 1548. Page 250.

destroyed. On 21st December, however, they reached Sandal Castle, with 6,000 men, and kept Christmas there, notwithstanding that the enemy under the Duke of Somerset and the Earl of Northumberland, were close by at Pontefract." Worcester has it that the Duke of York was out foraging for supplies when he was surprised by Somerset and the Lancastrians with far superior numbers. [276]

A Milanese ambassador reported back to his Duke… "Some of the lords of the queen's party, rendered desperate by the victory of the lords here, and especially by the Earl of Warwick, assembled a force in the northern parts, eighty miles from London, to come and attack their opponents here who are with the king, and get back the king into their power, as they had him before. Accordingly, the Duke of York, with two of his sons and Warwick's father, the Earl of Salisbury, went out to meet them. And it came to pass that, although they were three times stronger, yet from lack of discipline, because they allowed a large part of the force to go pillaging and searching for victuals, their adversaries, who are desperate, attacked the duke and his followers. Ultimately, they routed them, slaying the duke and his younger son, the Earl of Rutland, Warwick's father and many others. This news caused great alarm in these parts, although it seems Warwick was not there." [277]

---

[276] *The Chronicles of The White Rose of York: A series of Historical Fragments, Proclamations, Letters and Other Contemporary Documents relating to the Reign of Edward IV* Edited by James Bohn. Published London 1845. Paperback Version Reprint 2012. Introduction Page lxxxiii.
[277] *Calendar of State Papers* Milan 1461 Letter of 9th January 1461 Antonio de la Torre to Francesco Sforza, Duke of Milan.

The Battle of Wakefield   30th December 1460

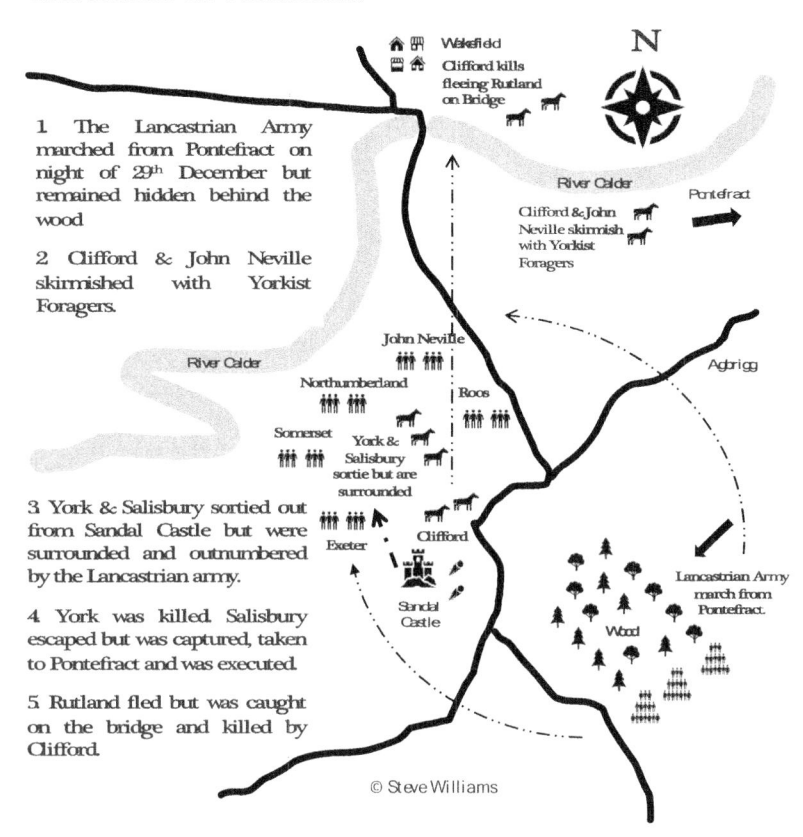

1. The Lancastrian Army marched from Pontefract on night of 29th December but remained hidden behind the wood

2. Clifford & John Neville skirmished with Yorkist Foragers.

3. York & Salisbury sortied out from Sandal Castle but were surrounded and outnumbered by the Lancastrian army.

4. York was killed. Salisbury escaped but was captured, taken to Pontefract and was executed.

5. Rutland fled but was caught on the bridge and killed by Clifford.

Map labels: Wakefield; Clifford kills fleeing Rutland on Bridge; River Calder; Clifford & John Neville skirmish with Yorkist Foragers; Pontefract; John Neville; Agbrigg; Northumberland; Roos; Somerset; York & Salisbury sortie but are surrounded; Exeter; Clifford; Sandal Castle; Wood; Lancastrian Army march from Pontefract.

© Steve Williams

Rutland, York's second son, was caught by Clifford attempting to flee across the bridge to Wakefield and was killed in revenge for the death of his father at Northampton. Hall has Rutland on his knees, begging for mercy, to which Clifford responds, "By God's blood, thy father slew mine, and so will I do thee and all thy kin". [278]

---

[278] *Hall's Chronicle: Containing the History of England*, by Edward Hall. Published by Forgotten Books 2018. Originally published by Richard Grafton 1548. Page 251.

Salisbury was captured and taken to Pontefract Castle where the English Chronicle tells us... "the common people of the country, which loved him not, took him out of the castle by violence and smote off his head". [279] The Bastard of Exeter, one of two illegitimate brothers of the Duke of Exeter, was the executioner.

The heads of York, Salisbury and Rutland were placed on spikes above Micklegate Bar at York. A paper crown was placed in a derisory fashion upon York's head. Tradition has it that Clifford was responsible. Now it was the turn of the Yorkist sons to seek retribution for the deaths of their fathers. The wheel of fortune was turning.

---

[279] *An English Chronicle* edited by J.S. Davies. Camden Society 1856.

St Albans 17th February 1461

> *… And quite in accordance with the doubtful issue of warfare, now the one and now the other, for the moment gained the victory, while fortune was continually shifting her position…* [280]

News of the **death and defeat of the Duke of York and his father, Salisbury** reached Warwick in London on 2nd January 1461. It was news that Warwick was not expecting. Others of his family and retainers had been killed at Wakefield including his brother, Thomas, and his brother-in-law William Lord Harrington and the Neville knights Parre and Radford.

Warwick took action immediately. Fresh monies were loaned from the city Council who also helped him by setting free some of the Earl's servants arrested for a violent attack against the home of one Simon Briggeman in Bishopsgate. [281] Commissions and communications were issued to raise fresh troops and authorise defensive measures in advance of the expected movement south of Margaret's Lancastrian army. The town of Shrewsbury, for example, was ordered to guard its gates against the likes of Somerset, Devon and Northumberland, Roos, Clifford and Neville who had gathered wicked men to commit treason and crimes. No-one should help or assist them.

Warwick managed diplomatic relations by sending letters to Duke Philip of Burgundy, Pope Pius II and Duke Sforza of Milan reassuring them that all would be well. The letter to Pope Pius II was dated 11th January 1461 and told him… "Your Holiness must not be troubled if you have heard of the events in England and of the destruction of some of my kinsmen in the battle against our enemies. With the help of God and the king, who is excellently

---

[280] *Ingulph's Chronicle of the Abbey of Croyland:* with the continuations by Peter of Blois and Anonymous writers. Translated by Henry Riley. Published by Nabu Press 2014. Originally published 1854. Written 1486. Page 419.
[281] *The Life and Reign of Edward the Fourth King of England and of France and Lord of Ireland* by Cora L. Scofield. Volumes One and Two. Fonthill Media 2016. First Published 1923. Page 128.

disposed, all will end well. We shall obtain either a fair and sure peace or victory, especially if you confer the long-expected promotion on your legate. The people will then see that our adversaries, who daily scorn your authority and the legate's, and say the latter has no power and is no legate, adding marvellous falsehoods to make him unpopular, to the detriment of the Church and the king… do not desert me and the others, whom you formerly received as sons, for eventually you will see us end well and devoutly. [282]

Coppini wrote to Duke Sforza that he was not discouraged "as the Earl of Warwick is safe". Another letter dated 24th January to the Duke from Antonio de la Torre, English Envoy to the Papal Court spoke extremely highly of Warwick saying he "is like another Caesar in these parts." [283]

Margaret left Scotland and was in York with her successful Lords by 20th January 1461. It was not long before they made their way south leaving a trail of destruction in their wake which was picked up in most contemporary reports.

The Croyland Chronicler was horrified… "there was no one now who would care to resist their inroads, they swept onwards like a whirlwind from the north… and they irreverently rushed… into churches and other sanctuaries of God… and most nefariously plundered chalices, books and vestments, and unutterable crime! Broke open the pixes in which were kept the body of Christ". Anyone such as Priests who tried to bar their way were "cruelly slaughtered in the very churches or churchyards" They "proceeded with impunity… over a space of thirty miles in breadth… covering the whole surface of the earth like so many locusts". The Croyland monks hid what they could, fortified the natural and other defences around their monastery and prayed. Their prayers were answered. The "execrable and so abominable" army passed by within six miles

---

[282] *Calendar of State Papers* Milan 1461 Letter of 11th January 1461 Richard Neville, Earl of Warwick, to Pope Pius II.
[283] *Calendar of State Papers* Milan 1461 Letter of 24th January 1461 Antonio de la Torre, English Envoy to the Papal Court and to the Duke of Milan to Francesco Sforza, Duke of Milan.

and they were "saved from calamity... by divine grace and clemency... after adjoining counties had been given up to dreadful pillage and plunder". [284]

Others were certainly not so fortunate. Grantham, Stamford, Peterborough, Huntingdon, Royston and other towns suffered at the hands of the Lancastrian army. Such outrages played into the hands of the Yorkists. Warwick sent out communications warning that "the misruled and outrageous people in the north parties of this realm" were intent upon the "destruction and subversion of all our land" and asked for them to rise up and resist such enemies.

The Abbot of St Albans wrote that the "Queen and the Prince" and their army "made their way towards the southern parts and advanced without interruption... in every place... they robbed, plundered and devastated, and carried off with them whatever they could find. Or discover, whether clothing or money, herds of cattle or single animals, or any other thing whatsoever, sparing neither churches nor clergy, monasteries nor monks, chapels nor chaplains". [285]

The English chronicle said that "they of the north secretly gathered a great people and came down suddenly to the town of Dunstable, robbing all the country and people as they came, spoiling abbeys, houses of religion and churches, and bearing away chalices, books and other ornaments, as if they had been pagans or Saracens and not Christian men". [286]

Clement Paston wrote to John Paston on 23rd January 1461... "I have heard it said that the (northern) Lords will be here sooner than

---

[284] *Ingulph's Chronicle of the Abbey of Croyland:* with the continuations by Peter of Blois and Anonymous writers. Translated by Henry Riley. Published by Nabu Press 2014. Originally published 1854. Written 1486. Page 422.
[285] *Registrum Abbatiae Johannis Whethamstede* by Abbot J. Whethamstede. Edited by H.T. Riley. 1872.
[286] *An English Chronicle* edited by J.S. Davies. Camden Society 1856. Pages 107-110.

men expected, I have heard within three weeks… In this (southern) country every man is very willing to go with the Lords here, and I hope God will help them, for the people in the north rob and steal, and be agreed to pillage all this country, and give away men's goods and livelihoods in all the south country". [287]

Queen Margaret became aware of the reputational damage to her cause and wrote two letters to the citizens of London, one from herself and one purportedly from Prince Edward. The letter from Prince Edward spoke of the "horrible and falsely foresworn traitor, Richard, calling himself Duke of York, mortal enemy unto my Lord, to my Lady and to us" who had spread malicious lies and made unlawful assemblies against the true King. The letter stated that they did not intend the destruction of London for theirs was an honourable cause. The King looked to the support of the people of the good city. [288]

Warwick responded to the growing threat. A call to arms was issued in the name of the Privy Council against the "misruled and outrageous people in the north parties of this realm" who were on their way south "towards these parties, to the destruction thereof, of you, and subversion of all our land". [289] Warwick readied and prepared to do battle.

Edward, Earl of March, was in Wales where he had gathered around him loyal nobles and many armed men. The eldest son of the Duke of York celebrated Christmas in the town of Shrewsbury, in the Friary [290] and not at Gloucester as suggested by the Short English

---

[287] *The Paston Letters 1422-1509* edited by J. Gairdner. Chatto and Windus, London 1904. Volume 3. Page 250.
[288] *Harleian MS.* 543, f, 147b.
[289] *Privy Council Proceedings VI* Pages 307-310. *The Life and Reign of Edward the Fourth King of England and of France and Lord of Ireland* by Cora L. Scofield. Volumes One. Page 136.
[290] *Annales Rerum Anglicarum in Letters and Papers illustrative of the Wars of the English in France.* Edited by J. Stevenson. Rolls Series. Volume 2. Pages 774-775.

Chronicle. It was there that he probably received the news of the deaths of his father and brother.

Edward and his men were preparing to march to London when they received news that Pembroke and Wiltshire had landed in the south-west of Wales with Frenchmen, Bretons and Irishmen recruited to fight for Queen Margaret. Edward organised his forces accordingly and met them in battle at Mortimer's Cross, near Wigmore. The chroniclers recorded the battle, though with the usual discrepancy on numbers of combatants.

The English Chronicle tells us that "Edward, the noble Earl of March, fought with the Welshmen near Wigmore in Wales, whose captains were the Earl of Pembroke and the Earl of Wiltshire, he won a victory over his enemies, put the two Earls to flight, and slew *4,000* Welshmen. [291] The *Annales Rerum Anglicarum* says that "a battle was fought near Wigmore at Mortimer's Cross, where the Earl of March with *51,000 men* attacked the Earl of Pembroke with *8,000*, and there fled from the field the Earl of Pembroke, the Earl of Wiltshire and many others". [292]

The Short English Chronicle tell us of a curious natural phenomenon of a parhelion that took place. In the sky around ten o'clock in the morning, there appeared "three suns shining on him in the east". People were shocked but Edward told them it was a good sign and "he kneeled down on his knees and made his prayers and thanked God". [293]

---

[291] *An English Chronicle* edited by J.S. Davies. Camden Society 1856. Pages 107-110.
[292] *Annales Rerum Anglicarum* in *Letters and Papers illustrative of the Wars of the English in France*. Edited by J. Stevenson. Rolls Series. Volume 2. Pages 775-776.
[293] *Three Fifteenth Century Chronicles with Historical Memoranda* by John Stowe. Edited by J Gairdner for the Camden Society. Published by Nabu Press 2012. Originally published 1881. Page 77.

Gregory's chronicle tells us more about the aftermath of the battle... "Edward Earl of March, the Duke of York's son and heir, won a great victory at Mortimer's Cross in Wales, where he put to flight, the Earls of Pembroke and Wiltshire, and took and slew knights, squires and others to the number of 3,000. Owen Tudor was taken and brought to Hereford, where he was beheaded in the market place, his head was set on the highest pinnacle of the market cross. And a mad woman combed his hair, washed away the blood off his face, got candles, and set about him, burning more than a hundred". [294]

The Croyland chronicler was more succinct... "The Duke of York's eldest son, Edward Earl of March, campaigning against the Queen's supporters in Wales, won a glorious victory over them at Mortimer's Cross". [295]

Pembroke and Wiltshire did not remain long at Pembroke Castle. They made their way northwards to Brecon, via Camarthen and Llandovery, on their way to join the Queen. Edward defensively arrays his men around Mortimer's Cross on the old Roman Road up which Pembroke and Wiltshire chose to progress. The river Lugg covered their flank to the east. Archers were positioned on the rising ground and cavalry hidden in the forested slopes to the west. Wiltshire has not recruited well. The Welsh under Edward and his lieutenants fought for their lands but the Irish were not well equipped. It didn't take much before they along with their French and Breton colleagues sought flight in the face of overwhelming force. Pembroke and Wiltshire escaped. Edward, Earl of March, was victorious.

---

[294] *Historical Collections of a Citizen of London* in Gregory's Chronicle, edited by J. Gairdner. Camden Society 1876. Pages 211-214.
[295] *Ingulph's Chronicle of the Abbey of Croyland:* with the continuations by Peter of Blois and Anonymous writers. Translated by Henry Riley. Published by Nabu Press 2014. Originally published 1854. Written 1486. Page 456.

The Battle of Mortimer's Cross 3rd February 1461

1. The Lancastrian Army arrived and camped in Great West Field.

2. The Yorkist camp was at Mortimer's Cross, with the muster at Wigmore Castle.

3. The Lancastrians advanced to meet the Yorkists. Fierce fighting ensued.

4. The Yorkist Cavalry, hidden in the wooded hills, surprised the Lancastrian left flank.

5. The Lancastrians including Pembroke & Wiltshire fled. Owen Tudor was caught and executed at Hereford.

© Steve Williams

The Elizabethan poet John Daniel writes of Edward's successful ambush… "Now like the Libyan lion when with pain. The weary hunter hath pursued his prey, outrushing from his den rapts all away, so comes young March their hopes to disappoint."

The three suns spoken of in the chronicles are an optical phenomenon of luminous spots on each side of the sun caused by

Page 162

the effect of light refraction through atmospheric ice crystals. They are known as a parhelion or sun dogs and are most common in the winter. The happening is described by Shakespeare in Henry VI Part III…

"Three glorious suns, each one a perfect sun;
Not separated with the racking clouds,
But severed in a pale clear-shining sky.
See, see! They join, embrace, and seem to kiss,
As if they vowed some league inviolable:
Now are they but one lamp, one light, one sun.
In this the heaven figures some event."

The words set by Shakespeare though are spoken by the future Richard III who in fact is only eight years old at the time of the battle and is with his mother, the Duchess Cecily, in London.

The battle of Mortimer's Cross reportedly took place on 3rd February, St Blaise's Day. This is the view of William of Worcester, John Benet, the English Chronicle and an Italian merchant, Prospero Camulio, writing on 11th March 1461 to Duke Sforza of Milan. [296] This is the day after Candlemas Day which was on 2nd February in 1461. The English Chronicle, a writer well informed of Yorkist affairs, reported that the battle was fought "on the third day of February". The event of the three suns took place on "the Monday before the day of battle, that is to say the feast of the purification of our blessed lady Mary".

In London, preparations continued. Warwick's brother, John Neville, was created Lord Montagu. On 8th February Warwick was elected a knight of the Garter along with Sir John Wenlock, Sir Thomas Kyriell and Lord Bonville at a meeting of the order at the

---

[296] *Calendar of State Papers* Milan 1461 Letter of 11th March 1461 Prospero di Camulio, Milanese Ambassador to the Court of France, to Francesco Sforza, Duke of Milan.

Bishop of London 's palace. [297] Men, arms, provisions and supplies were being gathered in readiness for battle. The citizens of London held their collective breath. Some were conspicuous in their help for Warwick was a popular figure. Others went about their ways or else decided to vacate the capital for reasons of safety.

The Pope's legate, Coppini, sailed for Europe. The Italian merchant Prosper Camulio later reported that Coppini left after a falling out with Warwick because he had promised the Earl at Northampton that he would "excommunicate the enemy and give the benediction to the followers of Warwick, but seeing the bad weather and the Queen's power, and not feeling well, he did not go". [298] Warwick cannot have been too displeased with Coppini for he provided an escort for him as far as Gravesend, across the river from Tilbury from where he sailed. It was more likely that Coppini was briefing accordingly having overreached himself at Northampton.

On 12th February Warwick led his army out from London to meet the Queen's army taking the King with him. Warwick deployed his army defensively around St Albans thus blocking the Queen's expected path to London. A small forward force was sent to hold Dunstable. Archers were deployed strategically within the town. The Bars were strengthened and defended but the main army under Montagu encamped on Bernard's Heath to the north-east of the town by the road to Hatfield and Ware. Warwick himself camped further up the road near the village of Sandridge and Norfolk drew together his men further away still on an area known as Nomansland.

---

[297] *The Life and Reign of Edward the Fourth King of England and of France and Lord of Ireland* by Cora L. Scofield. Volumes One. Page 139. *Register of the Order of the Garter* II, 166-168.
[298] *Calendar of State Papers* Milan 1461 Letter from Prospero di Camulio, Milanese Ambassador to the Court of France, to Francesco Sforza, Duke of Milan.

Warwick set about arranging elaborate defences. Gregory wrote that… "The Lords in King Harry's party pitched a field and fortified it strongly… they had such instruments as would shoot both pellets of lead and arrows… and nets of great cords four fathoms in length and four feet wide, like a hedge, and at every second knot there was a nail standing upright… and body shields borne like a door." [299]

The Yorkist scouts reported incorrectly that the opposing army was still far distant. Gregory tells us that "their prickers came not back to them to bring them tidings how near the Queen was, save one who came and said that she was nine miles away".

The Lancastrian army diverted to Dunstable where they easily overcame the small Yorkist force and the townsfolk led by a butcher who subsequently hanged himself in disgrace according to both Gregory and Worcester. [300] They then made a surprise night march arriving at St Albans at three o'clock in the morning on Shrove Tuesday 17th February 1461 catching Warwick's men unaware. The vanguard, led most probably by Anthony Trollope, encountered little resistance crossing the river Ver by St Michael's mill and church until they reached the marketplace which was strongly defended by Yorkist archers. A second wave of attacks led by Somerset and armed men on horses breached the defences to the north and entered the town thus isolating the Yorkist archers.

The Lancastrians strengthened with further troops arriving down the road from Dunstable then attacked the main Yorkist force from the rear. This caused chaos amongst the Yorkist ranks. Some men from Kent, led by Sir Henry Lovelace, chose to flee triggering a full-

---

[299] *Historical Collections of a Citizen of London* in Gregory's Chronicle, edited by J. Gairdner. Camden Society 1876. Pages 211-214.
[300] *The Itineraries of William Worcester* edited by J.H. Harvey. Oxford 1969. Page 776.

scale flight. Warwick, for whatever reason, chose not to support his brother and retreated westwards to safety with the bulk of his men. Norfolk returned eastwards with his troops. Montagu was captured and later imprisoned. King Henry VI was found lightly guarded in the camp and taken to meet up once more with his wife, Queen Margaret, and his son, Prince Edward who was knighted by him in the field.

Abbot Whethamstede describes the battle… "The northern men, coming to the town of the said protomartyr, and hearing that the King, with a great army and some of his Lords, was lying near, immediately entered the said town, desiring to pass through the middle of it and direct their army against the King's army. However, they were compelled to turn back by a few archers who met them near the Great Cross, and to flee with disgrace to the west end of the town where, entering by a lane which leads from that end northwards as far as St Peter's Street, they had there a great fight with a certain small band of the people of the King's army. Then, after not a few had been killed on both sides, going out to the heath called Barnet Heath, lying near the north end of the town, they had a great battle with certain large forces, perhaps four or five thousand, of the vanguard of the King's army. [301] This "vanguard of the King's army" was in fact the rearguard of the Yorkist army which was turned by the surprise and unexpected direction of attack by the Lancastrians.

Gregory tells us that "before they (the Yorkists) were prepared for the battle, the Queen's party was at hand with them in the town of St Albans, and then everything was out of order… before the gunners and Burgundians could level their guns they were busily fighting, and many a gun of war was provided that was of little avail or none at all… but in time of need they could shoot not one of them, for the fire turned back on those who would shoot these

---

[301] *Registrum Abbatiae Johannis Whethamstede* by Abbot J. Whethamstede. Edited by H.T. Riley. 1872.

things…" Gregory's own opinion was that… "in foot soldiers is all the trust". [302]

The English Chronicle reports that "King Harry and his Lords. The Dukes of Norfolk and Suffolk, and the Earls of Warwick and Arundel, Lord Neville and others, left London and came with their people to the town of St Albans, not knowing that the people of the north were so near. When the King heard that they were so near him, he went out and took his field and saw his people slain on both sides. At the last, as a result of the withdrawal of the Kentishmen and also the indisposition of the people of the King's side, King Harry's party lost the field. The Lords who were with the King, seeing this, withdrew and went away." [303]

Another tale of King Henry was told by a foreign correspondent in his letter to the Duke of Milan… "We hear many strange things from England day by day and hour by hour. A letter written to *the Dauphin* by one who was at the great battle on Shrove Tuesday gives full particulars of the princes, the numbers engaged, the assaults, the blows, the wounded and the rumours circulating that day on one side and the other… The king was placed under a tree a mile away, where he laughed and sang, and when the defeat of the Earl of Warwick was reported, he detained upon his promise the two princes who had been left to guard him. Very soon the Duke of Somerset and the conquerors arrived to salute him, and he received them in friendly fashion and went with them to St. Albans to the queen, and on the morrow one of the two detained, upon his assurance, was beheaded and the other imprisoned." [304]

---

[302] *Historical Collections of a Citizen of London* in Gregory's Chronicle, edited by J. Gairdner. Camden Society 1876. Pages 211-214.
[303] *An English Chronicle* edited by J.S. Davies. Camden Society 1856. Pages 107-110.
[304] *Calendar of State Papers* Milan 1461 Letter of 9th March 1461 Prospero di Camulio, Milanese Ambassador to the Court of France, etc., to Francesco Sforza, Duke of Milan.

The Croyland Chronicler summarises events very succinctly… "The northerners invaded the southern parts until they reached St Albans, where they put to flight the Earl of Warwick, who had brought King Henry as if to make him fight against the Queen, his wife, and his son. The northerners failed to follow up their victory, leading the King and Queen back with them to the north". [305]

The *Annales Rerum Anglicarum* records that "the battle of St Albans was fought, where the Duke of Norfolk and the Earls of Warwick and Arundel and many others fled from the field. And King Henry was captured on the field… and the prince came to the King in the field, where the King, his father, dubbed him knight." [306]

Waurin places the blame on the traitorous Lovelace who had promised himself to the Queen's cause in exchange for being released after Wakefield. Lovelace not only revealed the Yorkist deployments to the Lancastrians but caused confusion in the ranks and gave up King Henry. Lovelace is not specifically mentioned by other accounts but is a very convenient scapegoat for Warwick who briefed Waurin accordingly. [307]

Abbot Whethamstede blames Warwick himself for not supporting Montagu's troops… "The southern men who were fiercer at the beginning… were broken very quickly afterwards, and the more quickly because looking back, they saw no-one coming up from the main body of the King's army, or preparing to give them help, whereupon they turned their backs on the northern men and fled."

---

[305] *Ingulph's Chronicle of the Abbey of Croyland:* with the continuations by Peter of Blois and Anonymous writers. Translated by Henry Riley. Published by Nabu Press 2014. Originally published 1854. Written 1486. Page 456.
[306] *Annales Rerum Anglicarum* in *Letters and Papers illustrative of the Wars of the English in France.* Edited by J. Stevenson. Rolls Series. Volume 2. Pages 775-776.
[307] *Recueil des Croniques et Anciennes Istories de la Grant Bretaigne* by J. de Waurin, edited by W. Hardy 1864-91. Page 263-266.

[308] The Abbot despite all his pleas was unable to save the town of St Albans from once more being subject to robbery and pillage. Both the town and abbey suffered at the hands of the northern army such that "not even the beggars were spared".

The road to London was now open for the victorious Queen and her Lancastrian supporters but London was not ready to welcome the northern army whose reputation for pillage and plunder was feared by all. The gates of London were locked shut and the citizens readied their defences. Guards were put in place. Shops were closed. The Queen was very aware of these fears and kept her army at St Albans whilst sending an embassy to London and a small force to Barnet ready to take the keys of the city once offered. The mayor sent the Dowager Duchesses of Buckingham and Bedford, together with the widow of Lord Scales to negotiate with the Queen.

The Queen withdrew her army to Dunstable but sought money and food in exchange. Money and food were sent as agreed. The food was seized by some citizens led by John Wenlock's cook according to Gregory's chronicle "but as for the money, I don't know how it was departed". [309] The citizens did not believe the promises of safety from pillage given by the King and Queen. The Queen's troops at Barnet sought entrance to London but were repulsed and put to flight.

The situation was tense. The Duchess of York sent her youngest two sons, George and Richard, overseas to Burgundy. Others too left the city, rather than remain and face the northern army. A letter of the 19th February 1461 written from London by C. Gigli to Michele Arnolfini of Bruges explains the situation… "When the news was known here, the mayor sent to the king and queen, it is

---

[308] *Registrum Abbatiae Johannis Whethamstede* by Abbot J. Whethamstede. Edited by H.T. Riley. 1872.
[309] *Historical Collections of a Citizen of London* in Gregory's Chronicle, edited by J. Gairdner. Camden Society 1876. Page 214.

supposed to offer obedience, provided they were assured that they would not be plundered or suffer violence. In the meantime, they keep a good guard at the gates, which they keep practically closed, and so through all the district they maintain a good guard, and those who are here, thank God, feel no harm or lack of governance. Yet the shops keep closed, and nothing is done either by the tradespeople or by the merchants, and men do not stand in the streets or go far away from home. We are all hoping that, as the queen and prince have not descended in fury with their troops, the gates may be opened to them upon a good composition, and they may be allowed to enter peacefully. God grant this may happen! otherwise … favour, and thus we are not without great fear, as … the least lack of control would ruin everything. God be our protector, and may He not consider our sins!" [310]

The *Annales Rerum Anglicarum* records that "The Aldermen of London sent the Duchesses of Bedford and Buckingham to sue to the Queen for grace and the peace of the city". [311] The English Chronicle reports that… "London, dreading the manners and malice of the Queen, the Duke of Somerset and others, lest they would have plundered the city, sent the Duchess of Buckingham and knowledgeable men to negotiate with them to show benevolence and goodwill to the city which was divided within itself. Some… promised a certain sum of money… certain spearmen and men at arms were sent by the duke to enter the city before he came: of these, some were slain, some sore hurt, and the rest put to flight… the commons took the keys of the gates and courageously kept and defended it from their enemies until the coming of Edward, the noble Earl of March". [312]

---

[310] *Calendar of State Papers* Milan 1461 Letter of 19th February 1461 written from London by C. Gigli to Michele Arnolfini of Bruges.
[311] *Annales Rerum Anglicarum in Letters and Papers illustrative of the Wars of the English in France*. Edited by J. Stevenson. Rolls Series. Volume 2. Pages 775-776.
[312] *An English Chronicle* edited by J.S. Davies. Camden Society 1856. Pages 107-110.

Richard Beauchamp, the Bishop of Salisbury, spoke of "that unlucky battle of St Albans" in writing some weeks later to Coppini telling him that the kingdom "was convulsed on every hand" and that few people felt secure, neither rich nor poor. [313] Chancery proceedings records tell us of one William Keynes who entrusted his fellow citizen, Thomas Trebolance, with the safe keeping of his jewels of silver and gold to the value of £74 10s 8d for he was "afraid for robbing by the late rebels that then were resorting towards the city to rob and spoil, like as they robbed and spoiled in other places". One month later when his fears had passed, he asked for his property back. Trebolance took sanctuary in St Martin's-le-Grand and Keynes's wife ran off with the jewels. [314]

There were rumours that Warwick had fled to Calais, but these were incorrect Warwick met up with Edward, Earl of March at Chipping Norton according to Worcester, or Burford according to Gregory. They then marched together to London. The gates that had been closed to Queen Margaret and her army were now opened amongst much relief and almost joy. Gregory captured the mood of the city... "Let us walk in a new wine yard and let us make a gay garden in the month of March with this fair white rose and herb, the Earl of March".

The London Chronicle reports that on Thursday 26th February 1461 "the Earl of March and the Earl of Warwick came to London with a great power and, on the Sunday afterwards, all the host mustered in St John's field and there was read among them certain articles and points in which King Harry VI had offended against the realm. Then it was demanded of the people whether Harry were worthy to reign still and the people cried 'Nay!' Then they were asked if they

---

[313] *Calendar of State Papers* Milan 1461.
[314] *The Life and Reign of Edward the Fourth King of England and of France and Lord of Ireland* by Cora L. Scofield. Volumes One and Two. Fonthill Media 2016. First Published 1923. Page 148.

Page 171

would have the Earl of March as King and they cried 'Yea!' Certain captains then went to the Earl of March's place at Baynard's castle, and many people with them, and told him that the people had chosen him as King: he thanked them and, by the advice of the archbishop of Canterbury, the Bishop of Exeter and the Earl of Warwick, and others, consented to take it upon him". [315]

Edward was acclaimed King by popular demand. Letters were sent out across the realm to let people know that the 4th of March 1461 was the first day of the reign of King Edward IV. The Croyland Chronicler relates that… "After proper deliberation with his council, it was decided, irrevocably, that since King Henry, by associating with the murderers of his father and endeavouring to annul the decree of Parliament, had broken the accord, the Earl no longer need observe his fealty to him". The Chronicle explains that Edward was received "with unbounded joy… for he was then of vigorous age, and well fitted to endure the conflict of battle, while, at the same time, he was fully equal to the management of the affairs of the state". These aspects were in sharp contrast to Henry VI. [316]

The English Chronicle explains that "Edward the noble Earl of March was chosen King in the city of London and began to reign" and that "thereafter King Harry, with Margaret his Queen and the northern men, returned homeward, doing harm innumerable, taking men's carts, horses and beasts, and robbing the people such that the men in the shires through which they passed had almost no beasts left to till their land". [317]

---

[315] *London Chronicle: Gough 10. Six Town Chronicles of England.* Edited by R. Flenley. Oxford 1911. Pages 161-162.
[316] *Ingulph's Chronicle of the Abbey of Croyland* Translated by Henry Riley. Published by Nabu Press 2014. Originally published 1854. Written 1486. Pages 456 and 425.
[317] *An English Chronicle* edited by J.S. Davies. Camden Society 1856. Pages 107-110.

Nicolo Darabatta wrote to Coppini on 4th March 1461... "By my last letter I advised your lordship of the news here and told you how at St. Albans on carnival day the forces of the queen and prince routed those of the king and Warwick, with a great slaughter, and that everyone believed that Warwick had gone to Calais. But it was not so, as he went to meet the Earl of March, and last Friday after dinner they came here with about 5,000 persons, including foot and horse. A great crowd flocked together and with the lords, who were there, they chose the Earl of March as their king and sovereign lord, and that day they celebrated the solemnity, going in procession through the place amid great festivities. It remains to see how King Henry, his son, the queen and the other lords will bear this, as it is said that the new king will shortly leave here to go after them." [318]

George Neville, Bishop of Exeter, wrote to Coppini one month later on the return of his brother Warwick to London and Edward, formerly Earl of March, replacing "that puppet of a King". Neville reported... "on the 25th they entered the city, and were joyfully received by all the people, and on the 4th of March he [Edward] was nominated and practically by force created king by the nobles and people universally, near Westminster". [319]

"Universally" was an exaggeration. It was a well-managed affair. George Neville addressed a large gathering in St John's Field on Sunday 1st March of committed supporters including soldiers and citizens of London. Edward's right and title to the throne was fully explained. Henry VI was unfit and unworthy to rule for he was weak in mind and had broken the agreement made before Parliament. The crowd gave their vociferous support for Edward to be their King. All the captains and *available* council members were brought on side.

---

[318] *Calendar of State Papers* Milan 1461 Letter of 4th March 1461 Nicolo Darabatta to Francesco Copino, bishop of Terni, Papal Legate to England and Flanders.
[319] *Calendar of State Papers* Milan 1461. Letter of 7th April 1461 George Neville, Bishop of Exeter, Chancellor of England, to Francesco Coppino, Bishop of Terni, Apostolic Legate in Flanders

Edward was acclaimed King by the city of London and his own supporters including Warwick. Many important and influential Lords were not present and thought otherwise. Edward was appointed "King of England and of France and Lord of Ireland" but in reality, he had yet to consolidate his new position. London may be his, but King Henry and Queen Margaret were in York with their Lancastrian Lords gathering men around them to take back the throne.

The Milanese Ambassador explained the position to his duke in a letter dated 27th March 1461… "the people of London, the leaders of the people of the island, together with some other lords, full of indignation, created a new king, Edward, son of the Duke of York, known as my lord of March. From what we have heard since, he was chosen, so they say, on all sides as the new king by the princes and people at London…

As is usual in common and great matters, opinions vary in accordance with men's passions. Those who support the claims of Edward and Warwick say that the chances in favour of Edward are great, both on account of the great lordship which he has in the island and in Ireland, and owing to the cruel wrongs done to him by the queen's side, as well as through Warwick and London, which is entirely inclined to side with the new king and Warwick, and as it is very rich and the most wealthy city of Christendom, this enormously increases the chances of the side that it favours. To these must be added the good opinion of the temper and moderation of Edward and Warwick.

Some, on the other hand, say that the queen is exceedingly prudent, and by remaining on the defensive, as they say she is well content to do, she will bring things into subjection and will tear to pieces these attacks of the people, who, when they perceive that they are not on the road to peace, will easily be induced to change sides, such being the very nature of the people, especially when free, and never to let things go so far that they cannot turn". [320]

Edward chose not to be crowned. There would be a time for him to be appointed King in the time-honoured fashion but not then. Warwick and Edward prepared to do battle once more.

---

[320] *Calendar of State Papers* Milan 1461 Letter of 27th March 1461 Prospero di Camulio, Milanese Ambassador to the Court of France, etc., to Francesco Sforza, Duke of Milan.

Towton 29th March 1461

> *...So about nine o'clock, on the 29th April, being Palm Sunday, both the hosts approached in a plain field, between Towton and Saxton. When each part perceived the other, they made a great shout, and at the same instant of time there fell snow, which by violence of the wind was driven into the faces of them, which were King Henry's part, so that their sight was somewhat blemished and diminished...* [321]

The new **King Edward** issued a proclamation and rallying call on 6th March 1461. The Lancastrian Lords had been "moved and stirred by the spirit of the Devil" to do wrong through their negligence, ambition and covetousness. They were committing heinous crimes. Men were being murdered and maimed... "in such detestable wise and cruelness as hath not been heard done among the Saracens or Turks to any Christian men... wives, widows, maidens, women also of religion, and other" were being sadly oppressed. Pembroke and Wiltshire were singled out for bringing into England "our enemy strangers, as well Frenchmen and Scots".

"He that calleth himself King Henry the Sixth, contrary to God and to his surety and promise made to such Lords and other persons as by his commandment went with him to the field, now late ungodly, cruelly and unmanly suffered certain of them to be murdered and destroyed". No-one was to give the "rebels and rioters" help or comfort in any way, nor commit crimes of robbery, rape or pillage, on pain of death or forfeiture. "Grace and Pardon of his life and goods" would be granted to any follower of Henry VI who tendered submission within ten days. Twenty-two Lancastrians were excluded from this offer, These included Anthony Trollope, John Morton, Gervase Clifton, Thomas Tresham, Clapham the Younger

---

[321] *Hall's Chronicle: Containing the History of England* by Edward Hall. Published by Forgotten Books 2018. Originally published by Richard Grafton 1548. Page 255.

and both the Bastards of Exeter. Prices were placed on their heads.[322]

Warwick left London on 7th March with "a great puissance of people" in order to bring order to the midlands and to array men before meeting up with Edward once more. Thomas, Bastard of Exeter, was captured at Coventry and executed. Norfolk travelled home to raise troops. Money was borrowed once more from the mayor and aldermen of London.

Warwick remained Captain of Calais, Constable of Dover Castle and the Cinque Ports and retained the office of Great Chamberlain left to him after the death of his father. He was given the Captaincy of Guines and Hammes. Warwick's brother, George Neville, was made Chancellor. Warwick's uncle, Lord Fauconberg, was made a Baron to serve on Edward's council. Viscount Bourchier continued as Treasurer. There was little time for much else.

Lord Fauconberg marched north from London on Wednesday 11th March at the head of the "foot people' of the army, mostly Welshmen and men from Kent. Sir John Wenlock and a small force of men were tasked with taking the castle of Thorpe Waterfield where a few Lancastrian supporters were holed up and causing trouble.

On 12th March Edward wrote for help and support from towns and cities such as Coventry... "for as much as we now be coming on our journey for the repressing of our adversaries and rebels and also enemies, strangers as Frenchmen and Scots, which by the stirring of our adversaries and rebels be coming into this our land for to destroy it, we will and straightly charge you that you make and ordain all defensible men that you can come and await upon us on our journey, not failing as our special trust is in you". Coventry

---

[322] *The Life and Reign of Edward the Fourth King of England and of France and Lord of Ireland* by Cora L. Scofield. Volumes One. Page 139. Close Roll 1 Edward IV m 38 dorso. Calendar of Charter Rolls 1461-68, Pages 54-56.

responded well by raising £80 which paid for 100 men to join Edward's army. [323]

Fabyan summarised events so… "Edward the eldest son unto the Duke of York, then was elected and chosen for King of England… the Saturday following, the Earl of Warwick with a great puissance of people, departed out of London northward; and upon the Wednesday following the King's footmen went toward the same journey; and the Friday next following, the King took his voyage through the city with a great band of men, and so rode forth at Bishopsgate… In which the self-same day, which was the twelfth of March, a grocer of London, named Walter Walker, for offence by him done against the King, was beheaded in Smithfield; but his wife which after was married to John Norland, grocer and alderman, had such friends about the King, that her goods were not forfeited to the King's use." [324] It was most fortunate that Walker's wife had friends about the King…

Edward left London with the remainder of his troops including a small number of Burgundians provided to him by Duke Philip. Progress was slow and deliberate in order to swell the ranks of armed men. It gave time for Warwick to organise matters in the Midlands and Norfolk in the East. Edward travelled north via Cambridge and Nottingham. Warwick met the young King near Doncaster about 27th March having journeyed from Coventry via Lichfield. They progressed onward to Pontefract.

Henry VI wrote out from his base in York on 13th March to rally support. Henry's letter to Sir William Plumpton survives… "for as much as we have knowledge that our great traitor, the late Earl of March, had made great assemblies of riotous and mischievously disposed people, and, to stir and provoke them to draw unto him, he has cried in his proclamations havoc upon all our true liege people and subjects, their wives, children and goods, and is now

---

[323] *Coventry Leet Book*. Edited by M.D. Harris. Early English Text Society 1907-13. Pages 314-315.
[324] *The New Chronicles of England and France* by Robert Fabyan. Edited by Henry Ellis London 1811. Forgotten Books 2018. Originally edition by Pynson 1516. Page 639.

coming towards us. We therefore pray you and also straightly charge you that, upon the sight hereof, you, with all such people as you may make defensibly arrayed, come to us in all haste possible to resist the malicious intent and purpose of our said traitor". [325]

[325] *Letter from Henry VI to Sir William Plumpton.* Plumpton Letters and Papers. Edited by J. Kirby. Camden Society 1996. Page 26.

The Yorkist Army encamped near Pontefract Castle around 27th March. An advance task force of "foreprickers" led by John Radcliffe, Lord Fitzwalter, was sent to take and hold the crossing at Ferrybridge over the River Aire. The Lancastrian army encamped outside Tadcaster blocking the route further north to York where King Henry and the royal family were staying.

Fitzwalter arrived at Ferrybridge to find the bridge destroyed by the Lancastrians and set his men to repair the damage. A narrow temporary bridge was put in place and the advance force camped overnight. Unbeknown to them, Lord Clifford and his mounted force launch an early morning surprise attack. Fitzwalter thought his men were quarrelling, wandered out of his tent without armour and was killed. Warwick's brother, the Bastard of Salisbury, was also slain in the melee.

Hall wrote that… "The Lord Clifford both being in lusty youth and of frank courage determined with his light horsemen to make an assay to such as kept the passage of Ferrybridge, and so departed from the great army on the Saturday before Palm Sunday, and early or his enemies were ware, gained the bridge and slew the keepers of the same, and all as would withstand him. The Lord Fitzwater hearing the noise, suddenly rose out of his bed, and unarmed, with a poleaxe in his hand, thinking it had been a fray amongst his men, came down to appease the same, but was slain and with him the Bastard of Salisbury, brother to the Earl of Warwick, a valiant young gentleman, and of such audacity…. When the Earl of Warwick was informed of this feat… he slew his horse with his sword saying, 'let him flee that will, for surely I will tarry with him that will tarry with me', and he kissed the cross of his sword". [326] Hall's story about Warwick killing his horse is a direct translation from the French chronicler Du Clercq. [327]

---

[326] *Hall's Chronicle: Containing the History of England* by Edward Hall - Published by Forgotten Books 2018. Originally published by Richard Grafton 1548. Page 255.
[327] *Memoires de la Regne de Philippe le Bon*, Duc de Bourgogne Brussels 1835-6, iii, Page 118.

Warwick retook the crossing. Gregory's Chronicle tells us that Warwick sustained a leg wound in the fighting at Ferrybridge… "Lord Fitzwalter was slain at Ferrybridge, and many more with him were slain and drowned. And the Earl of Warwick was hurt in his leg with an arrow. [328]

Fauconberg, Sir William Blount and Robert Horne led a mounted force of men three miles upstream to Castleford where they crossed and made their way north along the old Roman road before turning eastwards towards Saxton cutting off Clifford's retreat at Dinting Dale. Clifford was killed by an arrow to the throat according to Hall. The Lancastrian army were unable or unwilling to assist perhaps fearing it was the vanguard of the main Yorkist army which was still some ten miles south making slow progress in crossing the now undefended River Aire. They moved up towards Saxton where they camped in fields to the south and prepared for battle.

Most accounts report that the fighting at Ferrybridge occurred on Saturday 28th March, the day before Towton. Some argue though that all the fighting occurred on Sunday 29th March based on a letter from George Neville to Coppini which stated that "on Palm Sunday, near a town called Ferrybridge, there was a great conflict, which began with the rising of the sun, and lasted until the tenth hour of the night". [329] The poem "Rose of Rouen" says that the main battle at Towton did not start until mid-afternoon… "On Palm Sunday, after the none (3 o'clock), they met us in the field". It could have all happened on the Sunday, but timing and distances would suggest the different phases of the battle took place over the whole weekend.

---

[328] *Historical Collections of a Citizen of London* in Gregory's Chronicle, edited by J. Gairdner. Camden Society 1876. Pages 216-19.
[329] *Calendar of State Papers* Milan 1461 Letter of 7th April 1461 George Neville, Bishop of Exeter, Chancellor of England, to Francesco Coppino, Bishop of Terni, Apostolic Legate in Flanders.

The Battle of Towton 29th March 1461

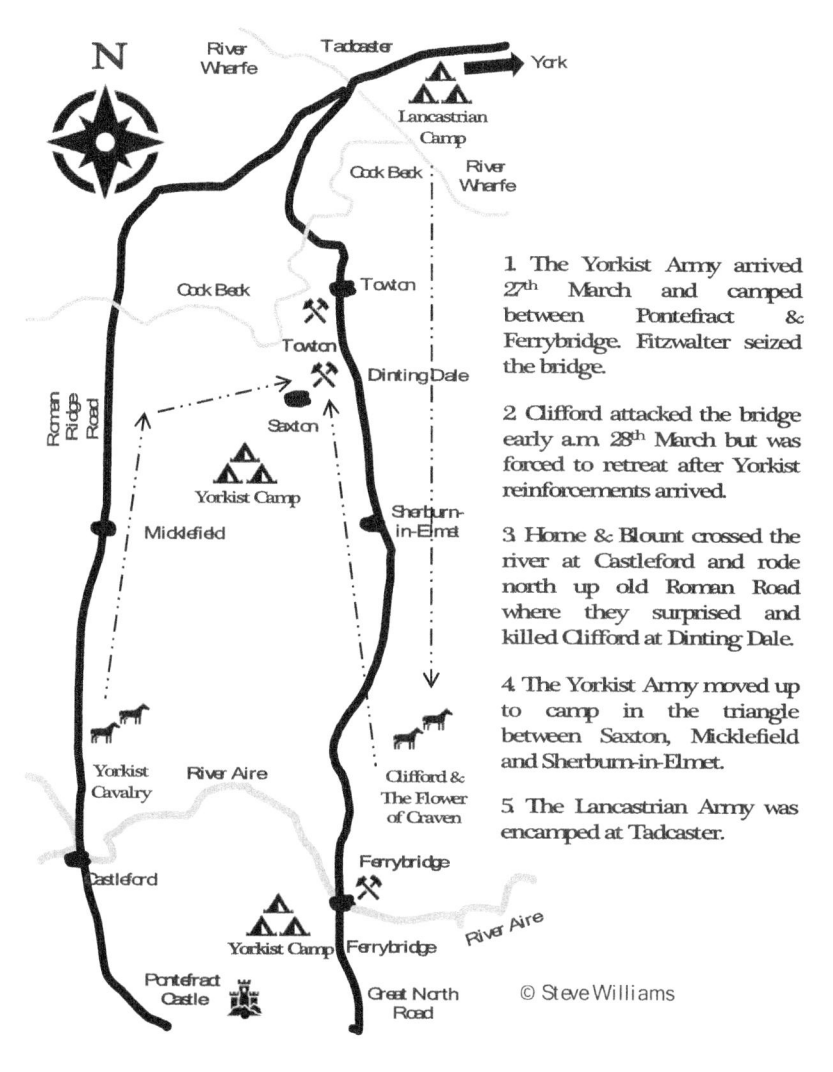

1. The Yorkist Army arrived 27th March and camped between Pontefract & Ferrybridge. Fitzwalter seized the bridge.

2. Clifford attacked the bridge early a.m. 28th March but was forced to retreat after Yorkist reinforcements arrived.

3. Horne & Blount crossed the river at Castleford and rode north up old Roman Road where they surprised and killed Clifford at Dinting Dale.

4. The Yorkist Army moved up to camp in the triangle between Saxton, Micklefield and Sherburn-in-Elmet.

5. The Lancastrian Army was encamped at Tadcaster.

© Steve Williams

It was bitterly cold as dawn broke on Palm Sunday on 29th March 1461. We know that from the reports of snow falling. This was more winter than spring. The Yorkist army moved up towards the plateau at Towton where the Lancastrians were mustered after leaving their camp at Tadcaster. Visibility was poor. Hall wrote how the Yorkist

Page 182

exploited the poor conditions… "The Lord Fauconberg, who led the forward of King Edward's battle, and of much experience in martial feats, caused every archer under his standard, to shoot one flight and then made them to stand still. The northern men, feeling the shots, but by reason of the snow, not well viewing the distance between them and their enemies, like hardy men shot their sheaf of arrows as fast as they might, but all their shots were lost and their labour in vain for they came not near the southerners by 40 yards. When their shot was almost spent, the Lard Fauconberg marched forward with his archers, who not only shot their own arrows but also gathered the arrows of their enemies and let a great part of them fly against their own masters, and another part they let stand on ground which sore moved the legs of the owners when the battle joined". [330]

Battle was joined. Fighting was fierce. All accounts are agreed in this respect, but they vary as to the details of battle itself and where individual Lords and their retinues fought. It is generally agreed that the Yorkists initiated the fighting but then were very pressed. Waurin alone mentions 200 Spearmen hidden in Castle Hill Wood.[331] The Lancastrians gained an advantage by an overlapping movement on one of the flanks, perhaps by Somerset and Rivers. This movement caused the two armies to pivot 45 degrees. The Brief Latin Chronicle reports that many of the Yorkist soldiers "turned their backs".

Edward was forced to lead from the front and played a significant and well publicised role. Waurin is not the only source who gives prominence to Edward IV in leading his troops. Hall wrote that the battle "ebbed and flowed" and that Edward "so courageously

---

[330] *Hall's Chronicle: Containing the History of England* by Edward Hall - Published by Forgotten Books 2018. Originally published by Richard Grafton 1548. Pages 255-256.
[331] *Recueil des Croniques et Anciennes Istories de la Grant Bretaigne* J. de Waurin, ed. by W. Hardy 1864-91.

comforted his men, refreshing the weary, and helping the wounded" that the Lancastrians were at last "discomforted and overcome". [332]

Bishop Richard Beauchamp wrote to Coppini on 7th April… "On Palm Sunday last King Edward began a very hard-fought battle near York, in which the result remained doubtful the whole day, until at length victory declared itself on his side, at a moment when those present declared that almost all on our side despaired of it, so great was the strength and dash of our adversaries, had not the prince single-handed cast himself into the fray as he did so notably with the greatest of human courage." [333]

It was the Duke of Norfolk's late arrival with fresh troops up the road from Ferrybridge which surprised the Lancastrian left flank and turned the tide of battle. Lancastrian nobles fearing the worst fled. Others quickly followed and it was soon a rout as the Yorkists chased down the fleeing troops. The geography saw many Lancastrians seeking flight either killed by Yorkist lances or by drowning in the flooded River Cock. "Bloody Meadow" earned its name. The bridge at Tadcaster over the River Wharfe was destroyed to delay pursuit by Yorkist horsemen but it only added to the confusion and deaths by drowning of those who had yet to cross.

---

[332] *Hall's Chronicle: Containing the History of England* by Edward Hall - Published by Forgotten Books 2018. Originally published by Richard Grafton 1548. Page 256.

[333] *Calendar of State Papers* Milan 1461 Letter of 7th April 1461 Richard Beauchamp, Bishop of Salisbury, to Francesco Coppino, Bishop of Terni, Apostolic Legate in Flanders.

The Battle of Towton   29th March 1461

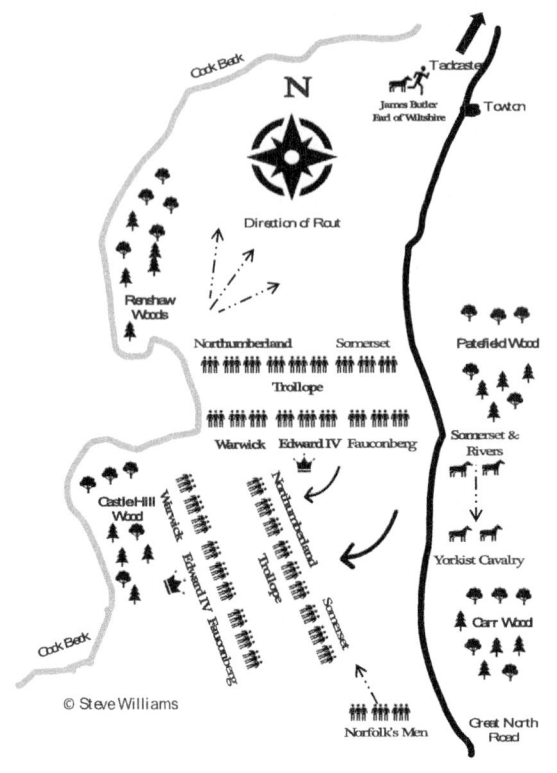

6. Palm Sunday 29th March 1461. Snow fell. Yorkist Archers fired at the advancing Lancastrian army. Fierce fighting erupted.

7. Somerset & Rivers pressed the Yorkist right flank and chased Yorkist horsemen down the Great North Road.

8. Battle lines pivoted to east to west. Yorkists were pressed back against Castle Hill Wood.

9. Norfolk's men arrived late to the battle up the Great North Road and surprised the Lancastrian left flank.

10. Lancastrians fled the field, a rout. Many were caught trying to cross the swollen Cock Beck. Yorkists chased after them in a killing spree.

Hearne's Fragment records ... "about four o'clock at night, the two battles joined, and fought all night till on the morrow at afternoon; when about noon John, Duke of Norfolk, with a fresh band of good men of war, came to the aid of the newly elected King Edward. This field was sore fought. For there was slain on both parts 33,000 men, and all the season it snowed. There were slain the Earls of Northumberland and Westmorland withy others and Sir Anthony Trollope; and taken the Earls of Devonshire and Wiltshire and beheaded there; and the deposed King Harry, his Queen, with

Henry, Duke of Somerset, and others, in great haste fled into Scotland". [334]

Gregory's Chronicle lists those that lost their lives and heads… "Palm Sunday the King met with the Lords of the north… the names of the Lords that were slain in the field in King Harry's party: the Earl of Northumberland, the Lord Clifford, the Lord Neville, the Lord Welles, the Lord Mauley and many more… the whole number is 35,000… The Earl of Devonshire was sought, taken and beheaded. And the Earl of Wiltshire was taken and brought unto Newcastle to the King. And there his head was smote off and sent unto London to be set upon London bridge. [335]

The Great Chronicle reminds us of the great divisions caused by civil war even amongst families, an tells us that Edward "journeyed northwards, he came upon a village named Sherborn near York where, on Palm Sunday he encountered with King Henry's host, which was a great multitude and in it many Lords of name, with knights, and other men of honour. But that notwithstanding, after a sore and long and unkindly fight – for there was the son against the father, the brother against brother, the nephew against nephew – the victory fell to King Edward, to the great loss of people on both sides… When the field was thus won by King Edward and word thereof brought to King Henry and Queen Margaret, being then at York, anon they fled towards Scotland with such small company as they had, among which were the Duke of Somerset and the Lord Roos… And upon the next morn King Edward with great triumph and joy entered into the city of York, and there kept his Easter tide". [336]

Waurin writes of "a great slaughter that day at Towton and for a long time no one could see which side would gain the victory, so

---

[334] *The Chronicles of The White Rose of York:* Edited by James Bohn. Published London 1845. Paperback Version Reprint 2012. Hearne's Fragment. Page 9.
[335] *Historical Collections of a Citizen of London* in Gregory's Chronicle, edited by J. Gairdner. Camden Society 1876. Pages 216-19.
[336] *Great Chronicle of London.* Edited by A.H. Thomas and I.D. Thornley. London 1938. Pages 196-197.

furious was the fighting. But at last, the supporters of the King, Queen and Duke of Somerset were utterly defeated". [337]

The Croyland Chronicler writes of divine providence. Edward "found an army drawn up in order of battle, composed of the remnants of the northern troops of King Henry. They, accordingly, engaged in a most severe conflict, and fighting hand to hand with sword and spear, there was no small slaughter on either side. However, by the mercy of Divine clemency, King Edward soon experienced the favour of Heaven, and, gaining the wished-for victory over his enemies, compelled them either to submit to be slain or to take to flight. For, their ranks being now broken and scattered in flight, the King's army eagerly pursued them, and cutting down the fugitives with their swords, just like so many sheep for the slaughter, made immense havoc among them for a distance of ten miles, as far as the city of York... the blood, too, of the slain, mingling with the snow which at this time covered the whole surface of the earth, afterwards ran down in the furrows and ditches along with the melted snow". [338]

William Paston wrote to John Paston on 4th April 1461... "our sovereign Lord (Edward IV) has won the field and on the Monday after Palm Sunday, he was received into York with great solemnity and procession... King Harry, the Queen, the Prince, the Dukes of Somerset and Exeter are fled into Scotland, and they be chased and followed". [339]

Perhaps most interesting is the letter to Coppini some five weeks later from Warwick's brother George Neville, Bishop of Exeter and Lord Chancellor...

---

[337] *Recueil des Croniques et Anciennes Istories de la Grant Bretaigne* J. de Waurin, ed. by W. Hardy 1864-91.
[338] *Ingulph's Chronicle of the Abbey of Croyland* Translated by Henry Riley. Published by Nabu Press 2014. Originally published 1854. Written 1486. Pages 425-426.
[339] *The Paston Letters 1422-1509* edited by J. Gairdner. Chatto and Windus, London 1904. Volume 3. Page 267.

"On the 15th of February, as I think your lordship will have learned from others, we had an action with the enemy to our loss, near St. Albans, the details of which would be equally painful and lengthy to narrate, and everyone who heard of it must have been much astonished…

In the meantime, our King Edward, then commonly known as the Earl of March, betook himself with an army of 30,000 men to London. With him went my brother the Earl of Warwick, as he had departed from the first battle and gone to join him. On the 25th they entered the city, and were joyfully received by all the people, and on the 4th of March he [Edward] was nominated and practically by force created king by the nobles and people universally, near Westminster. They postponed the celebration of his coronation only for most urgent reasons. Then on the 12th of March he set out towards the North with a large and magnificent army, having previously, on the 7th, sent on my brother to the West to collect troops. The king, the valiant Duke of Norfolk, my brother aforesaid and my uncle. Lord Fauconberg, travelling by different routes, finally united with all their companies and armies near the country round York.

The armies having been re-formed and marshalled separately, they set forth against the enemy, and at length on Palm Sunday, near a town called Ferrybridge, about sixteen miles from the city, our enemies were routed and broken in pieces. Our adversaries had broken the bridge, which was our way across, and were strongly posted on the other side, so that our men could only cross by a narrow way which they had made themselves after the bridge was broken. But our men forced a way by the sword, and many were slain on both sides. Finally, the enemy took to flight, and very many of them were slain as they fled.

That day there was a great conflict, which began with the rising of the sun, and lasted until the tenth hour of the night, so great was the pertinacity and boldness of the men, who never heeded the possibility of a miserable death. Of the enemy who fled, great numbers were drowned in the river near the town of Tadcaster, eight miles from York, because they themselves had broken the bridge to cut our passage that way, so that none could pass, and a great part of the rest who got away who gathered in the said town and city, were slain and so many dead bodies were seen as to cover an area six miles long by three broad and about four furlongs.

In this battle eleven lords of the enemy fell, including the Earl of Devon, the Earl of Northumberland, Lord Clifford and Neville with some cavaliers; and from what we hear from persons worthy of confidence, some 28,000 persons perished on one side and the other...

O miserable and luckless race and powerful people, would you have no spark of pity for our own blood, of which we have lost so much of fine quality by the civil war, even if you had no compassion for the French! If it had been fought under some capable and experienced captain against the Turks, the enemies of the Christian name, it would have been a great stroke and blow. But to tell the truth, owing to these civil discords, our riches are beginning to give out, and we are shedding our own blood copiously among ourselves, while we were unwilling to give help in men and money to the army of his Holiness against the infidel Turks, despite all the instances of his Holiness and your Reverence. But the limitations of writing do not permit me to state my mind on all these things.

Let us now return to our puppet who, with the aforesaid Margaret, his son, the Duke of Somerset, and some others, took refuge in a new castle about sixty miles north of York. By two letters written here to two individuals we hear that they have been taken by some cavaliers of those parts, friends of ours. I cannot, however, state this absolutely as I have no certainty, but I do not think they will get out thence so easily as they would like. Of the behaviour of the king, the valiant Duke of Norfolk, my brother and my uncle in this battle in fighting manfully, in guiding, encouraging and re-forming their forces, I would rather your lordship heard it from others than me. Our King Edward entered York peacefully on the last day of March with his army. My brother, Lord Montacute, who remained in the city when the enemy fled, with my Lord of Barnes went to the king to ask pardon for the citizens. Here they think that the king will remain for some days to reform the state of those parts, and I have recently received commands from his Majesty to go to him immediately.

After so much sorrow and tribulation I hope that grateful tranquillity and quiet will ensue, and that after so many clouds we shall have a clear sky, and after such shipwrecks we shall be brought to our desired haven…

May God grant us prosperity and send your Reverence back to us here safe and sound, when the opportunity arrives. Written in great haste. London, the 7th April, 1461." [340]

Historians have long argued about Towton. The exact details, dates of the fighting, numbers involved and killed are all subject to interpretation. Many fought at Towton, and many were killed there. Contemporary sources report very significant numbers in both categories. Towton is not known as England's "Bloodiest Battle" for nothing, and it is still referred to as England's largest battle. [341] Views differ. Scofield explains… "the battle of Towton… was a very bloody one, for on that all authorities are agreed; but it is difficult to arrive at any satisfactory conclusions in regard to the size of the two armies engaged in it or in regard to how many men were killed, as the numbers mentioned by the chroniclers are all too large for acceptance… all that can be safely said is that Henry and Margaret had the larger army and also the larger representation of the nobility". [342]

---

[340] *Calendar of State Papers* Milan 1461 Letter of 7th April 1461 George Neville, Bishop of Exeter, Chancellor of England, to Francesco Coppino, Bishop of Terni, Apostolic Legate in Flanders.
[341] *Battles of the Wars of the Roses* by David Cohen. Pen & Sword 2023.
[342] *The Life and Reign of Edward the Fourth* by Cora L. Scofield. Fonthill Media 2016. Volume One Page 165.

One thing is clear from all accounts. Towton was a terrible event. Towton has been called "Britain's most brutal battle".

George Neville lamented the great loss of blood.

Gregory completed his account of the battle with a prayer for the dead…

"Jesu be thou merciful unto their souls. Amen". [343]

---

[343] *Historical Collections of a Citizen of London* in Gregory's Chronicle, edited by J. Gairdner. Camden Society 1876. Pages 216-19.

Everything in this Kingdom

...They say that everyday favours the Earl of Warwick, who seems to me to be everything in this kingdom, and as if anything lacks, he has made a brother of his, Lord Chancellor... [344]

Edward was King but there was no doubt in many people's minds who was the power behind the new throne particularly for those foreign correspondents and diplomats reporting to their Duke or King on affairs in England. Warwick was "everything in this Kingdom". This can be seen in many contemporary accounts and letters.

John Rous was full of praise for Warwick... "A famous knight and excellent greatly spoken of throughout the most part of Christendom... He had all England at his leading and was dreaded throughout many lands. And though fortune deceived him in the end, yet his knightly acts had been so excellent that his noble and famous name could never be put out of laudable memory." [345]

The Great Chronicle of London tells us that Warwick "was ever had in great favour of the commons of this land, by reason of the exceeding household which he daily kept in all counties wherever he sojourned or lay; and when he came to London, he held such a house that six oxen were eaten at a breakfast, and every tavern was full of his meat, for whoever had any acquaintance in that house should have as much as he might carry on a long dagger". [346]

Jean de Waurin in his Chronicles of the Wars of the Roses commented that "The Earl of Warwick had in great measure the

---

[344] *Calendar of State Papers Milan 1461* Letter of 31st July 1461 from Giovanni Pietro Cagnola of Lodi to Francesco Sforza, Duke of Milan.
[345] *Warwick the Kingmaker* by Michael Hicks. Blackwell Publishers 1998. Page 3. *Rous Roll* Numbers 56,57.
[346] *Great Chronicle of London.* Edited by A.H. Thomas and I.D. Thornley 1938. Reprinted Gloucester 1983. Pages 212-213.

voice of the people, because he knew how to persuade them with beautiful soft speeches; he was conversible and talked familiarly with them – subtle, as it were, in order to gain his ends. He gave them to understand that he would promote the prosperity of the kingdom and defend the interests of the people with all his power, and that as long as he lived, he would never do otherwise. Thus, he acquired the goodwill of the people to such an extent that he was the prince whom they held in the highest esteem, and on whom they placed the greatest faith and reliance." Warwick knew how to improve his standing with those of influence. Waurin also wrote "I went to see the Earl of Warwick, and he kept me nine days in all honour and kindness, when I took leave of him, he paid all my expenses and gave me an excellent saddle horse." [347]

Philippe de Commines noted that "the leading supporter of the House of York was the Earl of Warwick (who) could almost be called the King's father as a result of the services and education he had given him". Commines recounts that "the Earl of Warwick governed King Edward in his youth and directed his affairs. Indeed, to speak the truth, he made him King and was responsible for deposing King Henry". Commines explains that "it was a factional dispute in the household of King Henry, who was hardly sane, which made the Earl of Warwick serve the House of York against King Henry of Lancaster." Queen Margaret of Anjou was at fault as she "supported the Duke of Somerset against the Earl of Warwick". [348] Commines was clear that Warwick "made him King".

Sir Thomas More would later write that Edward deposed King Henry "mostly by the power of the Earl of Warwick… a wise man and a courageous warrior, and of such strength, what with his lands, his allies, and favour with all the people, that he made Kings and

---

[347] *Edward IV From Contemporary Chronicles, Letters and Records* by Keith Dockray. Fonthill Media Limited 2015. Page 87. Jean de Waurin Chronicles of the Wars of the Roses. Edited by E. Hallam Page 244.
[348] *Philippe de Commynes Memoirs, The Reign of Louis XI 1461-83* Published by Penguin Books 1972. Translated and introduced by Michael Jones. Written 1498. Pages 180-181 and 143.

put down Kings almost at his pleasure… and reckoned it a greater thing to make a King than to be a King". [349] Shakespeare would refer to him as "thou setter-up and plucker-down of Kings". [350]

The Governor of Abbeville in a letter to Louis XI joked that England has "two rulers, Monsieur de Warwick and another whose name I have forgotten". [351]

Letters from that time give the impression that it was Warwick versus the Lancastrians and are revealing as to how news travelled abroad in the days and weeks after Towton. Prospero di Camulio, Milanese Ambassador in France, wrote to Francesco Sforza, Duke of Milan, on 12th April 1461… "I wrote to your Excellency *nine days ago* about the news of England and how we were celebrating rejoicings at Calais, and then soon afterwards, how the affair became doubtful. I now advise your Excellency that letters have come from London this day relating that fifteen days ago a battle was fought near York, 170 miles from London. King Edward and Warwick came off victors; the total slain was 28,000 and more, all reckoned by certain heralds. **On Warwick's side** there fell 8,000 and upwards and four nobles, on King Henry's side 20,000 and 14 nobles. King Henry, the queen, the prince and the Duke of Somerset, with two other nobles retreated to a castle on the coast near Scotland, whither the victors have sent 20,000 men to besiege it. After the sealing the news reached London that the castle was taken with those within. Bruges, 12th April 1461." [352]

News was often confused as typified by a letter of 13th April to Coppini from his physician… "I must advise your reverence that immediately I arrived here at Bruges I found authentic news brought by Genoese merchants staying at the court of the Duke of

---

[349] *The History of Richard III*. Sir Thomas More. Edited by R.S. Sylvester. Complete Works II Yale 1963. Pages 65-66.
[350] *King Henry VI*. Part 3. Act II. Scene III. Shakespeare.
[351] *Warwick the Kingmaker* by Michael Hicks. Blackwell Publishers 1998. Countdown to Civil War 1456-9. Page 256. Vaesen. *Lettres de Louis XI* iii 155.
[352] *Calendar of State Papers Milan 1461* Letter of 12th April 1461 from Prospero di Camulio, Milanese Ambassador in France to Francesco Sforza, Duke of Milan.

Burgundy, that the King of England had won a victory; 30,000 men are killed on both sides, almost all the nobles on the other side are slain except King Henry, his wife and son, Somerset and Ros, who are in a castle whose name I do not know, but it is surrounded they say, so that escape is impossible. On our side it is said that King Edward and the Earl of Warwick are wounded, and four nobles slain, whose names are not reported as yet." [353]

A few days later on 17th April, Coppini wrote to update the Duke of Milan… "Just now, although matters in England have undergone several fluctuations, **yet in the end my lord of Warwick has come off the best** and has made a new king of the son of the Duke of York, the Earl of March, who, together with Warwick, returned with me to England. Thus, things are turning out so that if assistance is given, such as has been frequently mentioned and solicited, noteworthy and most glorious things may be done in these parts, such as have not been for five hundred years, for this new king is young, prudent and magnanimous. If your lordship takes the matter up warmly, we shall see notable and great things, with my assistance and due reputation, as a reward for all our anxieties and my labours." [354]

On the same day the Duke of Milan wrote to Prospero Camulio, his Ambassador to the French Court with changed priorities… "Letters have arrived to-day from Bruges of the 10th inst., stating how the new King of England, **King Edward, and the Earl of Warwick** have routed the queen's army, and doubtless the new king will obtain the state. That being the case, we desire you to take leave of the dauphin and go to the said king, offering your services and commending yourself to him as you think most fitting, consulting my lord, the legate, and informing yourself fully of all the affairs of

---

[353] *Calendar of State Papers Milan 1461* Letter of 13th April 1461 Master Antonio, Physician to Francesco Coppino, Bishop of Terni, Apostolic Legate to the said Legate.

[354] *Calendar of State Papers Milan 1461* Letter of 17th April 1461 from Francesco Coppino, Bishop of Terni, Papal Legate, to Francesco Sforza, Duke of Milan.

those parts, sending us a full account of everything immediately, and you shall return to us as soon as possible." [355]

This letter must have crossed with another update from Camulio sent on the 18th April as information arrived from different sources… "We have news of English affairs hour by hour. Two days ago, letters arrived here from English merchants of repute, and we have also heard by way of Calais, that it is true that King Henry, the queen, the Prince of Wales, their son, the Duke of Somerset, Lord Ros, his brother, the Duke of Exeter were taken, and of these the Duke of Somerset and his brother were immediately beheaded. When the same fate was about to befall the Duke of Exeter, there came a message to let him off, and they say he escaped because he is related to King Edward, whose sister he married. However, as he is fierce and cruel, it is thought that they will put him to a more honourable death…"

Camulio was wrong about Somerset losing his head but was correct in foretelling a fall out between Warwick and Edward IV… "I postponed writing about this to see if it would be confirmed; if it is, then **before long grievances and recrimination will break out between King Edward and Warwick,** King Henry and the queen will be victorious, and he who seemed to have the world at his feet will provide a remarkable example of what prudent men, in excuse for human errors, have called Fortune".

Camulio wrote from Bruges where he was staying and reported the arrival of Edward's younger brothers, George and Richard, sent to safety in Burgundy by their mother Duchess Cecily… "Since I wrote to-day the two brothers of King Edward have arrived, one eleven and the other twelve years of age. The duke, who is most kind in everything, has been to visit them at their lodging, and showed them great reverence. Bruges, 18th April, 1461." [356]

---

[355] *Calendar of State Papers Milan 1461* Letter of 17th April 1461 from Francesco Sforza, Duke of Milan to Prospero di Camulio, Milanese Ambassador to the French Court.
[356] *Calendar of State Papers Milan 1461* Letter of 18th April 1461 from Prospero di Camulio, Milanese Ambassador in France to Francesco Sforza, Duke of Milan.

On 27th April Coppini wrote to Duke Sforza with another update and copies of letters from George Neville and Richard Beauchamp… "I now enclose copies of letters from England, principally from this Chancellor, brother of the Earl of Warwick, and from two other bishops, from which you will learn of the final and marvellous victory of the Earl of March, who is made the new king, of Warwick and the cruel battle, in which the total loss amounted to 28,000 men, including ten of their greatest lords, truly our king only lost one baron and 800 others…" The change in England increased the chance of it allying with Burgundy so putting pressure on France which was deemed good for Milan… "Things are disposed in favour of a change for the better, and never was there a better opportunity for his Holiness and your Lordship, if things are properly understood…" [357] A further letter of 8th May 1461 explained it more clearly… "this victory of King Edward is a great blow to the King of France, in the opinion of everyone, and might possibly induce that monarch to turn to the Dauphin rather than let his enemies gain the day…" [358]

Coppini and Camulio both dined with an ambassador of Warwick's in early May at St Omer. Coppini wrote to Duke Sforza on 6th May… "I have written fully to your Excellency of late about the state of England and all the affairs of the west… there was an ambassador here of the Earl of Warwick; he dined with me, Messer Prospero also being present, and, at the ambassador's departure, to give some comfort and advice to King Edward and the Earl of Warwick at this time when their position is not very solid… St. Omer, the 6th May, 1461. [359]

Camulio updated Duke Sforza on 9th May… "With regard to English affairs, I can confirm what I reported to your Excellency so far as the battles are concerned. It is true that I find that the capture

---

[357] *Calendar of State Papers Milan 1461* Letter of 27th April 1461 from Francesco Coppino, Bishop of Terni, Papal Legate, to Francesco Sforza, Duke of Milan.
[358] *Calendar of State Papers Milan 1461* Letter of 8th May 1461 from Francesco Coppino, Bishop of Terni, Apostolic Legate to Francesco Sforza, Duke of Milan.
[359] *Calendar of State Papers Milan 1461* Letter of 6th May 1461 from Francesco Coppino, Bishop of Terni, Papal Legate to Francesco Sforza, Duke of Milan.

of King Henry and the Queen is not correct, but I remember I said it was doubtful… it seems advisable to your Excellency to turn England against France, yet as we have a well-disposed pope, it might be well to pay attention to certain human weaknesses, since no man living can see far ahead at present in the affairs of England. I should recommend his increasing the authority of the said legate, because reputation often achieves what cannot be done by reason, and also that ships should be provided as above, to strengthen the force of the Earl of Warwick. This is what the legate and I discussed together. This is the thirty-first letter that I have written to your excellency, and I have received no reply or advice of receipt. St. Omer, 9th May, 1461…"

Camulio continued with news of matters more local to where he was staying in St Omer… "As regards matters here, a fortnight ago the Duke of Burgundy arrived here, and about the same time 1,500 horse of the King of France also approached to within little more than half a day's journey from the country of the Duke of Burgundy, though they stayed without doing any harm, and he sent a herald to them, and, according to what they say, he learned from them that they had come to raise the siege of a castle near here, attacked by those of Calais, which is holding out for King Henry and Somerset, and, on learning that the siege was raised, they went back. Two days ago, they returned again to the same neighbourhood, quite 12,000 strong, and relations between the Duke of Burgundy and the King of France are very strained. St. Omer, 9th May, 1461." [360]

As a Papal Legate as well as a Milanese Ambassador, Coppini had two "direct reports" and on 1st June he sent a letter to Pope Pius II… "The affairs of England are in the following position. Edward has not yet made himself supreme over the whole kingdom or reduced it to peace, because Henry, the late king, with his wife and son and the Duke of Somerset and Lord de Ros are with the Scots. There it is announced they have married the daughter of the late King of Scots and sister of the present little king to the son of the

---

[360] *Calendar of State Papers Milan 1461* Letter of 9th May 1461 from Prospero di Camulio, Milanese Ambassador to the Court of France to Francesco Sforza, Duke of Milan.

said Henry, King of England. They have received from the same Henry the town of Berwick, on the frontiers of Scotland, which the Scots have long claimed as their right from the English, as the excellently well-furnished guardian of their frontiers, and the place to which King Henry repaired as an asylum after the battle. Hence it is suspected on all sides, that something fresh is in preparation for Edward to chew, and that these Scots are about to break into England with Henry, his son and wife to recover the realm. And because of the ancient alliance by which the Scots are united with the French, it is thought that the French also will assist, and render support both by land and sea, because they also are inflamed against the English, especially under these new conditions, for old-standing reasons well known to all". [361] On 2nd June, Coppini sent Duke Sforza a copy of this letter to the Pope.

Camulio also on 2nd June sent a letter to Duke Sforza with similar news of King Henry taking refuge in and seeking help from Scotland but also further detail on France sending men in support. Camulio explains why the French will attack up the eastern coast of Britain rather than the western side however he retains confidence in the leadership of England by Edward and Warwick… "The force of 20,000 Frenchmen has left Normandy and gone to England… It is said that they have taken the route outside the island in the Gulf of Bristol and accordingly it is thought to assemble the people of Wales, who are said to love the queen. Nevertheless, Bristol is a strong city, and for coasting along the island from thence towards Scotland, it is not easy to navigate any vessels besides the small ships for transit of the country, owing to a tide that lasts six hours. Accordingly, it is thought that they cannot get any nearer to Scotland from that direction. In the direction of the strait of Dover and Calais, which is eighteen miles, Warwick is said to have a fleet, not so much to give battle to the French one in the open sea, but merely to prevent them from landing in the island and to guard that passage. Owing to the favour and kinship of the Scots and this strong encouragement from the French, they are afraid here that there may be some attack and battle. If that be the case, it will certainly involve the rest of the community and this kingdom of

---

[361] *Calendar of State Papers Milan 1461* Letter of 1st June 1461 from Francesco Coppino, Bishop of Terni, Papal Legate to Pope Pius II.

England. In any case, **King Edward and Warwick have the whole of the island and kingdom in their power** and are attending to such provisions as are necessary. King Edward is at present going to London. I fancy in order to make arrangements for consolidating the kingdom and to strengthen himself against the dangers which may crop up. It is true, most illustrious lord, that these English have not the slightest form of government unless they have it in some leader, and this they have in King Edward and the Earl of Warwick… [362]

Camulio sent a further update four days later… "we hear by letters of merchants of London to those here how the fleet of the French has struck at the coast of Cornwall. It did some damage by pillage and burning, and then sailed back towards Normandy, as they were short of eighteen bertons, which had not joined the fleet up to that moment. Also, that King Edward has gone to London for his coronation, and, as I said in my previous letter, to set the kingdom in order. Thus, he has commanded that a general parliament shall meet in London on the 6th of July. This is all we have heard up to the present; if there is anything more, I will keep your Excellency regularly advised. Bruges, 6th June 1461." [363]

The Duke of Milan was an important ally for Yorkist England. Both Edward and Warwick sent him letters carried by the envoy Antonio della Torre. We do not have these letters, but we do have those written in response by Duke Sforza which confirm Warwick's status and importance as viewed by those on the continent.

Letter of 14th June 1461 Francesco Sforza, Duke of Milan to Edward IV, King of England

---

[362] *Calendar of State Papers Milan 1461* Letter of 2nd June 1461 Prospero di Camulio, Milanese Ambassador to the Court of France to Francesco Sforza, Duke of Milan.
[363] *Calendar of State Papers Milan 1461* Letter of 6th June 1461 Prospero di Camulio, Milanese Ambassador to the Court of France to Francesco Sforza, Duke of Milan.

"After the receipt of your Majesty's letters by Master Antonio della Torre, your servant and envoy, we learned quite recently from our servant Prospero Camulio, the memorable victory, whereby, through consummate military skill and personal valour, your Majesty obtained that kingdom of England, and have arrived at the royal seat. We have always been anxious for your glory and exaltation, as you will have heard from Messer Prospero. We have expressed our joy to Master Antonio della Torre, who is now returning to your Majesty. Be pleased to give him credence touching this matter, the good-will of the pope and the state of affairs in Italy. Milan, 14th June 1461." [364]

Letter of 14th June 1461 Francesco Sforza, Duke of Milan to **Richard, Earl of Warwick and Salisbury**

"We have received your lordship's letters by the hands of Master Antonio della Torre, the King's servant and fully furnished. We have also heard what was reserved for him to say by word of mouth, under the guarantee of those letters. We have answered Messer Antonio fully upon all these things, as you will hear at length from his relation. He is returning to your parts fully informed about our deep affection for your lordship and upon Italian affairs, and of how desirous we are that Francesco, Bishop of Terni, legate of the apostolic see, whom we love exceedingly, may be beloved and acceptable to his Majesty and your lordship. We also beg you to give full confidence to the relations of Messer Prospero di Camulio, our servant, whom we have instructed by our letters, because if there is anything we can do to gratify your lordship, we shall always be delighted to do it. Milan, 14th June 1461." [365]

---

[364] *Calendar of State Papers* Milan 1461 Letter of 14th June 1461 Francesco Sforza, Duke of Milan to Edward IV, King of England.
[365] *Calendar of State Papers* Milan 1461 Letter of 14th June 1461 Francesco Sforza, Duke of Milan to Richard, Earl of Warwick and Salisbury.

Camulio wrote to Duke Sforza on 18th June to confirm matters. It appears that the ambassador did not have a high opinion of the English … "With regard to England, I can affirm what I have written that everything is in subjection to King Edward. King Henry, the queen, the Prince of Wales, the Duke of Somerset, and Lord Ros his brother, with the few left of that party who remained steadfast to them, have withdrawn to Scotland… In favour of that king there was a most powerful French fleet at sea, to attack England, so that Henry's party cherished great hopes. I sent word about this, their plans, the course of this fleet, its attack and return. Since then, we have heard from England, how in the attack made by the fleet on the coast of Cornwall, which is opposite to Spain, the French were repulsed, and lost some say 4,000, some say 2,000. **The truth cannot be obtained from England, owing to the stupidity of the people there…"**

Camulio had a further update on the whereabouts of Warwick and his focus of activities… "We have heard since that King Edward has gone to assemble his parliament on the 6th of July at London. The Earl of Warwick remained on the frontiers of Scotland, and it was arranged in Ireland, a savage country and an island near the Scots, that if the Scots sallied forth to help King Henry in England, 20,000 Irish should cross from Ireland to Scotland to do them hurt. This arrangement, with the garrisons of the Earl of Warwick, is accounted good and not only sufficient, but an advantageous provision against any chance wind that may blow from Scotland. At the same time, they are endeavouring to prevent this by embassies and other efforts…" [366]

Further news on Warwick was provided to Duke Sforza by Giovanni Pietro Cagnola of Lodi, one of the Milanese envoys sent to England to build relations with the new government. On 31st July

---

[366] *Calendar of State Papers* Milan 1461 Letter of 18th June 1461 Prospero di Camulio, Milanese Ambassador to the French Court to Francesco Sforza, Duke of Milan.

Cagnola wrote... "By my letters of the 9th I related how we had arrived here, and the honours shown us by the king at our entry, which continued throughout the day. As you may wonder at our remaining here, I report that the Count Ludovico has had the gout but is now free. The king yesterday rode to a castle of his called Windsor for hunting; we shall go there to-morrow. The king's desires seem to me to be directed towards having some sort of pleasure. It is true that he tries hard to afford every kind of pleasure that he can to the earl, both festivities of ladies and hunting...

...I have no news from here except that the Earl of Warwick has taken Monsig. de Ruvera (Rivers) and his son and sent them to the king who had them imprisoned in the Tower. Thus, **they say that every day favours the Earl of Warwick, who seems to me to be everything in this kingdom,** and as if anything lacked, he has made a brother of his, the archbishop, Lord Chancellor of England. They declare that the Duke of Exeter, who is cousin of this king and a great lord, who has always been a friend of King Henry, now wishes to return and ask pardon, and the king will grant it as well as to many other lords, whose names I cannot learn. **Everyone here rejoices at the death of the King of France."** [367]

Cagnola wrote again on 28th August... "By my letter, dated London, the last day of July, I acquainted you with what was passing in England. I now add for your further information that the **Earl of Warwick has gone towards Yorkshire**, a province opposed to that king and very friendly to King Henry. I believe it will submit to King Edward, seeing that favour fails King Henry on every side, and seeing at their backs the Earl of Warwick, who does them great mischief, and but for whom those people would have joined King Henry and taken the field again; but Warwick has prevented this nor can they now succour the king or do anything further." [368]

---

[367] *Calendar of State Papers* Milan 1461 Letter of 31st July 1461 Giovanni Pietro Cagnola of Lodi to Francesco Sforza, Duke of Milan.
[368] *Calendar of State Papers* Milan 1461 Letter of 28th August 1461 Giovanni Pietro Cagnola of Lodi to Francesco Sforza, Duke of Milan.

The Winning of the North

...My lord of Warwick lies at the castle of Warkworth, but three miles out of Alnwick, and he rides daily to all these castles for to oversee the sieges; if they want victuals, or any other thing, he is ready to purvey it to them to his power... [369]

Edward marched triumphant into York on 30th March the day after Towton. Warwick was probably by his side as they saw the heads of their respective fathers and Edward's younger brother still high on the city gates. These were quickly taken down and taken to Pontefract to be buried with their bodies. Warwick's own younger brother John, Lord Montagu, was released from jail where he had been held since his capture at St Albans.

Easter 5th April 1461 was spent in York. Warwick and Edward mixed vengeance with mercy according to their want. The Earl of Devon who was "sick and might not void away" was put out of any misery he might have been suffering. This was not a merciful act.

Surrounding towns submitted to Edward. The town records for Beverley [370] give us a useful picture. Fauconberg was received with grace and bread, fish, capons and more. Some townsfolk were sent to York to negotiate a "safeguard for the commonalty". The King's Treasurer received a gift of a horse which perhaps tempered his request for armed men and limited it to only twenty-four. Beverley had previously supplied men to fight for King Henry.

Warwick was at Middleham on 20th April but back with the new King in Durham two days later on 22nd April and may have journeyed with him to Newcastle where the Earl of Wiltshire, fresh

---

[369] *Paston Letters 1422-1509.* Edited by J. Gairdner. 1904. 6 Volumes. Reprinted one volume Gloucester 1983.
[370] *The Antiquities and History of the Town of Beverley* by Poulson. London 1829. Pages 238-242. *The Life and Reign of Edward the Fourth* by Cora L. Scofield. Volume One. Page 167.

from his capture at Cockermouth, was executed and his head sent to be placed on London Bridge.

Warwick played host to Edward at Middleham between 5th and 7th May before moving to York where they stayed on 10th and 11th May. Warwick was already warden of the east and west marches and was appointed to commissions of array in the northern counties. Edward had determined that he needed to return to London. Warwick would be left in charge in the North particularly with trouble brewing with the Scots.

Hearne's fragment tells us… "The feast of Easter accomplished, King Edward rode to Durham, and setting all things in good order in the north parts, he left behind him there the Earl of Warwick to have the oversight and governance there, and the King returned southwards and eastwards to his manor of Sheen". [371]

Edward had written to request of King James of Scotland that "Harry, late usurper King of our realm, Margaret, his wife, and her son, and other traitors and rebels" be given up. Margaret however promised Scotland much for its help and support including Berwick. Rumours were rife that Scotland would begin with a siege of Norham Castle. The expected incursion did not happen but on 12th June a mixed Scottish and Lancastrian force attacked and took Carlisle. It was quickly relieved by a force under Warwick's brother and lieutenant, Montagu. Warwick joined him shortly thereafter on 24th June to agree ongoing arrangements for its safety and security. Warwick looked after the North and could not attend the formal coronation of his young cousin as "Edward IV King of England, France and Lord of Ireland".

"King Edward removed from Sheen towards London and, on the way, received the mayor and his brethren, all in scarlet, with 400

---

[371] *The Chronicles of The White Rose of York:* Edited by James Bohn. Published London 1845. Paperback Version Reprint 2012. Hearne's Fragment. Page 10.

commoners well horsed and clad in green, and so advancing themselves, passed the bridge and through the city, they rode straight to the Tower of London, and rested there all night. On the morrow he made thirty-two new knights of the Bath, departing from the Tower in the afternoon, in like good order as they came thither, these thirty-two new knights proceeding immediately before the King in their gown and hoods, and tokens of white silk upon their shoulders, so in goodly order he was brought to Westminster where, on the morrow, he was solemnly crowned by the hands of the Archbishop of Canterbury, with great triumph and honour". [372]

As Edward was being "solemnly crowned" a number of Lancastrian Lords including Lord Roos, Sir Humphrey Dacre, Sir John Fortescue, Sir William Tailboys, Sir Edmund Mountfort and Thomas and Humphrey Neville of Brancepeth had crossed from Scotland to cause trouble in around Ryton, near Newcastle, and Brancepeth, near Durham, in areas loyal to the Percy's. Bishop Booth supported by local levies of men restored order.

Warwick assisted by his brother Montagu and his uncle Fauconberg sought to extend their control in the North. Warwick was confirmed once more as warden of the east and west marches and authorised on 2nd August to deal with the Scots. The castle of Alnwick was taken on 13th September and placed in the hands of Sir William Bowes. Sir Ralph Percy soon thereafter surrendered Dunstanburgh. Percy pledged himself to Edward and was retained in control of the coastal stronghold.

Warwick was fully occupied in the North. Others were tasked with keeping Calais secure, but the Channel Isles were taken by the Frenchman De Breze. Edward himself initially planned to confront

---

[372] *The Chronicles of The White Rose of York:* Edited by James Bohn. Published London 1845. Paperback Version Reprint 2012. Hearne's Fragment. Page 10.

Pembroke and Wiltshire in Wales but then left it to the very able and capable William Herbert.

Warwick found time to attend Edward's first parliament in November 1461. Parliament opened on 4th November and listened to his brother George as Chancellor preach on the text "Make good your ways and your habits". Sir James Strangeways was appointed speaker, a position gained through his Neville connections. God was thanked for granting the victory. Edward was praised for putting his life at risk to rescue the realm "to our greatest joy and earthly consolation".

Henry VI had broken the accord of 1460 and had worked "continually by subtle imaginations, frauds, deceptions and exorbitant means to the extreme and final destruction" of the rightful heirs to the throne in the House of York.

Warwick was appointed Steward of England on 3rd December in order that he might pronounce sentence on Henry VI and the Lancastrian Lords for their treacherous and treasonable actions. Warwick was exempted from the Act of Resumption and the Neville family benefited from reversals of judgement on the Earl of Cambridge 1415 and on Salisbury and Dispenser in 1400. Warwick's mother and wife could now take up their respective inheritances.

Warwick remained in London. He sent a letter to the Duke of Milan on 11th January 1462. Reappointments to "keep the sea" and as Captain of Calais saw him visit Sandwich and Dover and possibly a visit to Calais before returning to London and his King. Preparations were made to attack France by sea and regain control over the channel. On 18th March Warwick was granted commission of array in Hampshire but it was his uncle, Fauconberg, who conducted the raids by sea. Affairs in the North warranted his attention.

Alnwick was retaken by Sir William Tailboys, Naworth by Sir Humphrey Dacre. The Lancastrians conducted raids from their bases in Scotland. Warwick on behalf of Edward conducted diplomatic discussions with Scotland to agree an alliance and thus neutralise the old enemy. Mary of Guelders was Queen Dowager and Regent for her young son James III. There was even talk of a possible marriage between Mary and Edward, but this was rejected by her advisors such as Bishop Kennedy.

Warwick gathered troops and led a raid into Scotland which led to negotiations at Carlisle. A short-term truce was agreed until August 1462. A letter to John Paston advised him that "my Lord of Warwick hath been in Scotland and taken a castle of the Scots, and upon this there came the Queen of Scots with other Lords of her country in embassy to my said Lord of Warwick, and a truce is taken betwixt this and Saint Bartholomew's day in August". [373]

This allowed renewed focus on taking control of the region. Warwick's brother Montagu regained Naworth. Alnwick surrendered at the end of July to Sir Ralph Grey and Lord William Hastings who had recently become Warwick's brother-in-law following his marriage to Katherine Neville.

Margaret of Anjou was in France to secure help. Louis XI was plotting to destabilise England. Calais was once more under threat. There were rumours of "two hundred in Calais sworn contrary to the King's will" and that "Queen Margaret was ready at Boulogne with much silver to pay the soldiers… the soldiers are so wild there that they will not let in any man but the King or my Lord Warwick". [374] Fauconberg's raids on the northern coast of France saw Louis

---

[373] *Selections From the Paston Letters* transcribed by Sir John Fenn. Edited by Alice Greenwood. London 1920. Forgotten Books. Page 213. Letter from J Daubeney to J Paston 29th June 1461.
[374] *Paston Letters* Book IV Pages 57-58.

and the Duke of Brittany go cool on helping Margaret. Louis feared England and Burgundy joining in arms to fight against him.

Margaret sailed from France in October 1462 with around 800 men under the command of Pierre de Breze. King Henry, Somerset and other Lancastrians were picked up from Scotland before they landed in Northumberland. Sir Ralph Percy reneged on his promises to Edward. Alnwick then fell to the Lancastrians and their French mercenaries. Warwick was commissioned to address the threat to the "peace of the realm". Edward raised money and set off north.

News reached Margaret of Edward and Warwick's approach. She took to her ships, discretion being the better part of valour. Misfortune saw storms wreck her boats. Some Frenchmen escaped to Lindisfarne but were given no mercy and killed despite taking refuge in a church. Edward advanced as far as Durham but fell ill with the measles. Warwick took over control of the troops.

John Paston, the younger, wrote in Newcastle to John Paston on 11th December 1462 "we had tidings here that the Scots will come into England within seven days… to rescue these three castles, Alnwick, Dunstanburgh and Bamburgh, which castles were besieged as yesterday. And at the siege of Alnwick lies my lord of Kent (Fauconberg) and the Lord Scales; and at Dunstanburgh castle lies the Earl of Worcester and Sir Ralph Grey; and at the castle of Bamburgh lies the Lord Montagu and the Lord Ogle… My lord of Warwick lies at the castle of Warkworth, but three miles out of Alnwick, and he rides daily to all these castles for to oversee the sieges; if they want victuals, or any other thing, he is ready to purvey it to them to his power. The King commanded my lord of Norfolk to conduct victuals and the ordnance out of Newcastle unto Warkworth castle, to my lord of Warwick". [375]

---

[375] *Paston Letters 1422-1509*. Edited by J. Gairdner. 1904. 6 Volumes. Reprinted one volume Gloucester 1983.

No relief seemed forthcoming. Bamburgh gave themselves up on 26th December and Dunstanburgh a day later. Both were placed under Sir Ralph Percy as he pledged allegiance anew to Edward one more time. Somerset joined Warwick in the siege of Alnwick, but Pembroke and Roos took the offer of safe passage back to Scotland. A Scottish army appeared near Alnwick on 5th January. Warwick seeing the size of the army withdrew to more defensible ground allowing those within the castle to exit. The Scots then withdrew without a fight. Those remaining at Alnwick surrendered to Warwick. Edward was "possessed of all England except a castle in North Wales called Harlech" wrote Warkworth. [376]

A celebratory poem in the early part of Edward IV's reign praised Warwick "born of a stock that ever shall be true" as a "guiding star" for his help in subduing rebellious "castles, towns and towers" and thus helping and rescuing King Edward. [377]

Warwick's uncle, Lord Fauconberg and now the Earl of Kent died at Durham on 9th January 1463 and was buried at Guisborough Priory in north Yorkshire. Warwick's mother the Countess of Salisbury died also around this time. Warwick took the opportunity to find a final resting place for his father Salisbury and brother Thomas Neville killed at Wakefield and interred after Towton at Pontefract. Warwick and his brother, Montagu, accompanied the chariot drawn by six horses on its journey south to Bisham Abbey. The burial of Salisbury, the Countess and Thomas took place on 15th February. [378] They were joined at Bisham by another brother, George, Bishop of Exeter and Chancellor of England.

---

[376] *"Warkworth's" Chronicle: A Chronicle of the First Thirteen Years of the reign of King Edward the Fourth* John Warkworth edited by James Orchard. Halliwell Leopold Classic Library 2015. Written 1470-85. Page 3.
[377] *Warwick the Kingmaker Politics, Power and Fame* by A.J. Pollard. Continuum Books 2007. Page 168. *Political Poems and Songs relating to English History* edited by T. Wright. 1861. Page 270.
[378] *The Life and Reign of Edward the Fourth* by Cora L. Scofield. Fonthill Media 2016. Volume One. Page 269.

Whilst Warwick and his brothers were in the south, Ralph Percy handed back the castles of Bamburgh and Dunstanburgh to Queen Margaret of Anjou and her Lancastrian, French and Scottish supporters. Ralph Grey later opened the gates of Alnwick to Lord Hungerford. All three castles were once more back in Lancastrian hands.

John Neville, Lord Montagu, took over responsibility from his brother Warwick as warden of the east march. Warwick had other responsibilities to fulfil, and their uncle Fauconberg was no longer around to help. Montagu headed north to organise matters there. Warwick soon followed and after assessing the situation sought additional help. The Scots had entered England "with great puissance" according to a letter he wrote to the Archbishop of York.[379] Worcester was sent north with ships.

Edward left London accompanied by his newfound friend and captain of his bodyguard, Somerset. The contemporary Gregory was contemptuous of the appointment. It was as if "men should put a lamb among wolves of malicious beasts" he wrote. [380] The townsfolk of Northampton thought so too, and Somerset was nearly lynched before being sent away to a castle in Wales for his own safety by Edward. The King left a "tun of wine" in the marketplace for his good people to make merry.

Queen Margaret and an army of Scots crossed into England and laid siege to Norham. Such news allowed Edward to raise monies anew from his religious Lords and the council of London. Memories were still fresh of the army of Scotsmen who had marched south not too many years previously.

Warwick, and Montagu, raised the siege within eighteen days and followed the fleeing army into Scotland. They also caused Queen Margaret to flee from Bamburgh to the continent with her son, Prince Edward, Pierre de Breze, Exeter, Mountfort, Fortescue

---

[379] *The Life and Reign of Edward the Fourth* by Cora L. Scofield. Fonthill Media 2016. Volume One. Page 292. Raine, Priory of Hexham, I, cvii-cviii.
[380] *Gregory's Chronicle, The Historical Collections of a Citizen in London.* Edited by James Gairdner. Camden Society 1876. **Pages 221-222.**

Whittingham and Morton. King Henry VI was left in Edinburgh under the careful watch of the Bishop of St Andrews.

The "noble and valiant Warwick" with only the men of the marches had put the Scots to flight according to a letter written by William Hastings on 7th August 1463 to Jean Seigneur de Lannoy. Margaret and de Breze had fled overseas. The House of Lancaster had no future. [381]

The Scots were in disarray. England and France concluded a peace treaty. Mary of Gueldres died. England threatened an invasion. Scotland signed a truce on 9th December 1463. Warwick remained in the North to maintain pressure on the Scots. Edward had travelled no further than Yorkshire and Worcester's fleet had seen no active service.

Warwick had been unable to travel to St Omer and engage in the peace deliberations between England and France due to his northern commitments. This was much to the annoyance of Louis XI who it appeared wanted to meet or at least build a close relationship with him. Louis XI sent a servant of the Seigneur de la Barde to England in May 1463 to ask Warwick for a greyhound [382] We know from the French King's letters that Warwick and Louis communicated with each other through this period. [383]

Warwick together with Wenlock were appointed by Edward on 28th March 1464 to deal with Louis's ambassador, Seigneur de Lannoy and a new agreement was signed between the two countries. The discussions with France kept Warwick in London and away from continuing negotiations with Scotland. Fresh trouble was brewing.

Somerset "stole out of Wales with a privy many" and narrowly avoiding capture at Durham reached the safety of Bamburgh Castle.

---

[381] *The Life and Reign of Edward the Fourth* by Cora L. Scofield. Fonthill Media 2016. Volume One. Page 300.
[382] *The Life and Reign of Edward the Fourth* by Cora L. Scofield. Fonthill Media 2016. Volume One. Page 291. Lettres de Louis XI, II, 117-118.
[383] *Lettres de Louis XI, Roi de France*. Edited by Jos. Vaesen and others. Paris 1883-1909.

[384] Newly returned to the Lancastrian ranks, Somerset and Sir Ralph Percy took advantage of Warwick's absence to issue forth from Bamburgh and cause trouble. They captured Norham for a while and the castle of Skipton in the west riding of Yorkshire.

Responsibility for escorting the Scottish envoys to York fell upon Montagu who set off for the Scottish border with a small armed force. Montagu was aware of Lancastrian forces in the Newcastle area and changed his route to avoid a challenge from forces under the control of Humphrey Neville. Moving on from Alnwick, Montagu was confronted upon Hedgeley Moor by Somerset and Percy who had Hungerford and Roos with them. Gregory writes… "this meeting was upon St Mark's Day… and that same day was Sir Ralph Percy slain. And when he was dead, all the party was discomforted and put to rebuke. And everyman avoided and took his way with full sorry hearts". [385]

Montagu arrived at Hedgeley Moor, just north of Glanton village and seven miles south-east of Wooler, to find Somerset's army occupying the high ground in front of him and barring his passage to the north. Battle commenced with an exchange of arrows. Montagu advanced across 1,500 yards of moorland. The Lancastrian left flank, under the command of Lords Roos and Hungerford, faltered, broke and fled the field. Much of the rest of the Lancastrian forces fearing disaster did likewise. Somerset managed to rally some troops around Alnwick.

Sir Ralph Percy, who led the Lancastrian vanguard, made a last stand with his retainers. Local legend has it that Percy's horse leapt some thirty feet during the charge in which he was killed. Stones were later erected to mark the spot and are still visible in the small enclosure at the site known as "Percy's Leap". As he died, he is said to have uttered the enigmatic words: "I have saved the bird in my bosom". A square stone column, known as "Percy's Cross," stands near the site of the battle.

---

[384] *Gregory's Chronicle: The Historical Collections of a London Citizen.* Edited by James Gairdner. Camden Society 1876.
[385] *Gregory's Chronicle: The Historical Collections of a London Citizen.* Edited by James Gairdner. Camden Society 1876. Page 223-224.

Montagu proceeded to Norham, collected the Scottish envoys and returned to York.

The Battle of Hedgeley Moor 25th April 1464

1. John Neville, Lord Montagu, was sent north by Edward IV to escort Scottish Envoys back to York.

2. Henry Beaufort, Duke of Somerset, set an ambush near Newcastle but Montagu, was forewarned and evaded it.

3. Montagu arrived at Hedgeley Moor. Somerset's army occupied the high ground in front and barred his passage to the north.

4. Montagu's army advanced. The Lancastrian left flank, under Roos and Hungerford, broke up and fled. The rest did likewise. Somerset regrouped at Alnwick.

5. Sir Ralph Percy made a last stand. Local legend has it that Percy's horse leapt some thirty feet in the air. A square stone column, known as 'Percy's Cross' stands near the site of the battle.

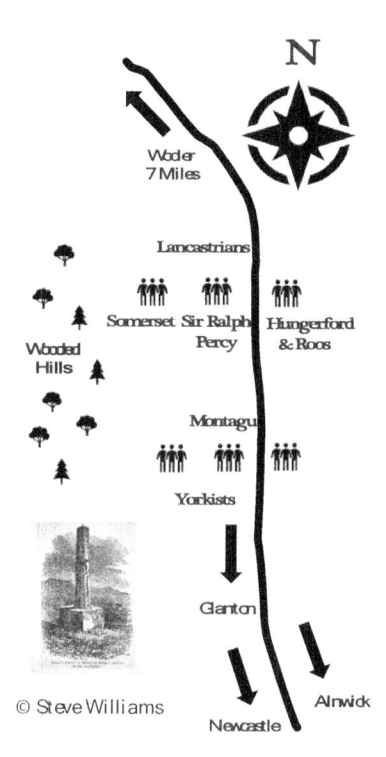

© Steve Williams

Somerset, Hungerford and Roos did withdraw to Bamburgh but advanced into the Tyne valley. They were eager to do battle. King Henry VI was lodged in nearby Bywell Castle for safety. Montagu did not wait for Warwick or Edward and supported by Lords Greystock and Willoughby, led his army out of Newcastle along the south bank of River Tyne to meet them. The Lancastrian army was encamped in three detachments near Linnel's Bridge with their back to Devil's Water, a fast-flowing stream set in a deep cutting, just to the south of Hexham.

The battle was brief but bloody. The Yorkist army charged from higher ground. The right division of the Lancastrian army, led by Lord Roos, gave way and fled across Devil's Water to escape. The remnants of Somerset's force were hemmed in and unable to manoeuvre. They were pushed back into Devil's Water. It was a rout. Men were drowned in the river, crushed as they climbed the steep banks or trapped and killed in West Dipton Wood.

Somerset attempted to fight his way out of the carnage. Unhorsed and badly wounded, he took shelter in a cottage but was discovered and was taken to Hexham Gaol. There he was executed, and his body was buried in Hexham Abbey. Hungerford and Roos were found within days in some nearby woods. They were taken to Newcastle and beheaded. Other Lancastrians were rounded up and justice meted out. It took another two months to find and execute Sir William Tailboys. The three thousand marks he carried to pay the Lancastrian troops proved to be a "very wholesome salve" for Montagu's men according to Gregory.

The Battle of Hexham 15th May 1464

1. Somerset advanced into the Tyne valley. John Neville, Lord Montagu, led his army out from Newcastle along south bank of River Tyne.

2. The Lancastrian army encamped near Linnel's Bridge with their back to Devil's Water.

3. The battle was brief but bloody. The Yorkist army charged from the higher ground. The right division of the Lancastrian army, led by Lord Roos, fled across Devil's Water to escape.

4. The remnants of Somerset's force were pushed back into Devil's Water. It was a rout. Men were drowned in the river, crushed as they climbed the steep banks or trapped in West Dipton Wood.

5. Somerset tried to fight his way out but was captured and taken to Hexham Gaol where he was executed. Somerset's body was buried in Hexham Abbey.

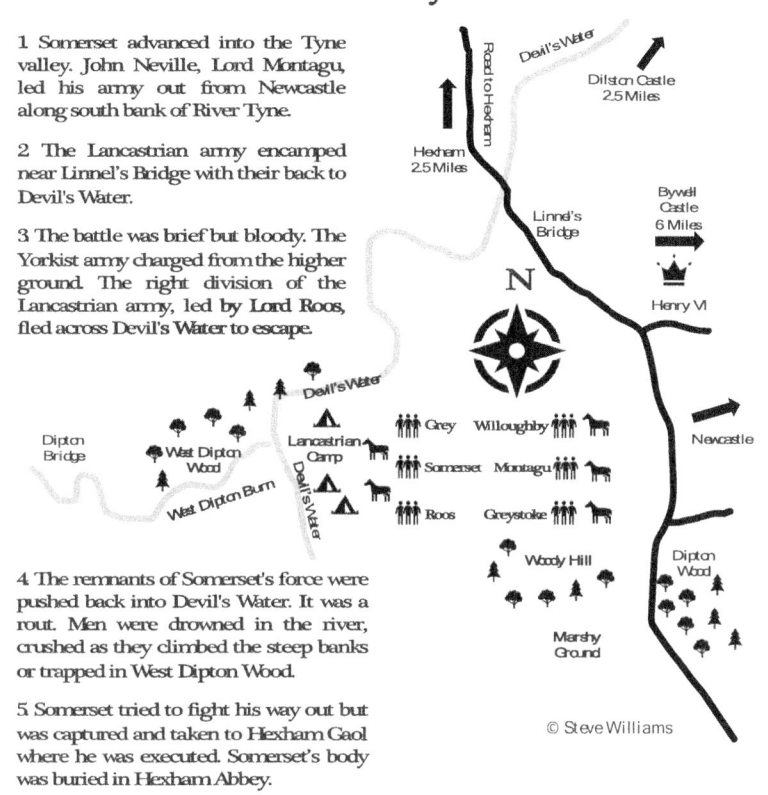

© Steve Williams

King Henry VI's bycocket (coronet) "garnished with two crowns of gold and fret with pearls and rich stones" was discovered in Bywell Castle along with three of his men "trapped in blue velvet" but the King himself was nowhere to be found. Montagu was made Earl of Northumberland on 27th May in York by a grateful King Edward who was in York to agree a truce with Scotland and to avoid an outbreak of the Plague which had hit London.

Warwick and Montagu were commissioned on 11th June to retake the castles on the coast. Warwick however appeared to be happy to leave this in the hands of his brother, given the latter's recent successes, and left for Calais and the continent. Montagu soon brought pressure on the remaining Lancastrians such that Alnwick and Dunstanburgh surrendered around 23rd June. Bamburgh took a little longer. An offer of pardon was turned aside. Guns were used to blast the walls. Sir Ralph Grey was badly injured. Humphrey Neville surrendered the castle. Grey was taken to Doncaster and executed.

The Neville brothers had won the North. Edward was "possessed of all England except a castle in North Wales, called Harlech". Somerset was dead. Margaret of Anjou was without money and support in France. Henry VI was in hiding. All seemed well.

The Falling Out

... In the ninth year of King Edward, being the year of our Lord, 1469, there arose a great disagreement between that King and his kinsman, Richard, the most illustrious Earl of Warwick, which was not allayed without the shedding of the blood of many persons... [386]

All may have seemed well but beneath the surface, relations between Warwick and his young cousin, Edward IV were starting to cool. The Neville's victory in the North made secure Edward's hold on his throne but it also made them less essential to the new King. Warwick and Edward drifted apart. Much has been written about the deteriorating relationship between the two cousins and the differences between them on issues of marriage, foreign policy and influence.

Ross writes that... "It is far from easy to trace with precision the development of the breach between the King and his most powerful subject." [387] One can see how the two of them were thrown together by events and through mutual loss and shared interests. Both saw the influence and importance of their families lessen as others took advantage of the weak King Henry VI. They fled the debacle of Ludford to Calais where Warwick became like a second father to Edward. They fought successfully together at Northampton but then lost their fathers at Wakefield. They went for broke in claiming the crown for Edward. They had no real choice. Edward needed Warwick. Warwick needed Edward.

Edward and Warwick won at Towton. Edward was crowned King. Warwick was his right-hand man, his sword in the north. Yet as they consolidated their hold on power, their reliance on each other

---

[386] *Ingulph's Chronicle of the Abbey of Croyland:* with the continuations by Peter of Blois and Anonymous writers. Translated by Henry Riley. Published by Nabu Press 2014. Originally published 1854. Written 1486. Page 445.
[387] *Edward IV* by Charles Ross. First Published 1974. Yale University Press 1997. The Burgundian Alliance Page 114.

lessened. Edward grew into his kingship, broadened his grasp on power and reduced his dependency upon Warwick.

Warwick who had tasted real power and prestige felt both starting to ebb away. The "over mighty" Earl was no longer so mighty. Certain events and happenings became almost like touchpoints for their relationship which deteriorated such that the two friends ultimately became foes.

* * * * *

The first such event was the King's marriage. Warkworth summarises it thus… "in the fourth year of King Edward, the Earl of Warwick was sent into France for a marriage for the King, for one fair lady, sister-daughter (niece) to the King of France, which was concluded by the Earl of Warwick. And whilst the said Earl of Warwick was in France, the King was wedded to Elizabeth Gray, widow… and when the Earl of Warwick come home and heard thereof, then he was greatly displeased with the King, and after that rose great dissonance ever more between the King and him." [388]

James Orchard Halliwell in his notes to Warkworth's chronicle writes that… "Gagvin, in his chronicon Franciae, informs us that the Earl (Warwick) was received by the King Louis XI at Rouen with great pomp; had secret conferences with him for twelve days consecutively; and was loaded with presents when he took his departure." [389]

Edward was the perhaps the most eligible bachelor in Europe in 1464. His marriage had been discussed far and wide since the age of three in 1445 when his father the Duke of York had raised the possibility of a marriage with the baby daughter of King Charles VII of France. More recently, possible marriage alliances had been the

---

[388] *"Warkworth's" Chronicle: A Chronicle of the First Thirteen Years of the reign of King Edward the Fourth* John Warkworth edited by James Orchard Halliwell Leopold Classic Library 2015. Written 1470-85. Page 3.
[389] *"Warkworth's" Chronicle: A Chronicle of the First Thirteen Years of the reign of King Edward the Fourth* John Warkworth edited by James Orchard Halliwell Leopold Classic Library 2015. Written 1470-85. Notes Page 35. P.3. l 17-8

subject of discussions with France, Burgundy, Spain and Scotland. Warwick had been party to many of these discussions as had others in the King's council.

Unbeknown to Warwick and others, Edward married a Lancastrian widow with two sons. Hearne's fragment records that "King Edward being a lusty Prince attempted the stability and constant modesty of divers ladies and gentlewomen, and when he could not perceive none of such constant womanhood, wisdom and beauty, as was Dame Elizabeth, widow of Sir John Grey of Groby late defunct, he then with a little company came unto the manor of Grafton, beside Stony Stratford, whereat Sir Richard Woodville, Earl of Rivers, and Dame Jacqueline, Duchess-dowager of Bedford, were then dwelling… early in a morning the said King Edward wedded the foresaid Dame Elizabeth there on the first day of May…" [390] Legend has it that Elizabeth waited under an old oak tree in Whittlebury Forest near her father, Lord Rivers' manor at Grafton Regis for the King to ride by. Later there would be claims of witchcraft.

The Chronicler Gregory reported that "on the first day of May our sovereign Lord the King, Edward IV, was wedded to the Lord River's daughter: her name is Dame Elizabeth… and this marriage was kept full secretly long and many a day, that no man knew of it; and men marvelled that our sovereign Lord was so long without any wife, and were ever feared that he had not been chaste in his living". [391]

The Croyland Chronicler explained that "King Edward, prompted by the ardour of youth, and relying entirely on his own choice, without consulting the nobles of the Kingdom, privately married the

---

[390] *The Chronicles of The White Rose of York: A series of Historical Fragments, Proclamations, Letters and Other Contemporary Documents relating to the Reign of Edward IV* Edited by James Bohn. Published London 1845. Paperback Version Reprint 2012. Pages 15-16, Hearne's Fragment.
[391] *Gregory's Chronicle: The Historical Collections of a Citizen of London* Edited by J Gairdner. Camden Society 1876. Pages 226-228.

widow of a certain knight, Elizabeth by name, who, though she had only a Knight for a father, had a Duchess for her mother". [392]

Mancini embellishes the story and tells that Edward… "found himself unable to seduce her whether by threats or inducements" and "there is a report that when Edward put a dagger to her throat to make her submit to his lust, she remained unperturbed and determined to die rather than live unchastely with him". Edward's ardour was such that he married this "lady of humble origin" and this marriage so incensed his mother that she was prepared to say that Edward was not her husband's son but conceived in adultery". [393]

The Chronicler Fabyan tells the fullest story… "in such past time, in most secret manner, upon the first day of May, King Edward spoused Elizabeth, late the wife of Sir John Grey… which vows were solemnized early in the morning at a town called Grafton, near unto Stony Stratford, at which marriage was no persons present but the spouse, the spowsesse, the Duchess of Bedford, her mother, and a Priest and two gentlewomen and a young man to help the priest sing. After… he went to bed, and so tarried there three or four hours, and after departed and rode again to Stony Stratford, and came in the manner that he had been hunting… and he sent to Lord Rivers, the bride's father to say he would lodge with him for four days. Each night she was brought to his bed in so secret a manner, that almost none but her mother knew." [394]

---

[392] *Ingulph's Chronicle of the Abbey of Croyland.* Translated by HT Riley. Lightening Source Press 2014. Pages 439-440.
[393] *Domenico Mancini de Occupatione Regni Anglie* Translated by Annette Carson. Imprimis Imprimatur 2021. Chapter Five. Page 43.
[394] *The New Chronicles of England and France* by Robert Fabyan. Edited by Henry Ellis London 1811. Forgotten Books 2018. Originally edition by Pynson 1516. Page 654.

Ross concludes that "even William, Lord Hastings, perhaps his closest friend, seems to have been kept in the dark." [395] Hastings as Lord Chamberlain was used to people approaching him for help or for access to the King. In mid-April 1464 he was approached by Dame Elizabeth Grey, nee Elizabeth Woodville, the widow of Lord Ferrers of Groby who had been killed fighting for the Lancastrians at the 2nd Battle of St Albans. She was in dispute with her mother-in-law, Baroness Ferrers, over her son's inheritance. Hasting's agreement was secured on 13th April. The price to be paid was high. It was to be a half share in the profits of the lands and a marriage between one of her sons and any future daughter born to William and his wife Katherine Neville. [396]

The appeal to Hastings by Elizabeth Woodville and his agreement to help suggests that as late as mid-April there was no expectation of the forthcoming marriage to the King on 1st May 1464.

The chronicler Gregory puts the marriage down to love. [397] Edward followed his heart and was loath to share news that others might not find agreeable. Perhaps though it was lust that then turned to love. We know that it may not have been the first time that Edward had married in order to bed an older woman. Eleanor Talbot (Butler) was the woman cited by Bishop Stillington as Edward's first wife thus making his children by Elizabeth Woodville illegitimate. [398] This was set out in an Act of Parliament "King Edward was and stood married and troth plight to one Dame Eleanor Butler, daughter of the old Earl of Shrewsbury". [399] Commynes reports it thus "King Edward being very enamoured of a certain English lady, promised to marry her, provided that he could sleep with her first,

---

[395] *Edward IV* by Charles Ross. Yale University Press 1997. The King's Marriage and the Woodvilles. Page 90.
[396] *Edward IV and Elizabeth Woodville, A True Romance* by Amy Licence. Amberley Publishing 2016. The Secret Wife, 1464. Page 107.
[397] *Gregory's Chronicle: The Historical Collections of a Citizen of London* Edited by J Gairdner. Camden Society 1876. Page 226.
[398] *The Secret Queen Eleanor Talbot, The Woman who put Richard III on the Throne*. John Ashdown-Hill. The History Press 2016.
[399] *Titulus Regius* Act of Parliament 1484.

and she consented. The bishop (Stillington) said that he had married them when only he and they were present". [400]

The secret of Edward's marriage to Elizabeth Woodville was maintained through the summer, despite or because of the international diplomacy seeking a marriage and peace treaty with France. Warwick was still being courted by Louis XI of France in order to draw England into his spider's web of influence.

Edward called a Council in Reading in September 1464. There were matters to discuss, such the peace negotiations with France and the need for a new coinage. The Council met on 14th September 1464. Peace with France was the agenda item. The brief for Warwick and Wenlock needed to be agreed ahead of a meeting in St Omer scheduled for 1st October 1464. The subject of a French marriage came up. Edward could remain silent no longer and confessed that he was already married.

Wenlock wrote to the Burgundian diplomat Lannoy and said that the announcement caused "great displeasure to many great Lords, and especially to the larger part of his council'. [401] Wenlock himself might have been displeased as he anticipated handsome gifts from Louis XI on the signing of a marriage and peace treaty.

The Burgundian Chronicler, Jean de Waurin, reported that the Council were none too pleased to hear the news… "they answered that she was not his match, however good and however fair she might be, and he must know well that she was no wife for a Prince such as himself; for she was not the daughter of a Duke or Earl". [402]

The Croyland Chronicler also reported that "the nobility and chief men of the Kingdom took amiss, seeing that he had with such

---

[400] *Memoires Philippe De Commynes*. Translated by M Jones. Pages 353-354.
[401] *Anchiennes Cronicques d'Engleterre by Jean de Waurin* Edited by E Dupont. French History Society Paris 1858-63. Page 326.
[402] *Anchiennes Cronicques d'Engleterre by Jean de Waurin* Edited by E Dupont. French History Society Paris 1858-63. Pages 327-328.

immoderate haste promoted a person sprung from a comparatively humble lineage, to share the throne with him". [403]

The Council may, or may not, have been pleased. They were surprised but there was nothing they could do. Warwick was probably put out by not being consulted by Edward and may also have been concerned with losing face with Louis XI. Warwick though still led the new Queen into the chapel of Reading Abbey on St Michaelmas Day when she was formerly introduced to the court. Elizabeth Woodville's grandfather may have been a squire. Her father had been paraded and pilloried before Warwick at Calais, but she was the Queen.

* * * * *

The marriage by itself may have disappointed and frustrated Warwick but of more concern was the waning of his influence with the King at a time when others, most notably the family of the Queen, were seeing their importance and influence grow.

The Queen's father, Richard Woodville, Lord Rivers, and "son of a squire" was made Treasurer of the Exchequer on 4th March 1466. A couple of months later on 24th May 1466 he was created Earl Rivers and on 24th August 1466 he was appointed Constable of England. Already a member of the King's council, the income from these offices of state equated to £1,330 per annum.

The Queen's brother, Antony Woodville, Lord Scales, in November 1466 became Lord of the Isle of Wight. The Queen's brothers, Richard and John Woodville, together with three of the Queen's brothers-in-law to be, were made Knights of the Bath on 23rd May 1465 at the occasion of the Queen's Coronation. The youngest brother, Lionel, was "archdeacon of Oxford at nineteen and Dean of Exeter at twenty-five but had to wait until he was twenty-nine before he was promoted to the bishopric of Salisbury". [404]

---

[403] *Ingulph's Chronicle of the Abbey of Croyland*. Translated by HT Riley. Lightening Source Press 2014. Page 440.
[404] *Edward IV* by Charles Ross. Yale University Press 1997. The King's Marriage and the Woodvilles. Pages 95-96.

It was not just the honours. Warwick had two daughters that he wanted to marry well. Yet the Queen's sisters were in 1466 given permission to marry some of the most eligible men in England. Katherine Woodville married Henry Stafford, heir to the Duke of Buckingham. Anne Woodville wed Viscount Bourchier, heir to the Earl of Essex. Eleanor married Anthony Grey, heir to the Earl of Kent. Mary Woodville was betrothed to William Herbert, heir to Lord Herbert.

The Queen's son by her first marriage, Thomas Grey wed Anne Holland, heiress to the Duchess of Exeter who was already betrothed to Warwick's nephew. The Queen's younger brother, John Woodville, aged twenty, married the very wealthy sixty-five-year-old dowager Duchess of Norfolk in January 1465. It was not for love alone! [405]

The Croyland Chronicler believed that the loss of influence at the expense of the Queen's family was the prime cause for the falling out of Warwick and Edward… "In the ninth year of King Edward, being the year of our Lord, 1469, there arose a great disagreement between that King and his kinsman, Richard, the most illustrious Earl of Warwick, which was not allayed without the shedding of the blood of many persons. The reason of this was, the fact that the King, being too greatly influenced by the urgent suggestions of the Queen, admitted to his especial favour all the relations of the said Queen, as well as those who were in any way connected with her by blood, enriching them with boundless presents and always promoting them to the most dignified offices about his person, while at the same time. He banished from his presence his own brethren, and his kinsmen sprung from the royal blood, together with the Earl of Warwick himself, and the other nobles of the realm who had always proved faithful to him." [406]

---

[405] *Edward IV* by Charles Ross. Yale University Press 1997. The King's Marriage and the Woodvilles. Page 93.
[406] *Ingulph's Chronicle of the Abbey of Croyland:* with the continuations by Peter of Blois and Anonymous writers. Translated by Henry Riley. Published by Nabu Press 2014. Originally published 1854. Written 1486. Page 445.

The Great Chronicle records that "many murmurous tales ran in the city between the Earl of Warwick and the Queen's blood". [407]

Yet Ross points out that "Edward did little to advance the material interests of the Queen's relatives… they never enjoyed the lavish patronage in land, wardship and profitable offices which so benefited the Neville family and men like Hastings and Herbert". [408]

* * * * *

Ross is clear that Warwick was treated well in material terms… "The impression (is) that Edward was excessively generous and **Warwick excessively greedy**. For the Earl was already by far the richest of Edward's subjects in his own right. Yet he appropriated for himself a disproportionately large share of the most valuable offices at the King's disposal and continued to acquire more as the reign wore on… Even by the standards of an acquisitive age **Warwick appears exceptionally grasping**. His private greed is swell illustrated by his efforts to expand his territorial influence not merely in the north of England but also in South Wales, where he sought to get control of the Duke of Buckingham's lordships adjoining his own Marcher holdings of Glamorgan and Abergavenny." [409]

Hearne's fragment states that Warwick's "insatiable mind could not be content, and yet before him was there none in England of the half possessions that he had… and yet he desired more". [410]

---

[407] *The Great Chronicle of London*. Edited by AH Thomas and ID Thornley. 1938. Page 207.
[408] *Edward IV* by Charles Ross. Yale University Press 1997. The King's Marriage and the Woodvilles. Page 95.
[409] *Edward IV* by Charles Ross. First Published 1974. Yale University Press 1997. The Establishment of the Yorkist Regime Page 71.
[410] *The Chronicles of The White Rose of York: A series of Historical Fragments, Proclamations, Letters and Other Contemporary Documents relating to the Reign of Edward IV* Edited by James Bohn. Published London 1845. Paperback Version Reprint 2012. Page 23, Hearne's Fragment.

Warwick and his Neville family were very well rewarded for their service and support. The Calendar of Patent Rolls [411] records the many appointments and awards made to them by his grateful and generous cousin King Edward IV. Perhaps the only omission was that Warwick was never made a Duke unlike Edward's brothers, George and Richard, who were created Dukes of Clarence and Gloucester respectively.

Richard Neville, Earl of Warwick – Appointments and Grants.

May 1461 - Great Chamberlain of England; Constable of Dover castle and Warden of the Cinque ports; Master of the King's mews and falcons; Steward of the lordship of Feckenham, Worcestershire; Custody of George, Lord Latimer during his idiocy; Castles, manors, lordships in Buckinghamshire, Northamptonshire, Warwickshire, Yorkshire and Westmorland formerly held by Henry Percy, Earl of Northumberland, John, Lord Clifford and James Earl of Wiltshire.

December 1461 - Steward of England at the trial of Henry VI and other rebels who murdered the King's father, Richard, Duke of York, at Wakefield.

April 1462 - Captain of Carlisle and Warden of the West Marches towards Scotland with fees of £2,500 p.a. in wartime and £1,250 in peacetime.

November 1462 - King's Lieutenant in the North.

December 1463 - Steward of the temporalities of the bishopric of Carlisle.

April 1465 - Castle, honour and lordship of Cockermouth; manors, lands in Cumberland, Westmorland, Yorkshire and elsewhere.

November 1466 - Custodian and Justice in Eyre of Royal Forests north of the river Trent, with annual fee of 100 marks.

---

[411] *Calendar of Patent Rolls Edward IV 1461-67*. Great Britain Public Record Office. Forgotten Books. 2018.

November 1467 - Custody of Francis, son and heir of Sir John Lovell, during his minority.

December 1468 - Custody with John Neville, Earl of Northumberland, and others of gold and silver mines north of the river Trent.

February 1469 – Manors in Cumberland and Warwickshire.

John Neville, Lord Montagu/Earl of Northumberland – Appointments and Grants.

May 1461 - Knight; Custody of the King's gold and silver mines in Devon and Cornwall.

July 1461 - Baron; Subsidy of ulnage of cloths in Hull, York and Yorkshire.

May 1462 - Manors and land in Leicestershire, Nottinghamshire and Lincolnshire.

May 1463 - Warden of the East Marches towards Scotland.

May 1464 - Earl of Northumberland with annuity of £20.

June 1464 - Forfeited Hull ship and merchandise.

March 1465 - Customs and Subsidies from merchandise in Newcastle upon Tyne and places adjacent, to the sum of £2,000 as part payment for expenses incurred as Warden of the East Marches towards Scotland.

November 1465 - Lordships and manors in Suffolk, Norfolk, Leicestershire, Nottinghamshire and Yorkshire.

July 1466 - Custodian and Sheriff of Northumberland.

William Neville, Lord Fauconberg/Earl of Kent – Appointments and Grants.

February 1462 - Earl of Kent; jointly with Laurence Booth, Bishop of Durham, the King's castle, manor and lordship of Wressle, Yorkshire.

July 1462 - Admiral of England.

August 1462 - Lordships and Manors in Cornwall, Devon, Dorset, Buckinghamshire, Suffolk, Nottinghamshire, Derbyshire, Lincolnshire and Yorkshire in the King's hands by forfeiture.

George Neville, Bishop of Exeter/Archbishop of York – Appointments and Grants.

May 1461 - Bishop of Exeter; Custody of the King's manor or lordship of Chilton Langley, Hertfordshire, and manors in Oxfordshire.

February 1462 - Lordships and manors in Devon, Buckinghamshire and Hertfordshire, in the King's hand by forfeiture.

July 1463 - Lordships and manors in Cornwall, Essex, Suffolk, Cambridgeshire and Oxfordshire during the minority of John de Vere, son and heir of John, Earl of Oxford.

September 1464 - Steward of the temporalities of the archbishopric of York.

George became Archbishop of York with Edward's support and in September 1465, hosted a lavish feast enjoyed (we presume) by twenty-eight peers, fifty-nine knights, ten abbots, seven bishops, numerous lawyers, clergy, esquires, and ladies. They consumed 4,000 pigeons and 4,000 crays, 2,000 chickens, 204 cranes, 104 peacocks, 1,200 quails, 400 swans and 400 herons, 113 oxen, 6 bulls,

608 pikes and bream, 12 porpoises and seals, 1,000 sheep, 304 calves, 2,000 pigs, 1,000 capons, 400 plovers, 2,400 ruffs, 4,000 mallard and teals, 204 kids and 204 bitterns, 200 pheasants, 500 partridges, 400 woodcocks, 100 curlews, 1,000 egrets, over 500 stags, bucks and roes, 4,000 cold and 1,500 hot venison pies, 4,000 dishes of jelly, 4,000 baked tarts, 2,000 hot custards with a proportionate quantity of bread, sugared delicacies and cakes, and all washed down with 300 tuns of ale and 100 tuns of wine. [412] Edward and Queen Elizabeth were not present, but it was attended by the King's young brother Richard who was at the time in Warwick's household. Warwick acted as Steward at the event.

Warkworth wrote of George, as Archbishop… "he and his brothers had the rule of this land and had gathered riches (over) many years". [413]

As the records show, Warwick and his family were very well rewarded for their active help and support. It was not for the want of more land and titles that relations broke down between Edward and Warwick.

* * * * *

Foreign Policy is another reason given by some for the falling out of Warwick and Edward. Warwick favoured closer ties with France. Edward was ever distrustful of the ancient enemy and preferred Burgundy.

The Croyland chronicler was one who believed a rift over foreign affairs was the real cause of dissension between them. The chronicler wrote about the marriage of Edward's sister, Margaret, to Charles, Duke of Burgundy… "at this marriage, Richard Neville, Earl of Warwick, who had for some years appeared to favour the party of the French against the Burgundians, conceived great

---

[412] https://en.wikipedia.org/wiki/George_Neville_(bishop) – *Antiquarii de rebus Britannicis Collectanea* Vol VI John Leland. Richardson Press 1752 London.
[413] *"Warkworth's" Chronicle: A Chronicle of the First Thirteen Years of the reign of King Edward the Fourth* John Warkworth edited by James Orchard. Halliwell Leopold Classic Library 2015. Written 1470-85. Pages 25-26.

indignation. For he would have greatly preferred to have sought an alliance for the said Lady Margaret in the Kingdom of France… it being much against his wish, that the views of Charles, now Duke of Burgundy, should be promoted by means of an alliance with England. The fact is, that he pursued that man with a most deadly hatred. This in my opinion, was really the cause of the dissensions between the King and the Earl, and not the one which has been previously mentioned – the marriage of the King with Queen Elizabeth." Warwick "continued to show favour to all the Queen's kindred, until he found that all her relatives and connections, contrary to his wishes, were using their utmost endeavours to promote the other marriage… of Charles and the lady Margaret".[414]

England was a much sought after ally. France under Louis XI was exerting more pressure upon subject states such as Brittany and Burgundy. Louis XI was seeking closer ties with England now Edward appeared to be secure on his throne despite the pleas for help from Margaret of Anjou. Warwick favoured France but Edward's preference was Burgundy.

On 28th March 1465 Warwick was commissioned to treat with "Lord Jakes" as the English called Jacques de Luxembourg, brother to Jacquetta de Luxembourg, the Queen's mother. Jakes wanted England to join a league including Brittany and Burgundy against France. Warwick led the negotiations. These led to nothing more than the Queen's Uncle being compensated for his trouble with £125 by way of expenses and jewels worth around the same amount.[415]

On 8th May 1465 Warwick was appointed to treat with France, Burgundy and Brittany for treaties of peace, friendship or commerce. Louis XI was otherwise engaged in hostilities with his dissident brother Charles. Edward was keen not to intervene.

---

[414] *Ingulph's Chronicle of the Abbey of Croyland:* with the continuations by Peter of Blois and Anonymous writers. Translated by Henry Riley. Published by Nabu Press 2014. Originally published 1854. Written 1486. Page 457.
[415] *The Life and Reign of Edward the Fourth* by Cora L. Scofield. Fonthill Media 2016. Volume One Page 373.

Margaret of Anjou was still trying to secure French help to restore her husband Henry VI to the throne of England. Warwick even missed the new Queen's coronation on Saturday 25th May and the celebratory tournament and banquets which followed. The talks came to nothing.

Warwick's return from Calais coincided with the capture of Henry VI who had taken refuge in a number of places in Lancashire and Yorkshire. Henry was brought south to London. Warwick rode out to Islington to meet him. "Henry of Windsor, late de facto and non de jure king of England" was led "through Cheapside and so through all London to the Tower". The Croyland Chronicler recorded that "Henry, lately styled King of England…was now taken prisoner… and led by a strong body of men to the Tower of London, where King Edward ordered all possible humanity to be shown towards him, consistently with his safe custody… supplied with all suitable necessaries and treated with becoming respect". [416]

On 22nd March 1466 Warwick was once again appointed to treat with France and Burgundy. This time the potential marriage of Edward's sister Margaret of York was on the table. [417] Discussions began with the Bastard of Burgundy at St Omer. The English party moved to Boulogne where they met directly with the heir to the Dukedom, Count Charles of Charolais. The talks did not go well. Warwick and Charles clashed. Warwick preferred an alliance with France in any case. The talks ended with no agreement.

Warwick then travelled to Calais where they met the French Ambassadors who included the new Constable of France, Louis de Luxembourg, Count of St Pol and Uncle to Elizabeth Woodville. On 24th May 1466 a short truce was signed by Warwick on land and sea to last until March 1468. They would meet again in October at Dieppe to treat for peace. A suitable French marriage for King Edward's sister would be found.

---

[416] *Ingulph's Chronicle of the Abbey of Croyland*. Translated by HT Riley. Lightening Source Press 2014. Page 439.
[417] *Edward IV* by Charles Ross. Yale University Press 1997. The Burgundian Alliance. Page 107.

Charles of Burgundy was very concerned with the closer links between England and France. In December 1466 a Burgundian Embassy led by Seigneur de la Gruthuyse arrived in London to discuss trade matters. No real progress was made. Duke Philip of Burgundy was reluctant to revoke his edict against English cloth.[418]

Warwick was in the North dealing with Scotland and alleged breaches of the truce but returned in February 1467 to receive an embassy from France. The French embassy stayed until May. King Edward picked up a bill of more than £500 including £152 for fine wines from Bourgogne according to the Treasurer's accounts. [419] Warwick accompanied the French ambassadors on their return and was lavishly entertained by Louis XI.

Parliament opened on 3rd June 1467. Warwick's brother, the Chancellor, George Neville, was absent and lost his job five days later on 8th June. Edward himself asked for the return of the Great Seal. Scofield [420] and Ross [421] both believe that George was tilting for a cardinal's hat in Rome. Matters between Edward and Warwick had deteriorated sufficiently that Edward felt able and willing to dismiss George. Warkworth's chronicle records that this was very significant… "and then the King put out of the Chancellorship, the Bishop of Exeter, the brother to the Earl of Warwick… after that the Earl of Warwick took to him in fee as many knights, squires, and gentlemen as he might, to be strong; and King Edward did that he might to feeble the Earl's power… they never loved together after." [422]

---

[418] *The Life and Reign of Edward the Fourth* by Cora L. Scofield. Fonthill Media 2016. Volume One. Page 410.
[419] *The Life and Reign of Edward the Fourth* by Cora L. Scofield. Fonthill Media 2016. Volume One. Page 413.
[420] *The Life and Reign of Edward the Fourth* by Cora L. Scofield. Fonthill Media 2016. Volume One. Page 416.
[421] *Edward IV* by Charles Ross. Yale University Press 1997. The Burgundian Alliance. Page 110.
[422] *"Warkworth's" Chronicle: A Chronicle of the First Thirteen Years of the reign of King Edward the Fourth* John Warkworth edited by James Orchard. Halliwell Leopold Classic Library 2015. Written 1470-85. Pages 3-4.

On 9th June 1467, Edward signed a treaty with Duke Francis of Brittany. Parliament was adjourned so all could attend the Great Tournament and see the guest of honour, the Bastard of Burgundy. The tournament was cut short. Duke Philip of Burgundy died on 15th June 1467. The Bastard left for home.

Warwick returned from meeting Louis XI of France accompanied by a French mission. They arrived on 24th June but were given little time by Edward according to Waurin. [423] Whilst the French ambassadors were in London, Edward concluded a treaty of Friendship with Burgundy and an alliance with King Henry of Castile. The French envoys returned home. Warwick escorted them to the coast and cannot have been happy with the treatment of his brother or his French guests. Warwick did not return to court but went home to Yorkshire.

On 20th September 1467 Edward sent envoys to Burgundy to seek peace and agree a marriage treaty. Warwick was not part of the embassy. Edward eased matters by agreeing to lift existing restrictions on Burgundian imports. Negotiations took place with Isabella of Portugal, the mother of the new Duke Charles. [424] The marriage treaty and alliance with Burgundy was signed in the Spring of 1468.

On 18th June 1468 the King's sister Margaret left London led by Warwick and other Lords. Margaret was joined by her three brothers, Edward, Clarence and Gloucester. They all made their way to the coast at Margate via Canterbury. Margaret married Duke Charles and became the Duchess of Burgundy on Sunday 3rd July 1468.

Margaret had an eventful wedding day. Hearne's fragment records that… "This 7th year, Margaret sister unto King Edward before said, departed from the King, and rode throughout London behind the Earl of Warwick, and rode that night to Stratford Abbey, and from

---

[423] *Anchiennes Cronicques d'Engleterre by Jean de Waurin* Edited by E Dupont. French History Society Paris 1858-63. Page 346-349.
[424] *The Life and Reign of Edward the Fourth* by Cora L. Scofield. Fonthill Media 2016. Volume One Pages 430-431.

thence to the sea-side, and went into Flanders to Bruges, where she was married with great solemnity: and after the feast done, the same night the Duke (of Burgundy) and she rode out of the town to a Castle called Male, one mile out of Bruges: and, when they were both in bed, the Castle was set on fire by treason, so that the Duke and she 'scaped narrowly." [425]

Commynes tells us that Warwick and Duke Charles were not good friends… "At this same time (April 1469) the Earl of Warwick visited the Duke of Burgundy, and neither were friends thereafter… [426] and… "The Earl of Warwick began to fall out with his master (Edward) about a year before the Duke of Burgundy besieged Amiens. The Duke of Burgundy encouraged this because he disliked the great influence which the Earl of Warwick exercised in England and they did not get on well together because the Earl of Warwick was always hand in glove with the King, our master" [427]

* * * * *

Edward trusted Warwick with the bringing up of his younger brother. Sometime between 1463 to 1465, the eleven to thirteen years old Richard was placed into the Warwick household to further his training and education as a noble. Warwick was paid £1,000 as reimbursement for the "costs and expenses incurred by him for the Duke of Gloucester, the King's brother". [428] Richard's time in his cousin's household lasted up to his sixteenth birthday in October 1468.

---

[425] *The Chronicles of The White Rose of York: A series of Historical Fragments, Proclamations, Letters and Other Contemporary Documents relating to the Reign of Edward IV* Edited by James Bohn. Published London 1845. Paperback Version Reprint 2012. Page 20, Hearne's Fragment.
[426] *Memoirs - The Reign of Louis XI 1461-83* by Philippe De Commynes Translated by Michael Jones Penguin Classics 1972 Page 145
[427] *Memoirs - The Reign of Louis XI 1461-83* by Philippe De Commynes Translated by Michael Jones Penguin Classics 1972 Page 181
[428] The National Archives E405/43

Some commentators have described it as Richard being "taken under the wing of Warwick". This is incorrect. Richard did not accompany Warwick on his travels, but he was treated as part of the domestic Neville family. He accompanied the Earl and Countess to Warwick College of St Mary in 1465 and York in 1468. Edward still paid for Richard's clothes. There is a wardrobe account [429] dated 20th March 1465 for "diverse robes, gowns, tunics, caps, hose, shoes". In addition, there is falconry gloves, four dozen bowstrings, twelve arrowheads, a bow case and riding equipment. The fletcher William Love is paid £20 6s 1d "for diverse sheaves of arrows and other chattels" delivered to John Younge, yeoman of the king's bows for "the use of our brethren the duke of Clarence and Gloucester". [430]

Warwick stood as Godfather to Edward and Elizabeth's first child, Elizabeth born on 11th February 1466.

As Warwick grew further distant to Edward, yet Warwick became closer to Edward's brother, George, next male heir in line to the throne, who subsequently became Warwick's son-in-law.

Hearne's fragment noted that Warwick "counselled and enticed the Duke of Clarence, and caused him to wed his eldest daughter, Isabel, without the advice or knowledge of Edward. Wherefore the King took a great displeasure with them both, and thereupon were certain unkind words betwixt them, in so much, that after that day there was never perfect love betwixt them." [431]

Ross believes that… "Warwick's plan to marry his eldest daughter to Clarence was a logical consequence of the series of Woodville

---

[429] The National Archives E361/6
[430] The National Archives E404/72/4/2
[431] *The Chronicles of The White Rose of York: A series of Historical Fragments, Proclamations, Letters and Other Contemporary Documents relating to the Reign of Edward IV* Edited by James Bohn. Published London 1845. Paperback Version Reprint 2012. Page 23, Hearne's Fragment.

marriages. The King's persistent refusal to approve this match merely added further to Warwick's mounting grievances." [432]

Warwick began to subvert Clarence with promises of making him King as early as during the visit of the French ambassadors in the summer of 1467 according to Jean de Waurin. The same account has Warwick blaming traitors around Edward causing the King to take away the role of Chancellor from his brother George Neville. [433]

Warwick's retreat to the North and away from Westminster to avoid the likes of the King's men, Rivers, Herbert and Scales was all very well but it did not help when a messenger from Margaret of Anjou was captured in the autumn of 1467 by William Herbert near Harlech and implicated Warwick along with others in a plot against the King. Herbert had worked for Warwick in Wales, but he had since tied his flag firmly to Edward's mast and been very well rewarded for the same. Herbert was Edward's right-hand man in Wales and was active in seeking further influence.

Edward's calls for Warwick to attend court and council to explain himself were refused and rejected. The court was dominated by the Queen's family, her father Lord Rivers and her brother Anthony Lord Scales and others such as the Lords Ferrers, Hastings, Herbert and Stafford. Warwick's feelings of insecurity and not being welcome, first experienced at the court of Henry VI and Queen Margaret, were once more aroused.

Warwick had no time for tournaments and lavish court dinners. As Pollard suggests... "Richard Neville had little time for the new Camelot. And perhaps the new Camelot had little time for him". [434] Warwick felt excluded from court and politics. Suspicions

---

[432] *Edward IV* by Charles Ross. First Published 1974. Yale University Press 1997. The King's Marriage and the Woodvilles Page 94.
[433] *Anchiennes Cronicques d'Engleterre by Jean de Waurin* Edited by E Dupont. French History Society Paris 1858-63. Introduction.
[434] *Warwick the Kingmaker, Politics, Power and Fame*. AJ Pollard. Continuum Books. 2007. England's Caesar. Page 57.

heightened, he was not going to be judged by those who had taken over from him in terms of influence and power.

It took the intervention of George Neville to persuade his brother Warwick to attend council in Coventry where matters seemed to be smoothed over, at least for a time. Warwick appointed his brother-in-law, William Hastings as his steward in Leicestershire, Rutland and Northamptonshire in April 1468. Hastings was a close friend of the King and his Lord Chamberlain. Warwick perhaps recognised his loss of influence and wanted someone on his side who had Edward's ear.

Warwick still pursued the marriage of his eldest daughter Isabel to Clarence despite Edward's opposition. Secret negotiations in Rome, facilitated by his brother and Archbishop George Neville, secured the necessary dispensation. Warwick "dissembled his fury" whilst he promoted discord through his intriguing, according to the Tudor writer Vergil.

* * * * *

Vergil wrote that Warwick fell out with Edward for "injury offered, or envy of authority" and came to judge Edward as unfit to be King. Warwick was "vexed in mind, moved and angry" by Edward's marriage to Elizabeth Woodville, the marriage of Margaret of York to Duke Charles of burgundy whom the Earl "hated worse than any man living" and that Edward had "tried to do some unhonest act" with a young lady "in the Earl's house." [435]

Most observers place the primary blame for the deterioration in the relationship on Warwick, aside perhaps from Charles Oman in his biography of Warwick. Edward is criticised more for his willingness to almost forgive and forget as evidenced by his treatment of Somerset. Ross is in no doubt… "The breach with Edward was

---

[435] *Three Books of Polydore Vergil's English History* by Camden Society. Edited by Sir Henry Ellis. Published by Forgotten Books 2012 Originally published 1844. Written 1510. Pages 117-118.

essentially of Warwick's own making and was the product of his inability to accept anything less than domination over the King." [436] Bicheno believes Warwick was an "unconstrained ego" and a "pioneer of mass propaganda" and for him… "The marriage and the matter of the Burgundian versus the French alliance were indeed the issues that led to war between Warwick and Edward – but because they were a trial of wills. Warwick could only be the power behind a throne occupied by a weak King." [437]

Whatever happened, for many the split between the two was inevitable. It was just a question of when, where and with what result…

---

[436] *Edward IV* by Charles Ross. First Published 1974. Yale University Press 1997. The Burgundian Alliance Page 116.
[437] *Blood Royale; The Wars of Lancaster and York 1462-1485* by Hugh Bicheno. Head of Zeus 2016.

The Commons of the North Rebel

...In this year the fall out between the King and the Earl of Warwick which had continued since the marriage of the Queen, began to appear; in so much that the Earl withdrew himself from the King and conspired with the Duke of Clarence, that before had married his daughter... whereupon the commons of the North began to rebel... [438]

Disturbances in the North were not new, but they set in trail several events which led to a full-scale breakdown of relations between Warwick and Edward. The Yorkshire rebellions suffer from confusion deriving from the bias and relative lack of interest of the mainly southern sources.

Most contemporaries focus upon the main rebellion. The Croyland Chronicler writes that "a whirlwind again came down from the north, in the form of a mighty insurrection of the commons of that part of the country. These complained that they were grievously oppressed with taxes and annual tributes by the said favourites of the King and Queen and having appointed one Robin of Redesdale to act as captain over them, proceeded to march, about *sixty thousand* in number, to join the Earl of Warwick". [439]

Yet there were at least two other uprisings, both put down by Warwick's brother, John Neville, the Earl of Northumberland at the bequest of the King. The first is mentioned in the Cambridge Fragment [440] and relates to an uprising at the end of April and in May by a "Robin de Redysdale or Robyn Mendall" who was seeking to "incite the minds of the county". The records of the Beverley Corporation tell us that archers were sent "to ride with the Earl of

---

[438] *The New Chronicles of England and France* by Robert Fabyan. Edited by Henry Ellis London 1811. Forgotten Books 2018. Originally edition by Pynson 1516. Page 657.
[439] *Ingulph's Chronicle of the Abbey of Croyland.* Translated by HT Riley. Lightening Source Press 2014. Page 445.
[440] *The Yorkshire Rebellions of 1469* by K.R. Dockray. The Ricardian 1983 Pages 246-57. At Page 252.

Northumberland to suppress Robin of Redesdale and other enemies of the kingdom on the morrow of St. Mark (26th April 1469) and were absent for some nine days". [441]

A more significant rebellion followed quickly led by Robin Hulderne or Robin of Holderness. This is covered by the Brief Latin Chronicle, Polydore Virgil and Edward Hall. [442] It was a local grievance based upon an ancient right claimed by St Leonard's Hospital to be able to tax farmers a "thrave" of corn. This right of "petercorn" had been confirmed by Henry VI's parliament and most recently by Edward IV following an investigation led by Warwick.

The rebels marched on York but being from the Percy family heartlands they added to their list of wants, the restoration of Henry Percy to the Earldom of Northumberland. Warwick's brother John, as the current Earl of Northumberland was not impressed and met the rebel forces outside the gates of York. They were defeated and their leader "Robin" was beheaded. [443]

On 22nd May 1469 a general commission of oyer and terminer "throughout the realm" was announced. Warwick was appointed with Hastings, Bourchier, Essex, Rivers and many others as Edward IV reacted to the lawlessness right across the country. [444]

The main rebellion arose in Yorkshire in June led by a Robin of Redesdale. There has been much discussion and debate as to who was "Robin of Redesdale". It was unlikely to be Robert Hulderne or Hilliard as he was from the East Riding and beholden to the Percy family, aside from having lost his head outside the gates of York.

---

[441] *Report on the Manuscripts of the Corporation of Beverley* Historical Manuscripts Commission HMSO 1900 Page 144.
[442] *The Yorkshire Rebellions of 1469* by K.R. Dockray. The Ricardian 1983 Pages 246-57. At Page 249.
[443] *Brief Latin Chronicle Three Fifteenth Century Chronicles*. Edited by J Gairdner. Camden Society 1881. Page 183.
[444] *Richard III Loyalty Binds Me* by Matthew Lewis Amberley Publishing 2018. Page 93.

Warkworth wrote that "Sir William Conyars knight was their captain and called himself Robyne of Riddesdale" [445] but his track record with first names is not good, mistaking James for John Conyers, and Roger for Richard Pigot, as two knights killed at the Battle of Edgcote. [446] William Conyers of Marske was also a relative junior member of the family.

Scofield wrote that "Robin lost many men, including his own son" and most commentators believe Sir John Conyers of Hornby to be Robin. Sir John was a "tried and trusted" retainer who had fought for Warwick's father at Blore Heath and Ludford and been subject to the subsequent order of attainder. [447] Sir John was of the stature and placing of someone who could lead the "commons of the North" and be followed by them.

This rebellion proved more troublesome. It became a large popular rising, "a great insurrection in Yorkshire, of diverse knights, squires, and commoners, to the number of twenty thousand" according to Warkworth. [448] Warwick was not behind the first two uprisings, but his fingers were very much on the third one. Warkworth was clear that the insurrection was "by the assignment" of Warwick, Clarence and the Archbishop of York. The uprising was based upon general grievances, but it was led and heavily influenced by members of the Neville family and those who served them.

Warwick understood how he might use the popular dissatisfaction with the regime to his advantage. In many respects, it was very similar to the position he found himself in during the reign of Henry VI, so he was not without prior experience of such things. As

---

[445] *"Warkworth's" Chronicle: A Chronicle of the First Thirteen Years of the reign of King Edward the Fourth* John Warkworth edited by James Orchard. Halliwell Leopold Classic Library 2015. Written 1470-85. Page 6.
[446] *The Yorkshire Rebellions of 1469* by K.R. Dockray. The Ricardian 1983 Pages 246-57. At Page 254.
[447] *The Yorkshire Rebellions of 1469* by K.R. Dockray. The Ricardian 1983 Pages 246-57. At Page 254.
[448] *"Warkworth's" Chronicle: A Chronicle of the First Thirteen Years of the reign of King Edward the Fourth* John Warkworth edited by James Orchard. Halliwell Leopold Classic Library 2015. Written 1470-85. Page 6.

previously his primary objective was to remove those "seditious persons" around the King with undue influence. Warwick did not set out to be a "Kingmaker".

Edward set off on a pilgrimage to Bury St Edmunds and Walsingham in early June. Preparations for riding North with an armed force were made. Warrants for Issues record the ordering of "banners, standards, coat-armours, pensils for spears, forty jackets of velvet, and of demask with roses, a thousand jackets of blue and murrey with roses, scutcheons, and such other stuff for the field as must needs be had at this time". [449]

Edward took his time and journeyed to Croyland and Fotheringay. It was early July before he pushed further North to Newark via Stamford, Grantham and Nottingham. Messengers advised that those with Robin of Redesdale were almost three times as strong in number as the King. Edward quickly retreated to Nottingham. Reinforcements were much needed. Calls for arms and men were sent to William Herbert and Humphrey Stafford. They made their respective ways north from Wales and the West country. The Woodvilles were sent to Wales and Norfolk for their own safety.

Warwick was at Sandwich where one of his boats the *Trinity* was blessed on 12th June. He was joined there by Clarence. They both travelled to London via Canterbury where on 28th June Warwick wrote to the townsfolk of Coventry advising that he and Clarence would be joining King Edward once Clarence and his daughter had married. [450] On 4th July they were back at Canterbury and two days later crossed to Calais where George, Duke of Clarence, was married to Isabel Neville. On 11th July 1469. The ceremony was performed by Warwick's brother, George Neville, Archbishop of York and the brides' uncle. Warkworth wrote "in the ninth year of the reign of King Edward, at midsummer, the Duke of Clarence passed (over) the sea to Calais to the Earl of Warwick, and there

---

[449] *The Life and Reign of Edward the Fourth* by Cora L. Scofield. Fonthill Media 2016. Volume One. Page 491.
[450] *The Life and Reign of Edward the Fourth* by Cora L. Scofield. Fonthill Media 2016. Volume One. Page 494. Note 1. Coventry Leet Book II Page 342.

wedded his daughter by the Archbishop of York, the Earl of Warwick's brother". [451]

The next day Warwick together with Clarence and the Archbishop of York issued a proclamation...

"Right trusty and well beloved, we greet you well. And well you know that our King our sovereign Lord's true subjects of diverse parts of this his realm of England have delivered to us certain bills of articles remembering the deceitful, covetous rule and guiding of certain seditious persons, that is to say, the Lord Rivers, the Duchess of Bedford his wife, Sir William Herbert Earl of Pembroke, Humphrey Stafford Earl of Devonshire, Lord Scales and Lord Audley, Sir John Woodville and Sir John Fogge, and others of their mischievous rule, opinion and assent, which have caused our said sovereign Lord and his said realm to fall into great poverty of misery, disturbing the administration of the laws, only tending to their own promotion and enrichment. The said true subjects, with piteous lamentations, calling upon us and other Lords for a remedy and reformation, we, thinking the petition comprised in the said articles reasonable and profitable for the honour and profit of our sovereign Lord and the common weal of his realm, fully purposed with other Lords to show the same to his good grace, desire and pray you to accompany us, with as many persons defensively arrayed as you can make, for by God's grace we intend to be at Canterbury upon Sunday next coming. Written under our signatures and signed the twelfth day of July 1469. [452]

Warwick openly supported the Yorkshire rebels, yet his opposition was firmly focused upon those around the King rather than the

---

[451] *"Warkworth's" Chronicle: A Chronicle of the First Thirteen Years of the reign of King Edward the Fourth* John Warkworth edited by James Orchard. Halliwell Leopold Classic Library 2015. Written 1470-85. Page 6.
[452] *"Warkworth's" Chronicle: A Chronicle of the First Thirteen Years of the reign of King Edward the Fourth* John Warkworth edited by James Orchard. Halliwell Leopold Classic Library 2015. Written 1470-85. Pages 46-47.

King himself. It was a call to arms for the Men of Kent and any others who wished to join them. Warwick was not to be disappointed and even managed to borrow a thousand pounds from the Mayor and Aldermen of London.

Edward was not pleased to hear that his brother George, Duke of Clarence, had defied his wishes and married Warwick's daughter. More concerning though was the open letter of discontent issued by Warwick supporting the rebel's petition and position. The manifesto issued by the rebels had the obvious influence, if not hand, of Warwick behind it. It railed against taxes and injustices. The blame was due to the bad advisors around Edward who were responsible for "the great poverty of misery" but comparisons were made with other Kings such as Edward II, Richard II and Henry VI who had lost their thrones due to similar errors of judgement and policy. [453]

A Newsletter from London in the Milanese State Papers wrote that "a captain rose in the northern parts of the kingdom, a base man with a following of 40,000 men, though some say many more. He said that the King did not have good ministers about him, and they wished to give him other ones and they wanted the heads of some of his ministers as well as some other articles which were all in favour of the people". [454]

The Rebels made their way south expecting to meet up with Warwick and his forces travelling north from London. Herbert's men clashed with the rebels near Northampton and fell back to Banbury. News was sent to Edward that his help was needed. Herbert and Stafford had a disagreement over lodgings according to some accounts. Stafford and his men withdrew many miles.

---

[453] *A Chronicle of the first Thirteen Years of the reign of King Edward IV* John Warkworth. Edited JO Halliwell. Camden Society 1839. Leopold Classic Library. Pages 46-51.
[454] *Edward IV From Contemporary Chronicles, Letters and Records* by Keith Dockray. Fonthill Media Limited 2015. Page 131. Milanese State Papers Newsletter from London, 16th August 1469.

Herbert camped his men on a hilltop at Edgcote. A skirmish took place on 23rd July as the rebel scouts clashed with the Welshmen under Herbert. Sir Henry Neville was killed. The next day on 24th July the rebels attacked. Herbert and his horsemen countered successfully. The rebels were then bolstered by the forward elements of Warwick's army led by Sir William Parr and Sir Geoffrey Gates. The arrival of another group under John Clapham was decisive. The Welshmen were routed. Welsh poems recall the loss of far too many brave Welsh warriors. [455]

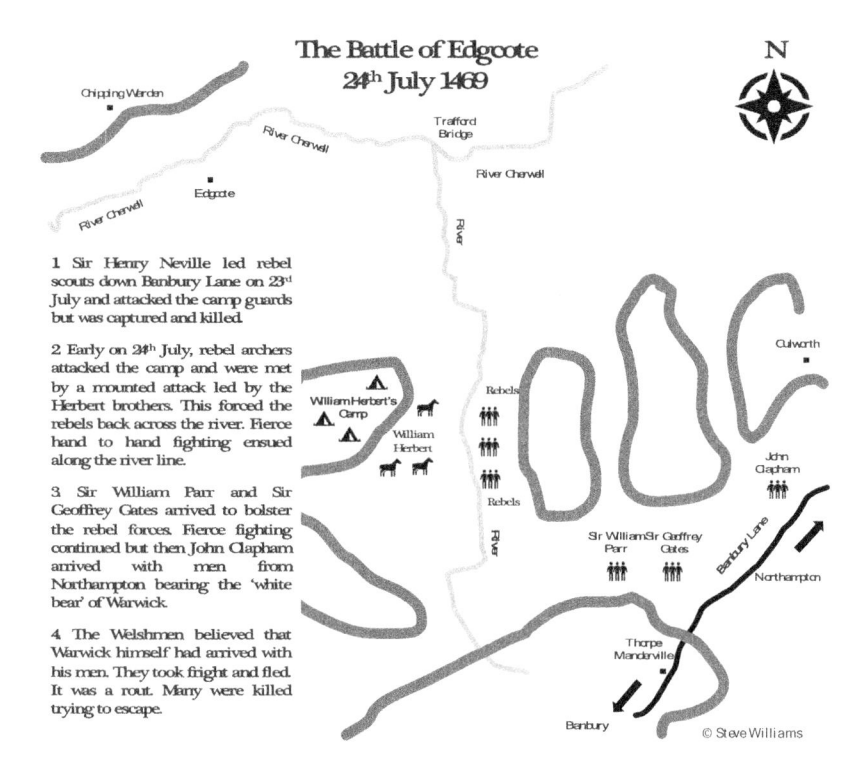

The Battle of Edgcote 24th July 1469

1 Sir Henry Neville led rebel scouts down Banbury Lane on 23rd July and attacked the camp guards but was captured and killed.

2 Early on 24th July, rebel archers attacked the camp and were met by a mounted attack led by the Herbert brothers. This forced the rebels back across the river. Fierce hand to hand fighting ensued along the river line.

3 Sir William Parr and Sir Geoffrey Gates arrived to bolster the rebel forces. Fierce fighting continued but then John Clapham arrived with men from Northampton bearing the 'white bear' of Warwick.

4 The Welshmen believed that Warwick himself had arrived with his men. They took fright and fled. It was a rout. Many were killed trying to escape.

© Steve Williams

William Herbert and his brother Richard were captured and later executed at Northampton on the strict orders of Warwick. "King Edward was taken prisoner at a certain village near Coventry, and,

---

[455] *The Battle of Edgcote 1469* By Graham Evans. Northamptonshire Battlefields Society. 2019. Excellent for a full review of the battle.

all his attendants being dismissed, was led thence to Warwick Castle, where he was detained in captivity." [456] Edward was taken into custody at Honiley and imprisoned by Warwick at Coventry and Warwick Castle before being moved to Middleham Castle. Kendall suggests that only William Hastings and Gloucester were with Edward in July 1469 when he was taken. [457] The other Yorkist Lords such as Mountjoy, Dinham, Ferrers and Howard were in London.

Warwick found himself rid of the remaining "evil councillors". Lord Rivers and his son, Sir John Woodville were captured at Chepstow and taken to Coventry where they were beheaded at Gosford Green on 12th August 1469. Queen Elizabeth lost her father and brother. [458] Stafford escaped back to the West Country but was killed by a mob in Bridgwater.

Warwick re-appointed William Hastings as Chamberlain of North Wales in August 1469 following the execution of William Herbert who had been granted the post by Edward in April 1468. This may have been an attempt by Warwick to win over Hastings and he was acceptable to both Warwick and Edward. [459] Sir John Langstrother replaced Rivers as Treasurer.

The Milanese State Papers Newsletter from London, dated 16th August 1469, reported that "The Earl of Warwick, as astute a man as ever was Ulysses, is at the King's side, and from what they say the King is not at liberty to go where he wishes." [460] The Milanese Ambassador to France wrote on 18th September that Warwick and Clarence were still in arms and "keep making a great gathering of

---

[456] *Ingulph's Chronicle of the Abbey of Croyland:* with the continuations by Peter of Blois and Anonymous writers. Translated by Henry Riley. Published by Nabu Press 2014. Originally published 1854. Written 1486. Page 458.
[457] *Warwick the Kingmaker* by PM Kendall. 1957. Page 247.
[458] *Coventry Leet Book.* The Early English Text Society edited by Mary Dormer Harris. 1907. Pages 340-346.
[459] *William Lord Hastings and the Crisis of 1483 Part 1* by W Moorhen. The Ricardian. September 1993.
[460] *Edward IV From Contemporary Chronicles, Letters and Records* by Keith Dockray. Fonthill Media Limited 2015. Page 131. Milanese State Papers Newsletter from London, 16th August 1469.

troops to constrain him (Edward) and deprive him of the crown". [461]

Warwick's victory though was short lived as he soon found that he lacked the authority to rule. Edward would not acquiesce. In the political vacuum, unrest broke out across the realm. Nobles took the opportunity to try and settle local disputes. There were riots in London. Far in the north men rebelled under Sir Humphrey Neville of Brancepeth and his brother Charles Neville, from the other branch of the Neville family. They called for the return of Henry VI. Warwick could only raise troops to quell the revolt by freeing Edward. The two rebel brothers were taken and executed at York on 29th September. Edward watched on but the tables had turned.

The Croyland Chronicler explained… "He (King Edward) did not so much make his escape, as find himself released by the express consent of the Earl of Warwick himself… for there was now a rising in England… The Earl of Warwick found himself unable to offer an effectual resistance to these, without first making public proclamation in the King's name that all the King's liege subjects must rise to defend him against the rebels…for the people seeing their King detained as a prisoner, refused to take notice of proclamations to this effect, until having been entirely set at liberty, he had made his appearance in the city of York." [462]

Edward returned to London and was met in early October by an impressive array of Lords. They did not include Warwick, Clarence and the Archbishop of York. Edward made some changes. Henry Percy was freed after swearing an oath of allegiance to the King. Percy was restored to the Earldom of Northumberland. John Neville, Lord Montagu, was compensated with land and his son George was given the Dukedom of Bedford and betrothed to Edward's oldest daughter Princess Elizabeth. Anthony Woodville

---

[461] *Calendar of State Papers* Milan 1469. Newsletter from France 18th September 1469.
[462] *Ingulph's Chronicle of the Abbey of Croyland:* with the continuations by Peter of Blois and Anonymous writers. Translated by Henry Riley. Published by Nabu Press 2014. Originally published 1854. Written 1486. Page 458.

Page 248

became Lord Rivers. A sorcery trial against the Queen's mother, Duchess Jacquetta, was stopped.

Edward appeared to be in a conciliatory mood but not everyone was fooled. Sir John Paston wrote that "the King himself hath good language of the Lords of Clarence, of Warwick, and my Lords of York and Oxford, saying that they be best friends... but his household men have other language". [463]

The Croyland Chronicler was another who wrote of deep-seated suspicions... "A grand Council of all the peers of the kingdom was summoned, and on a certain day which had previously been named, there appeared in the great chamber of Parliament, the Duke of Clarence, the Earl of Warwick, and the rest of their confederates; upon which, peace and entire oblivion of all grievances upon both sides were agreed to. Still however, there probably remained, on the one side, deeply seated in his mind, the injuries he had received, and the contempt shown to majesty, and, on the other, a guilty mind conscious of an over-daring deed..." [464]

Warwick had triumphed. A number of his rivals who were the King's favourites were no more. The Neville family were closer to the throne through the marriage of his daughter Isabel to Clarence and the betrothal of his nephew to Princess Elizabeth. Warwick though was further from power than for many years. Edward's trust in him was no more.

Cracks can be papered over but... they still remain.

---

[463] *Paston Letters V* Edited by J Gairdner. London 1904. Volume 5. Pages 63.
[464] *Ingulph's Chronicle of the Abbey of Croyland:* with the continuations by Peter of Blois and Anonymous writers. Translated by Henry Riley. Published by Nabu Press 2014. Originally published 1854. Written 1486. Page 459.

A Rebellion in Lincolnshire

…their cry was A Clarence! A Clarence! A Warwick! that time being in the field diverse persons in the Duke of Clarence's livery… they acknowledged and confessed the duke and earl to be partners and chief provokers of all their treasons. And this plainly, their purpose was to destroy the King, and to have made the duke (of Clarence) King… [465]

It did not take long for the fragile peace to be shattered. On this occasion disturbances arose in Lincolnshire. It all seemed to begin with a local quarrel between King Edward's Master of the horse, Sir Thomas Burgh of Gainsborough and Lord Willoughby and Welles, son of the Lord Welles killed at Towton and later attainted.

Warkworth wrote that "in the tenth year of King Edward's reign" Lord Willoughby and Wells, his son Robert and brothers-in-law Sir Thomas de la Lande and Sir Thomas Dymmock "drove out of Lincolnshire Sir Thomas Burgh, a knight of the King's house, and pulled down his place, and took all his goods and cattle, that they might find, and then gathered all the commons of the shire to the number of thirty thousand ad cried "King Henry" and refused King Edward". Warkworth is clear that "the Duke of Clarence and the Earl of Warwick caused all this, like as they did Robin of Redesdale to rise before that at Banbury field (Edgcote)". [466]

Edward had just arranged for a general pardon for all in Parliament upon application. The King determined to deal with the rebellion himself. Muster was set for Grantham in mid-March 1470. Rumours of the King's coming to exact vengeance poured oil on troubled waters. Tales were told that the King's judges would "sit and hang

---

[465] *Chronicle of the Rebellion in Lincolnshire.* Edited by J.G. Nichols. Camden Society 1847. Pages 10-11.
[466] *"Warkworth's" Chronicle: A Chronicle of the First Thirteen Years of the reign of King Edward the Fourth* John Warkworth edited by James Orchard. Halliwell Leopold Classic Library 2015. Written 1470-85. Page 8.

and draw great numbers of the commons". Messages of support purportedly from Clarence and Warwick were received by Lord Welles and his son, Sir Robert Welles. [467]

Welles and Dymmock were summoned to explain themselves. Both received a pardon, but this did not quieten Lincolnshire. Edward delayed his departure to meet with Clarence. Warwick was to join the King. Sir John Paston wrote to his brother… "I cannot tell you what will fall of the world, for the king is verily disposed to go into Lincolnshire, and men know not what will fall thereof, nor thereafter… my Lord of Warwick, as it is supposed shall go with the king into Lincolnshire; some men say that his going shall do good, and some say that it does harm". [468]

Edward was trusting of his brother and cousin. The Calendar Patent Rolls confirm that commissions of array were drawn up for Clarence and Warwick to raise men in Warwickshire and Worcestershire. [469] Then news reached him that Sir Robert Welles had arranged for announcements to be made in all churches in Lincolnshire in the names of Clarence, Warwick and himself for everyone in the shire to muster at Ranby Hawe to resist the King.

Edward sent for the recently pardoned Lord Welles and Dymmock. They were told that unless Sir Robert Welles stood down, they would die. Welles wrote to his son to explain his predicament. Sir Robert rushed to rescue his father rather than wait to join with Warwick as planned. Warwick and Clarence both sent Edward letters saying that they were at Coventry and would be with the King shortly.

---

[467] *The Life and Reign of Edward the Fourth* by Cora L. Scofield. Fonthill Media 2016. Volume One. Page 510.
[468] *The Paston Letters 1422-1509*. Edited by J. Gairdner. 1904. Gloucester reprint 1983. Volume 5. Page 70.
[469] *The Life and Reign of Edward the Fourth* by Cora L. Scofield. Fonthill Media 2016. Volume One. Page 512.

Edward by now was at Stamford. Scouts informed him that Sir Robert Welles and his army is some five miles from Stamford, beside the Great North Road just north of Tickencote Warren, near Empingham, in Rutland. They were arrayed for battle and had not laid down their arms. Edward positioned his men to the north of the rebel army and, in the space between the two forces, had Sir Robert's father, Lord Welles, and Sir Thomas Dymmock executed in sight of both armies.

The Battle of Losecote Field
12th March 1470

1. Edward IV's scouts advised that Sir Robert Welles's rebel army was 5 miles from Stamford, arrayed for battle, just north of Tickencote Warren, near Empingham, in Rutland. Edward had Sir Robert's father, Lord Welles, and Sir Thomas Dymmock executed in sight of both armies.

2. The rebels advanced with cries of *á Warwick* and *á Clarence*. Edward's men fired a single barrage of cannon balls and charged. The rebels broke and fled. Sir Robert Welles was captured, confessed his treason and named Warwick and Clarence as the "partners and chief provokers" of the rebellion. He was executed. Documents proved the involvement of Warwick and Clarence.

3. Legend was that many of Welles' men were wearing jackets displaying Warwick's and Clarence's livery. Many discarded their garments not wanting to be caught wearing them. The battle was thus called "Lose-coat". Contemporary accounts refer to the battle site as "Hornfield". A nearby woodland is called Bloody Oaks.

© Steve Williams

The rebels advanced with cries of *á Warwick* and *á Clarence*. A single barrage of cannonballs was fired by Edward's men and the King's men then charged the enemy. The rebels broke and fled. Documents in the form of "a casket of incriminating papers" were

Page 252

found proving the involvement of Warwick and Clarence. [470] Sir Robert Welles was captured, confessed his treason, and named Warwick and Clarence as the "partners and chief provokers" of the rebellion. He was executed at Doncaster on 19th March.

Legend has it that many of Welles' men were wearing jackets displaying Warwick's and Clarence's livery. The battle became known as "Lose-coat Field" for the fleeing rebels threw away their coats in a desperate bid to escape or not be caught wearing them. Contemporary accounts refer to the battle site as "Hornfield". A nearby woodland is called Bloody Oaks. Hearne's fragment records that "when the rebels heard of his (the King's) coming they left their field, and all their stuff, and fled as far as Scarborough, whereat they were beheaded, and that journey was called Lose cote Field". [471]

Much has been made of the confession by Sir Robert Welles and the Chronicle of the Lincolnshire Rebellion written in the mid nineteenth century to incriminate Warwick and Clarence. The argument is that they were dissatisfied with the outcome of the pardons and reconciliation and decided to incite and then exploit a local rebellion to place Clarence on the throne and Warwick back in power. Penny Tucker in a recent article on the rebellion [472] concludes from her analysis of the documents that "although Sir Robert Welles did write a confession, the document we have is not it". Therefore, we need to be cautious and more discerning about the chronicle itself which is lent reliability by it.

There are other possibilities. Charles Oman [473] argues that he provoked the rebellion to reassert his authority… "it is certainly in keeping with Edward's character to suppose that, finding himself at the head of a loyal and victorious army, it suddenly occurred to him

---

[470] *Edward IV* by Charles Ross. Yale University Press 1997. The Years of Crisis. Page 140.
[471] *The Chronicles of The White Rose of York*. Edited by James Bohn. Published London 1845. Paperback Version Reprint 2012. Hearne's Fragment Page 25.
[472] *The Lincolnshire Rebellion of 1470 Revisited* by Penny Tucker. *The English Historical Review*, Volume 136, Issue 578, February 2021.
[473] *Warwick The Kingmaker* by Charles W. Oman. First Published 1891. Ithink books. Lightning Source UK Ltd. Page 178.

that his position could be utilised to fall on Warwick and Clarence and take revenge for the death of Pembroke (William Herbert) and Rivers". It could have been an accident, suggests Tucker, an unfortunate result of Edward taking an army into Lincolnshire to confront an anticipated invasion on the coast there of supporters loyal to Henry VI. Tucker though argues that it all arose out of mistrust and misunderstanding between the key protagonists and that Edward then took advantage of the circumstances for his own ends to "bring down his brother and cousin".

Hearne's fragment speaks of "many secret conspiracies… in the winter" and tells the tale of Edward being invited "to a banquet at his Palace of the Moor besides Langley" by Warwick's brother, George Neville, Archbishop of York. John Ratcliffe, later Lord Fitzwalter "warned the King privily, and bade him beware, for there were ordained privily 100 men of arms, the which should take him and convey him out of the way. Wherefore the King, faining himself to make his water, caused a good horse to be saddled, and so with a small company rode to Windsor". Hearne says that this led to Warwick and Clarence fleeing with their wives to France where they landed at Honfleur. [474]

It does seem plausible that Warwick after unsuccessfully trying to be the power behind Edward on the throne decided that he would be better off seeking to replace him with his son-in-law Clarence. Warwick perhaps rightly concluded that Edward was simply biding his time and, at a point more to his choice, would seek to take retribution. In medieval times, perceived wisdom was that it was morally and spiritually wrong to kill a King anointed by God. However, if Edward should be killed in battle whilst trying to put down a rebellion, that was another matter entirely. Unfortunately for Warwick, Sir Robert Welles and his rebels were not up to the task.

Warwick was still at Coventry with Clarence when they both received a summons from Edward to set their men aside and meet him with only "a convenient number (of men) for their estates".

---

[474] *The Chronicles of The White Rose of York*. Edited by James Bohn. Published London 1845. Paperback Version Reprint 2012. Hearne's Fragment Page 26.

Warwick realised this was probably not the wisest thing to do having only just been pardoned for his part in the previous uprisings against the King. Word was sent via John Rufford and Henry Wrottesley of their good and loyal intentions. They would meet the King at Retford, but then they turned and made their way north via Burton-on-Trent and Derby to Chesterfield and then Sheffield towards Warwick's Yorkshire heartlands. [475]

Edward sent a messenger, Garter, to his brother Clarence. It carried a more direct command for him and Warwick to give themselves up. They had "laboured contrary to natural kindness and duty of liegance divers matters of great poise, and also how proclamations have been made in your name and our cousin of Warwick's to assemble our liege people, no mention made of us". Clarence was told that if he came to Edward "in humble wise" he would be treated appropriately "according to the nearness of our blood and our laws". If not, then he would need to be held to account for his misdeeds and punished. If blood was shed, the blame would rest with him. [476]

Warwick sent his chaplain. Clarence and himself would come "humble wise" subject to being safe conduct and a pardon. They feared execution or attainder. Edward was affronted that they were asking for so much, more than even his ancient enemies of France might ask. Clarence and Warwick needed to prove their innocence and if not, then they would be treated "rightwiseness with favour and pity". Harsh words were spoken such that Warwick's and Clarence's messengers were fearful and asked that the King send his message by his Garter king-of-arms rather than by them. [477]

Warwick and Clarence were unable to raise help from the Stanleys. And instead of turning north, they journeyed south. Warwick chose

---

[475] *Warwick the Kingmaker* by Michael Hicks. Blackwell Publishers 1998. Fortune's Second Wheel, 1470-1471. Page 285.
[476] *The Life and Reign of Edward the Fourth* by Cora L. Scofield. Fonthill Media 2016. Volume One. Page 515.
[477] *The Life and Reign of Edward the Fourth* by Cora L. Scofield. Fonthill Media 2016. Volume One. Page 516.

to take his previous path of escape via the west country to Calais undertaken in late 1459.

Edward was now strengthened with the retinues of the Dukes of Suffolk and Norfolk. John Paston wrote that never had England seen "so many goodly men and so well arrayed in a field." [478] Not an entirely accurate statement but enough to explain why Warwick chose to flee rather than fight.

Edward had moved to York to resupply and refuel his army. Proclamations called out the treason of Warwick and Clarence. [479] They had "before the feast of Christmas" been granted the King's pardon general of all offences committed and done against him… trusting thereby to have caused them to have shewed unto him their natural love, allegiance and duty". They had promised to help to subdue the insurrections and rebellions in Lincolnshire, yet had not done so, "unnaturally, unkindly and untruly intending his destruction, and the subversion of the realm". They had "dissembled… falsely and traitorously provoked and stirred… Sir Robert Welles…" and then attempted to raise men in Yorkshire for their own cause. They refused to subject themselves to the King's judgement and had fled. They must "come in humble and obeisant wise" and present themselves before the King by Wednesday 28th March, whereupon "his highness will be thereof right glad, and have them in his grace and favour". However, if they do not, the King declared them to be traitors and rebels. No-one should give them succour on pain of death. A just reward was placed upon them.

Orders were sent to Calais and Southampton that Warwick and Clarence and those with them should not be admitted. On 27th March Edward left York to give chase via Nottingham, Coventry and Wells. The King arrived in Exeter on 14th April only to learn that Warwick and Clarence had left the shores of England.

---

[478] *The Paston Letters 1422-1509*. Edited by J. Gairdner. 1904. Gloucester reprint 1983. Volume 5. Page 71.
[479] *The Chronicles of The White Rose of York*. Edited by James Bohn. Published London 1845. Paperback Version Reprint 2012. Last X Years of Edward IV. Pages 225-229. Close Rolls 10. Edward IV.

The Croyland Chronicler recorded that Warwick and Clarence "being fully conscious of their share in promoting this insurrection, consulted their safety flight, upon which, the king followed in pursuit of them, along their route from the county of Lancaster across the intervening counties, until they arrived at the city of Exeter in the county of Devon. Having arrived here before the King could come up with them, and finding a few ships in readiness, they embarked, and… pushed on with the utmost speed, and at length, with their confederates, landed safely in Normandy". [480]

Warkworth says that Warwick and Clarence "sailed towards Southampton, and intended there to have a great ship of the said Earl of Warwick's called the Trinity, but the Lord Scales, the Queen's brother, was sent there by the King's commandment, and others with him, and fought with the said Duke and Earl, and took diverse ships of theirs and many of their men therein, so that the Duke and Earl had to flee to the King of France where they were worshipfully received". [481]

Sir Geoffrey Gate and Clapham amongst others were captured at Southampton. Gate was pardoned for previous good service. Clapham was beheaded and more, no doubt for his intervention at Edgcote. Worcester as the new Constable of England meted out severe retribution to him and the other captives. Warkworth recorded that they were "hanged, drawn and quartered, and beheaded, and after that hung up by their legs, and a stake made sharp at both ends, whereof one end was put up their buttocks, and the other end their heads were put on, for the which the people of the land were greatly displeased, and ever afterwards the Earl of

---

[480] *Ingulph's Chronicle of the Abbey of Croyland:* with the continuations by Peter of Blois and Anonymous writers. Translated by Henry Riley. Published by Nabu Press 2014. Originally published 1854. Written 1486. Page 461-62.
[481] *"Warkworth's" Chronicle: A Chronicle of the First Thirteen Years of the reign of King Edward the Fourth* John Warkworth edited by James Orchard. Halliwell Leopold Classic Library 2015. Written 1470-85. Page 9.

Worcester was greatly hated". [482] In this manner, Worcester earned the nickname… "Butcher of England".

Hearne's Fragment is alone in recording a story that Lord Scales and Lord Audley were captured by Warwick and Clarence and imprisoned in Wardour Castle before being set free by "a gentlemen of Dorsetshire called John Thornhill". [483]

Warwick was hopeful of gaining entry to Calais with the help of Lord Wenlock who was there. Lord Duras was in command at Calais though and held the garrison to observe the King's orders that Warwick should not be permitted to land. Warwick was joined by his relative the Bastard of Fauconberg and they took the opportunity to commit piracy on some Burgundian and Breton ships. Warwick saw his eldest daughter Isabel give birth to a grandson whilst at sea, but unfortunately the baby died soon thereafter and was buried at sea just outside of Calais. Wenlock according to Commynes sent them two flagons of wine and presumably other fare. [484]

Warwick and Clarence landed at Honfleur in Normandy around 1st May 1470. The Croyland Chronicler tells us that they were "kindly received by King Louis and being after some difficulty admitted into the favour of Queen Margaret and her son, Prince Edward, made a promise that they would in future faithfully support their cause and that of King Henry…. Espousals were contracted between the said Prince, and the lady Anne, the youngest daughter of the said Earl of Warwick". [485]

---

[482] *"Warkworth's" Chronicle: A Chronicle of the First Thirteen Years of the reign of King Edward the Fourth* John Warkworth edited by James Orchard. Halliwell Leopold Classic Library 2015. Written 1470-85. Page 9.
[483] *The Chronicles of The White Rose of York.* Edited by James Bohn. Published London 1845. Paperback Version Reprint 2012. Hearne's Fragment Page 28.
[484] *Philippe de Commynes Memoirs, The Reign of Louis XI 1461-83* Published by Penguin Books 1972. Translated and introduced by Michael Jones. Written 1498. Page 182.
[485] *Ingulph's Chronicle of the Abbey of Croyland:* with the continuations by Peter of Blois and Anonymous writers. Translated by Henry Riley. Published by Nabu Press 2014. Originally published 1854. Written 1486. Page 462.

Warwick met with King Louis XI at Amboise on 8th June. Louis had delayed meeting them as Charles, Duke of Burgundy, was threatening to tear up the peace treaty of Peronne should Warwick and Clarence be allowed to remain in France given the hostilities inflicted upon Burgundian ships and men. The Milanese envoy Bettini wrote on 12th June of a great welcome, long discussions and feasting and dancing. [486]

Hearne's Fragment recorded that Warwick and Clarence hastened to see King Louis XI "at his castle of Amboise, beside Tours" where they met "with great feastings" and later held council with the former Queen of England, Margaret of Anjou where it was agreed "betwixt them to know by what manner they should return into England." [487] The Croyland Chronicler noted "They were kindly received by King Louis, and after some difficulty, admitted into the favour of Queen Margaret and her son Prince Edward, made a promise that they would in future faithfully support their cause and that of King Henry… espousals were contracted between the said Prince and the Lady Anne, the youngest daughter of the said Earl of Warwick." [488]

The meeting between the former enemies, Warwick and Queen Margaret, probably took some staging by Louis XI. Bettini wrote on 29th June that Louis XI "spent and still spends every day in long discussions with that Queen to induce her to make the alliance with Warwick". [489] The details of their meeting are set out in a document entitled "The Manner and Guiding of the Earl of Warwick at

---

[486] *Calendar of State Papers Milan* Edited by AB Hinds. London 1912. Volume I, 1385-1618. Pages 138-139.
[487] *The Chronicles of The White Rose of York*. Edited by James Bohn. Published London 1845. Paperback Version Reprint 2012. Hearne's Fragment Page 27.
[488] *Ingulph's Chronicle of the Abbey of Croyland:* with the continuations by Peter of Blois and Anonymous writers. Translated by Henry Riley. Published by Nabu Press 2014. Originally published 1854. Written 1486. Page 462.
[489] *Calendar of State Papers Milan* Edited by AB Hinds. London 1912. Volume I, 1385-1618. Pages 138-141.

Angiers from the 15th day of July to the 4th of August 1470". [490] "*First*, by means of the King of France, the said Earl of Warwick purchased a pardon of the Queen Margaret and of her son. *Secondly*, by the said mean was treated the marriage of the said Queen's son called Prince of Wales, and the Earl of Warwick's second daughter. Thirdly, there was appointed upon his passage over the sea into England with a puissance".

It was understandably not an easy meeting... "the said Queen was right difficult" for how could she pardon the person who had been most to blame for the fall of her husband? Queen Margaret had more to lose than gain from any pardon, amity or alliance". Warwick confessed that he was responsible for her and King Henry being "put out of the realm of England" but that he did so rightly to defend himself against the destruction of his body and goods intended by those who falsely counselled them. Warwick pledged to be loyal and faithful to the Queen and her son, the prince and looked to the King of France to vouchsafe for him, which he did for Louis XI feared the alliance of Edward and Charles, Duke of Burgundy. Warwick promised Louis that England would stand with France.

Shakespeare catches well the probable mood of the former Queen...

"QUEEN MARGARET
Peace, impudent and shameless Warwick,
Proud setter-up and puller-down of kings! I will not hence till with my talk and tears,
Both full of truth, I make King Lewis behold

---

[490] *The Chronicles of The White Rose of York*. Edited by James Bohn. Published London 1845. Paperback Version Reprint 2012. Last X Years of Edward IV. Pages 229-233. Stowe's Transcripts, MS Harleian 543. Page 168.

Thy sly conveyance and thy lord's false love,
For both of you are birds of self-same feather." [491]

Margaret pardoned Warwick but delayed on the question of the marriage of Prince Edward to Warwick's daughter, Anne. She shared with the King of France that Edward IV had written suggesting a union between her son and his daughter, Elizabeth. Finally, she agreed, subject to the marriage not being final until Warwick had restored King Henry to his throne.
Edward of Lancaster, Prince of Wales, and Lady Anne Neville were betrothed at a special service in Angers cathedral on 25th July 1470. Warwick swore allegiance just five days later "upon the very true cross in Saint Mary's Church of Angiers". Louis XI swore to help Warwick and Margaret promised to treat Warwick as a true and faithful servant of King Henry. [492]

The Milanese envoy Bettini wrote on 28th July, "the marriage of Warwick's daughter to the Prince of Wales is settled and announced… in two days, Warwick will leave for his fleet, to direct it under the auspices of St George to the enterprise of England. King Henry's brother, the Earl of Pembroke, is going with him, and if their affairs prosper, the King himself will immediately follow them". [493]

Clarence, it was agreed, would be given the duchy of York and would be next in line to the throne should Prince Edward die without an heir. It was quite a climb down from being promised the throne itself by Warwick. Clarence would have seen which way the wind was blowing whatever words of comfort and persuasion were used by his father-in-law.

---

[491] *Henry VI Part 3 Act 3 Scene 3* Shakespeare
www.folger.edu/explore/shakespeares-works/download/
[492] *Letters de Louis XI, Roi de France*. Edited by Jos Vaesen and others. Paris 1883-1909. Book IV. Page 131.
[493] *Calendar of State Papers Milan* Edited by AB Hinds. London 1913. Volume I, 1385-1618. Page 141.

Commynes tells a tale of intrigue saying that whilst he was at Calais negotiating with John Wenlock, he learned of a lady passing through who was "on her way to my Lady of Clarence in France. She was bearing an offer from King Edward to open peace talks". Commynes continues that "this woman's secret business was to persuade my Lord of Clarence not to be the agent of ruin of his family by helping to restore the Lancastrians to authority". [494]

---

[494] *Philippe de Commynes Memoirs, The Reign of Louis XI 1461-83* Published by Penguin Books 1972. Translated and introduced by Michael Jones. Written 1498. Page 185.

The Return of Warwick

...During the year following, England was a scene of fierce commotion; rebellion, fomented by the Earl of Warwick, spread on every side, till it drove the Yorkist monarch from his throne, and once more fixed the crown on the brow of Henry VI... [495]

Warwick and Clarence issued a letter from France before their return. [496] They complained of the poor treatment meted out to them and promised to take vengeance upon those "covetous and seditious persons, as have guided and been about the estate Royal of the Realm". The King's favourites were denounced and blamed for the ills of the world. There was no mention of blame attaching to the King.

Edward prepared as best he could. The new Earl Rivers was appointed Governor and Lieutenant of Calais on 11th June. Lord Howard became his deputy on 2nd July. The Earl of Arundel was put in charge of Dover and the Cinque Ports. Help on the seas was secured from Charles, Duke of Burgundy who was fearful of England falling to a pro-France Warwick.

Warwick sought to direct Edward's attentions elsewhere. Lord Fitzhugh who was married to Warwick's sister, Alice Neville, rose up with "many folks up in the north". Lord Percy was unable to deal with the revolt. Edward determined that he himself needed to go north as no news was forthcoming from Lord Montagu. London's defences were strengthened. The Exchequer accounts confirm that "great ordnance" was moved from Bristol and an order made for additional arms. Most importantly, his Queen, expectant with child, and daughters were placed in safety at the Tower of London.

---

[495] *The Chronicles of The White Rose of York*. Edited by James Bohn. Published London 1845. Paperback Version Reprint 2012. Last X Years of Edward IV. Page 30, Hearne's Fragment. Stapleton's Plumpton Family Page lxxv.

[496] *The Chronicles of The White Rose of York*. Edited by James Bohn. Published London 1845. Paperback Version Reprint 2012. Last X Years of Edward IV. Pages 235-239. Stowe's Transcripts, MS Harleian 543.

Edward marched north. He was at Leicester on 5th August and proceeded to York, and then Ripon. Fitzhugh and his rebels fled before him. Edward returned to York around 21st August and remained there until September despite rumours of Warwick's imminent arrival in the south. John Paston wrote on 5th August "the Lords Clarence and Warwick will assay to land in England every day as folks fear". [497]

Warwick and his fleet left France on 9th September. A storm put paid to the blockade of English and Burgundian boats and gave them a window of opportunity to cross the channel. Louis XI was pressing for them to leave his shores. Warwick accompanied by Clarence, Pembroke, Oxford and around sixty ships landed at Dartmouth and Plymouth. [498] Fabyan confirmed their arrival… "In the month of September, the foresaid Duke of Clarence, accompanied by the Earl of Warwick, of Pembroke and of Oxford, and many other gentlemen landed at Dartmouth and there made proclamations in the name of King Henry VI and so drew further into the land." [499]

All pretence was thrown away. Warwick, Clarence, Tudor and Oxford very publicly pronounced themselves in support of "the most noble and Christian Prince, our most dread Sovereign Lord, King Harry the Sixth, very true undoubted King of England and of France, now being in the hands of his rebels, and of the great enemy, Edward, late Earl of March, usurper, oppressor, and destroyer of our said Sovereign Lord, and of the noble blood of the realm of England, and of the true commons of the same, by his mischievous and inordinate new-found laws and profitless ordinances". They sought to deliver "our said Sovereign Lord out of his great captivity, and danger of his enemies, unto his liberty, and by grace of God to

---

[497] *The Paston Letters 1422-1509.* Edited by J. Gairdner. 1904. Gloucester reprint 1983. Volume 5.
[498] *The Life and Reign of Edward the Fourth* by Cora L. Scofield. Fonthill Media 2016. Volume One. Pages 535-536.
[499] *The New Chronicles of England and France* by Robert Fabyan. Edited by Henry Ellis London 1811. Forgotten Books 2018. Originally edition by Pynson 1516. Page 658.

rest him in his Royal estate, and crown of this his said realm of England". [500]

Edward, on hearing of Warwick's return, left York intending to secure London and challenge Warwick. Messages were sent to Burgundy to enlist the help of Duke Charles to prevent any return to France. At Doncaster, his sleep was disturbed by his chief minstrel who brought news. Montagu was not far away with his newly raised army and was coming as an enemy, not a friend. The bad news was confirmed by others who would not take up arms against their King.

Warkworth wrote that Montagu was enraged that his earldom of Northumberland had been taken away from him and he had only been given "a pye's-nest" to maintain his new position as Marquis of Montagu. Montagu would stand alongside his brother, Warwick. Edward knowing that he was vastly outnumbered chose flight rather than fight and slipped away quickly with his men and little else to Kings Lynn where they boarded ships to take them to safety in Flanders. Warkworth continued… "and then King Edward hastened to the town of Lynne and there took to his ships one Michaelmas day in the tenth year of his reign, with Lord Hastings, that was the King's Chamberlain, Lord Say with diverse other knights and esquires, and sailed to Flanders…" [501]

Commynes wrote that "when the Earl of Warwick landed, a great number of men joined him, and he was in a strong position. King Edward, as soon as he recognized the danger, began to look to his own affairs, although it was too late". Messengers arrived telling Edward that Montagu had thrown his lot in with Warwick, telling his men to shout, "Long live King Henry". Edward fled England in "two flat-bottomed boats and one of his own small ships, with seven or eight hundred followers who possessed no other clothes

---

[500] *The Chronicles of The White Rose of York*. Edited by James Bohn. Published London 1845. Paperback Version Reprint 2012. Last X Years of Edward IV. Page 239. Cotton Manuscript. British Museum No XVII.
[501] *Warkworth's Chronicle – A Chronicle of the First Thirteen Years of the Reign of King Edward the Fourth* Edited by James Orchard Halliwell. Camden Society 1839. Leopold Classic Library. Amazon 2015. Page 11.

than the ones they were fighting in; they did not have a penny between them and scarcely knew where they were going". [502]

Edward and his small group sailed for Burgundy on Tuesday 2nd October. They were nearly captured by ships of the Hanse but managed to land near Alkmaar and sought the protection of his friend Louis of Bruges, Duke of Gruthuyse who looked after them at his home in The Hague.

News of the King's departure led to general unrest. London shut its gates against those from Kent and around, who sought to take what they could. The Queen, her mother and her daughters sought sanctuary at Westminster. John Paston wrote from London to Margaret Paston on 12th October 1470 "The Queen that was, and the Duchess of Bedford, be in sanctuary at Westminster…" [503] Others close to Edward such as the chancellor and Bishop of Ely took refuge at St Martin's le Grand. [504]

The Archbishop of York arrived with armed men and took control of the Tower on Friday 5th October. The next day his brother Warwick arrived, riding alongside Clarence, Stanley, Shrewsbury, the Bastard of Fauconberg and others. Fabyan tells us that "the Duke of Clarence accompanied by the Earls of Warwick and Shrewsbury, and the Lord Stanley, rode to the Tower and there with all honour and reverence, set free King Henry and took him to the Bishops Palace at St Pauls." [505]

---

[502] *Philippe de Commynes Memoirs, The Reign of Louis XI 1461-83* Published by Penguin Books 1972. Translated and introduced by Michael Jones. Written 1498. Pages 186-187.
[503] *Edward IV From Contemporary Chronicles, Letters and Records* by Keith Dockray. Fonthill Media Limited 2015. Page 136. John Paston in London to Margaret Paston 12th October 1470.
[504] *Edward IV* by Charles Ross. Yale University Press 1997. The Years of Crisis. Page 153. Note 1.
[505] *The New Chronicles of England and France* by Robert Fabyan. Edited by Henry Ellis London 1811. Forgotten Books 2018. Originally edition by Pynson 1516. Page 659.

Warkworth wrote that Henry was not in a good way, he "was not worshipfully arrayed as a prince, and not so cleanly kept, as should seem such a Prince. They had him out, and new arrayed him, and did to him great reverence". Grafton's Chronicle tells us that Henry was "apparelled in a long gown of blue velvet". [506]

King Henry VI was paraded through London on 13th October. It was the feast day of St Edward the Confessor. Warwick and Oxford stood close as the crown of England was laid upon the head of Henry VI. Grafton says the people rejoiced and shouted out "God save the King". Warkworth suggests Henry's return was popular with many… "all his good lovers were full glad, and the more part of people". Henry had lost his throne "all because of his false lords, and never of him". Edward's promised peace and prosperity had not materialised, rather there was more taxes, battles and the "hurting of merchandize". Henry was King once more but was weak and frail with health problems. All knew that Warwick was the real power behind the throne.

Warwick stayed his hand. He had pressed for regime change and railed against cronyism in government. The rewards to his supporters were not excessive. Brother George became Lord Chancellor once more. The incumbent Stillington had sought sanctuary. There was nothing for his other brother John, Lord Montagu, nor others who had crossed the channel with him such as Oxford and Pembroke. The Prior of St Johns took over as Treasurer from Worcester who fled with money. Clarence was restored eventually as Lieutenant of Ireland. Warwick took back the captaincy of Calais.

Writs were sent out under Henry VI's seal for Parliament to meet on 26th November 1470. Warwick wanted to govern with consent and through the normal channels. Few Lords failed to receive a summons. Only those who had fled overseas with Edward such as Hastings, Gloucester, Say and Rivers did not receive invites. Warwick did not seek vengeance. The unpopular "butcher"

---

[506] *The Chronicles of The White Rose of York*. Edited by James Bohn. Published London 1845. Paperback Version Reprint 2012. Last X Years of Edward IV. Warkworth's Chronicle. Page 117 & Note 41 below.

Worcester, executed on 18th October, was the only leading Yorkist casualty of the readeption. [507]

Fabyan records "In this year (1470), in the readeption of King Henry… the third day of November, Queen Elizabeth, being, as before said, in Westminster sanctuary, was delivered of a fair Prince. And within the said place the said child, without pomp, was after christened, whose godfathers were the Abbot and prior of the said place, and Lady Scrope." [508]

The Burgundian writer Georges Chastellain painted a poor picture of life in London under Warwick's rule. Merchants and those close to Edward's regime suffered badly according to his writings… "the King was a subject there and ordered like a crowned calf". Yet Warwick ruled justly ordering those seeking trouble to return home. Those in sanctuaries were left untroubled. A general pardon was issued on 18th December. Warwick sought stability. Even Sir Richard Woodville, brother to the former Queen, benefited from his forbearance. [509]

Warwick was in regular correspondence with his sponsor, Louis XI of France. Louis was so pleased to hear that Edward had been driven from the English shores and Henry was once more upon the throne. Louis let it be known of the alliance signed between France and England with Queen Margaret. A general holiday was declared in celebration. [510] French ambassadors were soon making their way across the channel to bring words of praise from Louis to Warwick but also to press action on their alliance against Burgundy. Louis enquired as to who in England needed persuading of their plans and with what inducements. English merchants were already the subject

---

[507] *Edward IV* by Charles Ross. Yale University Press 1997. The Years of Crisis. Page 155.
[508] *The New Chronicles of England and France* by Robert Fabyan. Edited by Henry Ellis London 1811. Forgotten Books 2018. Originally edition by Pynson 1516. Page 659.
[509] *Oeuvres de Georges Chastellain*. Edited by M. le Baron Kervyn de Lettenhove, Brussels. 1863-1865. V Pages 489-90.
[510] *Letters de Louis XI, Roi de France*. Edited by Jos Vaesen and others. Paris 1883-1909. Book IV. Page 143-44.

of a campaign by the French King to try and ease the traditional hostilities between the two nations.

Warwick was kept very busy with internal and external affairs of state. It had been easy to promise Louis assistance in his relations with Burgundy in order to gain his sponsorship, and support to persuade Queen Margaret and Prince Edward of Lancaster to throw in their lot with him. Now Warwick had to walk the delicate tightrope of diplomatic relations. Too much support for France against Burgundy would result in Duke Charles lending direct aid to his brother-in-law Edward. Yet he needed Louis to continue to push for Margaret and Edward to return to England.

There was already talk of the former King Edward seeking to return. Warwick's brother, Montagu, was commissioned to raise men from the northern counties on 21st December. Seven days later, Warwick, Clarence, Oxford and Scrope were issued with papers to raise men in defence of the realm.

The French Ambassador Monypenny wrote back to France on 19th January 1471 with optimism. Another ambassador, the Bishop of Bayeux had more concrete news to impart in his letter of 6th February. The English King and Parliament had agreed to a ten-year truce with France and an alliance against Burgundy. Warwick would himself lead an army of English archers from Calais and there was agreement on how the spoils of war would be divided up. Warwick sent a covering letter confirming matters. [511]

News of the growing closeness of relations between England and France made up the mind of Duke Charles of Burgundy. Charles was torn between support for his kinsman Henry VI and his brother-in-law Edward. Commynes wrote…"the day when the Duke of Burgundy heard the news of King Edward's arrival in Holland, I had just joined him from Calais at Boulogne… The Duke of Burgundy had first been informed that Edward was dead. This did not disturb him greatly because he had always had more

---

[511] *The Life and Reign of Edward the Fourth* by Cora L. Scofield. Fonthill Media 2016. Volume One. Page 562 Legrand Collections, MS Francais 6977. Pages 32-33.

affection for the Lancastrian family than for the Yorkist… but he was scared of the Earl of Warwick…" [512]

Exiled Lancastrian lords such as Somerset and Exeter were at the Burgundian court. Edward had been held at arms-length. Seigneur de la Gruthuyse had played host to his friend Edward at the Hague. Charles now met with Edward who then met up with his sister. Somerset and Exeter returned to England. Charles publicly proclaimed that Edward as to be given no support but in private money, ships and men were provided to him.

Charles soon had more to worry about. Louis tore up the treaty of Peronne, declared war and invaded Picardy. Warwick wrote to Louis XI on 13th February 1471… "I have learnt that now war has begun between you, your adversary and ours (Charles, Duke of Burgundy), I pray to Almighty God to give you victory. In the matter of beginning the war at Calais, I have sent instructions to start it… As soon as I possibly can I will come to you to serve you against this accursed Burgundian". [513]

Warwick though did not go public on his declared intent to make war on Burgundy with France. The arrival of Queen Margaret and Prince Edward was imminent. The Prior of St Johns was sent over the channel to help escort them back to London. Storms and bad weather delayed their departure. Fabyan wrote "And on the 27th day of February, rode the said Earl of Warwick through the city toward Dover, for to have received Queen Margaret; but he was disappointed, for the wind was to the contrary, and she lay at the sea-side tarrying for a convenient wind from November until April." [514]

---

[512] *Memoirs - The Reign of Louis XI 1461-83* by Philippe De Commynes Translated by Michael Jones Penguin Classics 1972 Page 190
[513] *English Historical Documents IV 1327-1485*. Edited by A.R. Myers. London 1969. Page 307.
[514] *The New Chronicles of England and France* by Robert Fabyan. Edited by Henry Ellis London 1811. Forgotten Books 2018. Originally edition by Pynson 1516. Page 660.

Warwick prepared as much as he could to prevent or obstruct Edward's return. Defences everywhere were strengthened. Loyal fleets of ships patrolled the seas. The Duke of Norfolk was recalled from his home county and leading gentry with suspect loyalties were placed in prison or freed under sureties. [515] Edward with Burgundian support soon returned. Warkworth wrote "In the second week of March… in the tenth year of the reign of King Edward IV, the same King Edward took to his ship to Flanders and had with him Lord Hastings and Lord Say and 900 Englishmen and 300 Fleming men with handguns, and sailed to England…" [516]

---

[515] *History of the Arrival of Edward IV in England and the Final Recovery of the Kingdoms from Henry VI* Transcribed by John Stowe. Edited by John Bruce. Camden Society 1838. Kessinger Publishing 2007. Written 1471. Page 2.
[516] *Warkworth's Chronicle – A Chronicle of the First Thirteen Years of the Reign of King Edward the Fourth* Edited by James Orchard Halliwell. Camden Society 1839. Leopold Classic Library. Amazon 2015. Page 13.

Edward's Travels 1470 - 1471

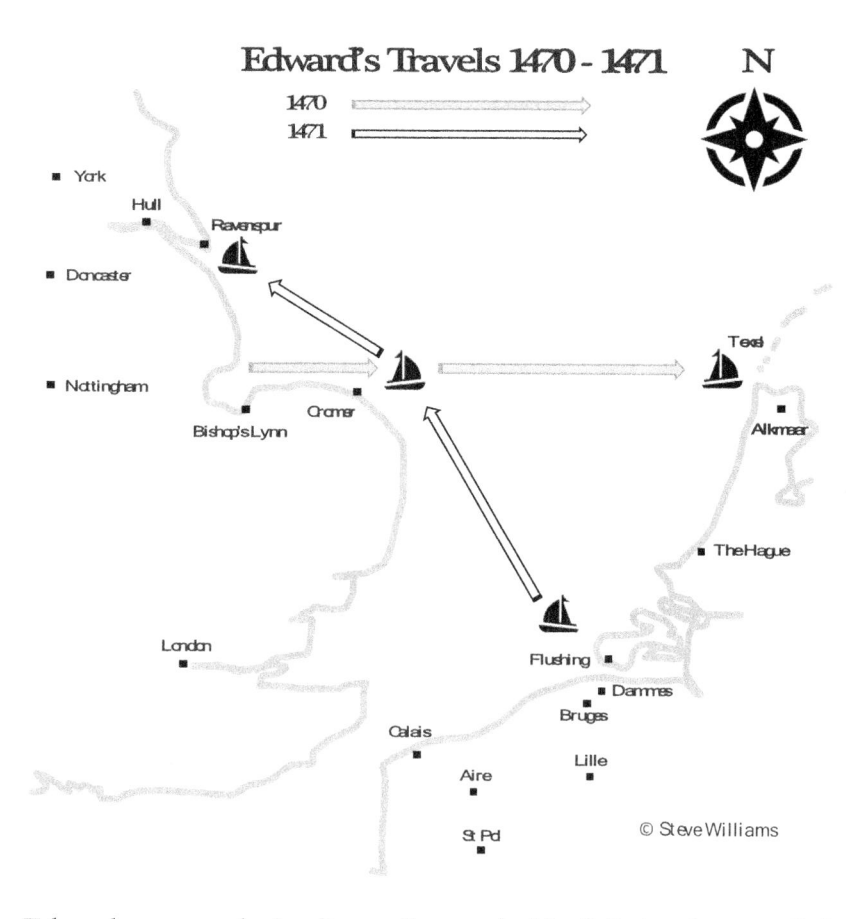

Edward attempted a landing at Cromer in Norfolk, but it was called off due an unwelcome reception from unfriendly men of the Earl of Oxford. Edward and his small fleet of ships sailed on up the eastern coast beset by storms and high winds. The *Arrival* documented that "the King... with Lord Hastings, his chamberlain, and others of his well-chosen men, landed within Humber, at a place called Ravenspur". [517] Gloucester landed further up the coast. Rivers chose to land further inland up the Humber estuary. The *Arrival* admitted that Edward's arrival was not well received... "as

---

[517] *History of the Arrival of Edward IV* Transcribed by John Stowe. Kessinger Publishing 2007. Page 2.

Page 272

to the folks of the country there came but right few to him, or almost none... notwithstanding the love and favour they had borne his father, the Dule of York".

Edward and his few supporters made their way to York where entry was gained for a limited few with great reluctance. Edward had it be known that he just wanted the return of his duchy of York and nothing more. Once at York, messengers were sent out to call for men and support. Edward set off south via Tadcaster, Wakefield and Doncaster. The Earl of Northumberland, "sat still" giving tacit but not public support to Edward. Percy had been restored to his earldom by Edward and would be reluctant to raise arms against him for Warwick and the Nevilles.

Warwick's brother Montagu at Pontefract was unable to rouse his men and let Edward pass. The *Arrival* was unsure whether this was down to "goodwill or not, men may judge at their pleasure" but considered that Montagu was afraid to do battle due to insufficient numbers, uncertainty as to the loyalty of Percy and the historic support locally for the House of York.

Edward continued south gaining more men along the way at Doncaster and Nottingham turning aside towards Newark on hearing Exeter, Oxford and Beaumont were nearby. They retreated north towards Montagu leaving Edward free to continue his journey south. Warkworth wrote... "and there came to him Sir William Stanley with 300 men and Sir William Norris, and diverse other men and tenants of Lord Hastings..." [518] The *Arrival* documents the welcome arrival of men stirred by messages from Hastings via his "servants, friends and lovers". [519].

Warwick had stationed himself in the Midlands at Coventry where he sought to raise men. Henry Vernon and others were summoned to fight "yonder man Edward, the King our sovereign lord's great

---

[518] *Warkworth's Chronicle – A Chronicle of the First Thirteen Years of the Reign of King Edward the Fourth* Edited by James Orchard Halliwell. Camden Society 1839. Leopold Classic Library. Amazon 2015. Page 14.
[519] *History of the Arrival of Edward IV* Transcribed by John Stowe. Kessinger Publishing 2007. Pages 8-9.

enemy, rebel and traitor" by personal letters "my very singular trust is in you… Henry, I pray you fail not now as ever I may do for you". [520]

Warwick, the "Great Rebel" as Edward referred to him, learnt of Edward's approach and withdrew with his forces behind the fortified defences of Coventry. Time was on his side, or so he thought. Warwick's brother, John Lord Montagu, together with Exeter, Oxford and Beaumont were making their way south to him. Warwick's son-in-law, Clarence, was raising men in the south-west and had written telling him to await his arrival before committing to battle. Warkworth tells us… "But the Earl of Warwick had a letter from the Duke of Clarence, that he should not fight till he came himself". [521]

Edward sent messages three days running that he "desired him to come out, with all his people, into the field, to determine his quarrel" but Warwick refused to do so. Edward according to the *Arrival* was willing to grant Warwick his life and more "which seemed reasonable" considering his "great and heinous offences". Warwick "would not accept the said offers, nor accord thereunto".

Clarence delayed at Wells and sent messages to his friend Henry Vernon to enquire of developments for he did not want to reveal his intentions prematurely. Vernon was gratefully thanked for his news and help. Clarence had been turned. The *Arrival* relates that William Hastings acted as a go between for Edward and his brother Clarence… "so that a perfect accord was appointed, accorded, concluded and assured betwixt them". Clarence agreed to "aid and assist (Edward) against all his enemies". [522] Warwick's deal with Louis and Margaret had seen him demoted in succession and importance. There was no real place for a Yorkist Prince in the

---

[520] *Warwick the Kingmaker* by Michael Hicks. Blackwell Publishers 1998. Fortune's Second Wheel, 1470-71. Page 308.
[521] *Warkworth's Chronicle – A Chronicle of the First Thirteen Years of the Reign of King Edward the Fourth* Edited by James Orchard Halliwell. Camden Society 1839. Leopold Classic Library. Amazon 2015. Page 14.
[522] *History of the Arrival of Edward IV* Transcribed by John Stowe. Kessinger Publishing 2007. Pages 10-11.

Lancastrian court. Clarence was open to the whisperings of Hastings, and his mother Cecily and his sister Margaret.

Clarence met up with his two brothers, Edward and Gloucester near Banbury… "And when they were together within less than half a mile, the King set his people in array the banners and left them standing still, taking with him his brother of Gloucester, the Lord Rivers, Lord Hastings, a few others, and went towards his brother of Clarence" and there was "right kind and loving language between them two, with perfect accord knit together for ever here after, with as heartly loving cheer and countenance". [523]

News of the reunion of the two brothers would have filtered through to Warwick at Coventry. There was even more reason for him to remain within the city walls now despite having been joined by Montagu, Oxford and Exeter. Clarence was "right desirous to procure a good accord between the King and the Earl of Warwick, not only for the Earl, but also to reconcile thereby unto the King's good grace many Lords and noble men of his land, of whom many had largely taken part with the Earl". Warwick refused to accept any arrangement. The *Arrival* states that reasons were various. Perhaps Warwick could see no prospect of accord with Edward or else he wanted to stay true to the oaths sworn to "the French King, Queen Margaret and her son, Edward". Warwick may have already had his escape route planned or else others such as the Earl of Oxford persuaded him not to accept the King's grace.

Edward left the Midlands on 5th April. The *Arrival* records a miracle at the shrine of St Anne in Daventry before he moved on to Northampton. Letters were sent to his wife in sanctuary and to his "true Lords, servants, and lovers" in London. Warwick also sent letters to the Mayor, Aldermen and commons of London asking for the gates to be closed to Edward. Warwick's brother George, Archbishop of York was charged with raising men to keep London from Edward for a few days. Warwick "promised that he would not fail to come with a great puissance… to distress and destroy him".

---

[523] *History of the Arrival of Edward IV* Transcribed by John Stowe. Kessinger Publishing 2007. Page 11.

Somerset and Devon left London for the South-West to welcome Queen Margaret and Prince Edward. They had little time for Warwick and preferred to link up once more with their Queen and Prince and other Lancastrian Lords from exile. It was to be a strategic mistake to split up the Lancastrian forces but one understandable given the history between Somerset and Warwick. Commynes commented "you can see therefore, how ancient divisions survive, how much they are to be feared and how great are the losses they can cause". [524]

George Neville gathered together what men he could and led Henry VI in procession from the Bishop's Palace near St Paul's through the city of London and back again. The sight of the weak and feeble Henry had the opposite effect of what was intended. The London Chronicle commented "this progress was held more like a play than the showing if a prince to win men's hearts; for by this means he lost many and won none or right few". [525]

The news that Edward was nearby at St Albans with his army also weighed heavily on the minds of the leading citizens. The Mayor, Aldermen and Merchants agreed that the city should be open to Edward. Messages of welcome were sent. Even George Neville "sent secretly unto him desiring to be admitted to his grace". [526]

Commynes wrote of three factors why London changed its mind and supported the return of Edward: first the men, who were in the sanctuaries, and his wife, the Queen, who had given birth to a son; secondly the great debts he owed in the city, which made his merchant creditors support him; thirdly several noblewomen and

---

[524] *Philippe de Commynes Memoirs, The Reign of Louis XI 1461-83* Published by Penguin Books 1972. Translated and introduced by Michael Jones. Written 1498. Restoration of Edward IV. Page 196.
[525] *The Great Chronicle of London.* Edited by A.H. Thomas & I.D. Thornley. Gloucester 1983. Pages 214-216.
[526] *History of the Arrival of Edward IV* Transcribed by John Stowe. Kessinger Publishing 2007. Page 16.

Page 276

wives of rich citizens with whom he had been closely and secretly acquainted won over their husbands and relatives to his cause". [527]

Men loyal to Edward took over the Tower and on Thursday 11th April, he rode into London to St Pauls and the Bishops Palace where George Neville handed over Henry VI. Thanksgiving at Westminster followed and at last Edward met up with his wife, Elizabeth and his newly born son. Edward and his family lodged with his mother, the Duchess of York, at Baynard's Castle.

---

[527] *Philippe de Commynes Memoirs, The Reign of Louis XI 1461-83* Published by Penguin Books 1972. Translated and introduced by Michael Jones. Written 1498. Restoration of Edward IV. Page 194.

Barnet 14th April 1471

...In the morning a dreadful engagement took place, in which there fell various nobles of either party. On the side of those who were of king Henry's party, there fell those two most famous nobles, the brothers Richard, Earl of Warwick, and John, Marquis of Montagu ... [528]

The road to Barnet was long but some would say inevitable. The two cousins, Warwick and Edward could not settle their differences in any other way.

The Barnet Campaign 1471

Edward ⇨   Warwick ⬛➡
Clarence ⇨   Montagu ⇨
            Exeter, Oxford & Beaumont ⇨

1. King Edward landed at Ravenspur on 14th March and marched via York, Wakefield, past Montagu at Pontefract Castle, to Doncaster and then to Nottingham by 25th March.

2. Edward turned east to Newark to attack Exeter, Oxford and Beaumont but they retreated north to join Montagu.

3. Edward advanced to Leicester and by 29th March to Coventry. Warwick remained within the Castle awaiting reinforcements.

4. Clarence met with Edward at Banbury on 3rd April. Warwick still did not fight or make peace. Edward reached London 12th April.

5. Warwick, now joined by Montagu, Oxford & others, marched south to St Albans.

6. Edward set out on 13th April to confront Warwick. There was a skirmish around Barnet. Battle commenced early morning on Easter Sunday 14th April.

© Steve Williams

---

[528] *Ingulph's Chronicle of the Abbey of Croyland.* Translated by HT Riley. Lightening Source Press 2014. Page 464.

The *Arrival* stated that "The Earl of Warwick, calling himself lieutenant of England, and so constituted by the pretence of the authority of King Henry, being at Coventry, and understanding well that the King would much do to be received in at London... issued out of Coventry with a great puissance... and so, he (Edward) took in his company to the field, King Henry; and so, that afternoon he rode to Barnet, 10 miles out of London, where his afore-riders found the afore-riders of the Earl of Warwick's host and beat them, and chased them out of the town, more some-what than a half mile away, where under a hedge-side were ready assembled a great people, in array, of the Earl of Warwick." [529]

Warwick had rejected Edward's offers of peace or battle at Coventry, but he now headed south to confront him. He must have felt confident enough to do so rather than wait for Margaret and Prince Edward and the men they might bring or rally to their sides. Perhaps he expected London to hold out against Edward or else he wanted to catch his cousin whilst he celebrated Easter. Perhaps it was the news that Louis XI had signed a truce with Burgundy.

Warwick and his army moved to St Albans and then on to Barnet. We have the benefit of a contemporary account by the representative of Cologne, called Gerhard von Wesel, to understand what happened next. [530] "On Easter Eve around seven o'clock in the evening, as King Edward marched away from here and came into the vicinity of Hornsea Park, six miles from London, Warwick's vanguard encountered him and they had a skirmish thereabouts and they chased each other in the dark as far as a village called Barnet, ten miles from London. Warwick and his Lords and companions who had been in Coventry pitched their battle a mile beyond the said village, just beside the highway to St Albans on a broad green plot, and King Edward's people, not knowing in the night where the

---

[529] *History of the Arrival of Edward IV in England and the Final Recovery of the Kingdoms from Henry VI* Transcribed by John Stowe. Edited by John Bruce. Camden Society 1838. Kessinger Publishing 2007. Written 1471. Page 18.
[530] *Gerhard von Wesel's Newsletter from England.* 17th April 1471. Hannes Kleineke. *Blood Royale* Hugh Bicheno 2016. Page 187.

Page 279

opposing parties were, also in the night rode onto the same plot and set up their camp on the other side of the afore-said highway, just opposite Warwick, in a hollow and marsh".

Saturday saw Edward's army mustered in St John's field to the north of the city of London before they moved north to meet Warwick. There were some light skirmishes at Barnet. The weather was poor. Both sides settled down for the night closer to each other than they thought due to the lack of visibility due to darkness and fog. Warwick's guns fired through the night but overshot Edward's men.

Warwick organised his men with Oxford on the right, Exeter on the left and Montagu in the centre. Warwick himself remained to the rear. Edward had Gloucester on his right and Hastings on his left. Edward commanded the centre where he could keep a close eye on the newly returned Clarence.

Dawn saw an early start to the battle. It was Easter Sunday 14th April 1471. Archers fired arrows on both sides. Gloucester pushed forwards on the right of the Yorkist army and outflanked Exeter. The fighting was so fierce that a couple of esquires were killed. Gloucester was injured.

It was a different story on the left where Hastings was outflanked by Oxford. Hasting's men were pushed back towards and beyond Barnet. Some escaped as far as London. The news was that "the King was distressed, and his field lost". [531]

The Arrival reports that Edward fought "manly, vigorously and valiantly" and "with great violence, beat and bare down afore him all that stood in his way." [532] The Yorkist centre held firm, but the axis of fighting had turned from north-south towards east-west as Gloucester continued pressing on the right.

---

[531] *History of the Arrival of Edward IV* Transcribed by John Stowe. Kessinger Publishing 2007. Page 19.
[532] *History of the Arrival of Edward IV* Transcribed by John Stowe. Kessinger Publishing 2007. Page 20.

Oxford's men lost discipline. Some chose to plunder Barnet. It was some time before they regrouped. On their return to battle they were mistaken for Yorkist troops by the Lancastrian centre in the poor visibility. Shouts of "Treason" rang out. Feelings were running high. The Lancastrians stood uneasily alongside Warwick. Clarence had deserted them. Montagu was under suspicion. The day was soon lost.

Warkworth provides useful detail… "On Easter Day in the morning, right early, each of them came upon the other, and there was such a mist that neither of them could see the other properly. They fought from 4 o'clock in the morning until 10 o'clock. And divers times the Earl of Warwick's party had the victory and supposed that they had won the field. But it happened so, that the Earl of Oxford's men had upon them their Lord's livery, which was a star with streams, which was much like King Edward's livery, the sun with streams; and the mist was so thick, that a man might not profitably judge one thing from another; so that the Earl of Warwick's men shot and fought against the Earl of Oxford's men… and the Earl of Oxford's men cried Treason! Treason! And fled away from the field…

…The Lord Marquis of Montagu… put upon himself King Edward's livery; and a man of the Earl of Warwick saw that, and fell upon him, and killed him. And when the Earl of Warwick saw his brother dead, and the Earl of Oxford fled, he leapt on horseback, and fled to a wood, by the field of Barnet, where there was no way forth; and one of King Edward's men had espied him, and came upon him and killed him, and despoiled him naked. And so, King Edward won the field…" [533]

---

[533] *"Warkworth's" Chronicle: A Chronicle of the First Thirteen Years of the reign of King Edward the Fourth* John Warkworth edited by James Orchard. Halliwell Leopold Classic Library 2015. Written 1470-85. Page 16.

The Battle of Barnet 14th April 1471

1. Edward arrayed his forces on evening of 13th April near those of Warwick. No fires were lit. Warwick's guns shot overhead through the night. Visibility was poor in the early morning mist.

2. Battle commenced. Oxford's men overlapped and overcame Hasting's men who fled south past Barnet. Some of Oxford's men looted Edward's baggage train and Barnet town. Oxford's men regrouped and returned.

3. Gloucester overlapped Exeter and pushed him back. This together with the collapse of Edward's left flank saw the lines of battle turn anti clockwise.

4. Oxford's returning men were mistaken by Montagu's men for Edward's army and were attacked. There was chaos and shouts of 'treason'. Edward & Richard pressed forward. Warwick's lines broke.

5. The battle was won. Montagu dies. Warwick sought his horse but was killed. Fleeing men lost their lives, many in the area known as Deadman's bottom.

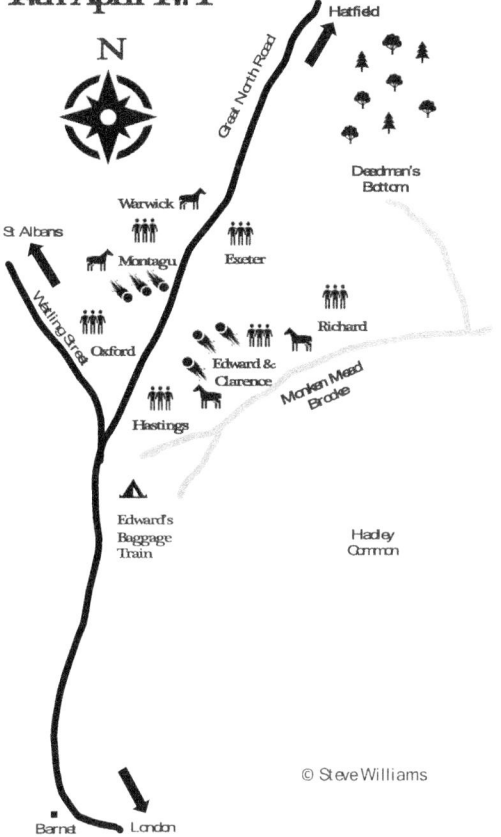

© Steve Williams

The *Arrival* records… "in this battle was slain the Earl of Warwick, somewhat fleeing". Montagu was killed in plain battle. Exeter was badly wounded but escaped. Oxford fled to Scotland. King Henry VI who had been taken to Barnet was returned to the Tower where he remained under lock and key until his death.

The *Arrival* understandably gave a good account of Edward in battle… "trusting verily in God's help, our blessed ladies and St George, took to him great hardiness and courage to suppress the falsehood and treachery of those who so falsely and traitorously had conspired against him, where through he manfully, vigorously and valiantly assailed them in the midst and strongest of their battle… so that he won the field there". [534]

The Croyland Chronicler was pleased but surprised writing that Edward "won a marvellous, glorious and unexpected victory" and recorded those who lost their lives on both sides. For the Lancastrians Warwick and Montagu were dead. Exeter, Oxford and Beaumont escaped. For the Yorkists, Lord's Say and Cromwell died, as did Sir William Blount. [535]

Sir John Paston's brother, also John, was "hurt with an arrow on his right arm beneath the elbow" but "he shall be all whole within a right short time" according to the letter sent to his wife Margaret on 18th April 1471. [536]

Fabian's chronicle spoke of a "long and cruel fight" where King Edward obtained the upper hand" and "of the commons of both parties were slain 1,500 men and more". [537]

Commynes blamed Warwick's demise on being on foot rather than on horseback… "if the battle was going well for him, he would throw himself into the fray but if it was going badly, he would make an early escape". It was his brother, Montagu that persuaded him to "dismount and send away his horses". [538]

---

[534] *History of the Arrival of Edward IV in England and the Final Recovery of the Kingdoms from Henry VI* Transcribed by John Stowe. Edited by John Bruce. Camden Society 1838. Kessinger Publishing 2007. Written 1471. Page 19.
[535] *Ingulph's Chronicle of the Abbey of Croyland. Translated by HT Riley. Lightening Source Press 2014. Page 465.*
[536] *Paston Letters 1422-1509.* Edited by J. Gairdner. 1904. Gloucester 1983. Volume 5. Pages 99-100.
[537] *The New Chronicles of England and France* by Robert Fabyan. Edited by Henry Ellis London 1811. Forgotten Books 2018. Originally edition by Pynson 1516. Page 661-2.
[538] *Philippe de Commynes Memoirs, The Reign of Louis XI 1461-83* Published by Penguin Books 1972. Translated and introduced by Michael Jones. Written 1498. Restoration of Edward IV. Page 195.

Epilogue

...Undone on land and on the quiet sea, Earl Richard,
You'll lie unburied on an unknown beach! ... [539]

"On the morrow after, the King commanded that the bodies of the dead lords, the Earl of Warwick, and his brother the Marquess, should be brought to St Paul's Church and openly showed to all the people..." It was important that everyone should know that the "great rebel" was no more... "people should not be abused by feigned seditious tales... that the Earl of Warwick was yet alive... to cause new insurrections and rebellions... for right many were towards him". [540]

The bodies were subsequently handed over to their brother George and they were buried in the Neville family vault at Bisham Priory in Berkshire. Nothing of the chapel and tomb remains today thanks to Henry VIII's destruction of the abbeys. The Editor of Warkworth's Chronicle however, notes that "The brass matrix of the seal of the Earl of Warwick, taken from him when he was slain, is in the British Museum; an impression may be seen among the charters xxxiv.33." [541]

Warwick was survived by his son-in-law Clarence and his daughter Anne who would later become the Queen of England that Warwick at one time expected his eldest daughter Isabel to become. Warwick's great offices and wealth were shared between King

---

[539] *Jeane Mielot: On the Earl of Warwick, 1470.* L. Visser-Fuchs. Drinker of Blood, A Burgundian View of England 1471. The Ricardian, Volume 7. No 92. 1986. Page 217.
[540] *History of the Arrival of Edward IV in England and the Final Recovery of the Kingdoms from Henry VI* Transcribed by John Stowe. Edited by John Bruce. Camden Society 1838. Kessinger Publishing 2007. Written 1471. Pages 20-21.
[541] *"Warkworth's" Chronicle: A Chronicle of the First Thirteen Years of the reign of King Edward the Fourth* John Warkworth edited by James Orchard. Halliwell Leopold Classic Library 2015. Written 1470-85. Notes. Page 64.

Edward's two brothers, Clarence and Gloucester. The returning and widowed Countess of Warwick though lost her inheritance and independence.

Warwick's demise met mixed reviews. Burgundian poems were not praiseworthy of the man who promised to carve up their country with Louis XI of France.

Jeane Mielot in his poem "On the Earl of Warwick, 1470" wrote…

"Undone on land and on the quiet sea, Earl Richard,
You'll lie unburied on an unknown beach!
Where else but to death are you rushing?! You,
Who venture on things too great for your powers.
Hot blood and your ignorance troubles you,
Fierce and stiff necked as you are, but wherever you come,
Traitor, to break up the league between brothers,
Through strife, deceit, by vice and fraud and snares,
Your fierceness leads you to folly and the savage fates,
Are spinning your last thread: unhappy will your life,
Through thin air sink to hell and leave your body here.
Keep, then, the arms in which you had such joy, drinker of blood,
You shall be miserable dust, a wraith and nothing but a tale." [542]

A Burgundian Ballad of Barnet Field celebrates the downfall of Warwick at the same time as taunting the French King…

"Now time his schemes have eaten,
And his coin, yes, there's the sting,
For Warwick's dead and beaten
Ha! What a sly dog is the King!

Frenchmen, one to another,

---

[542] *Jeane Mielot: On the Earl of Warwick, 1470.* L. Visser-Fuchs. Drinker of Blood, A Burgundian View of England 1471. The Ricardian, Volume 7. No 92. 1986. Page 217.

Rain tears and drip alarms,
For Warwick, your sworn brother,
Is crushed by force of arms." [543]

However, the short poem "The Battle of Barnet" is written more in sorrow rather than anger… and in the expectation and hope of reconciliation, for "right many were towards him".

"Turn away and fear your King…
He is gone…
…that great division is dead…

'Allas!' may he sing that caused all this,
Sorrow and care caused many a day.
Pray for his soul, that he may come to bliss,
You that are his friends, you Priests, to pray." [544]

Warwick lived and died in a violent world, but he is not forgotten. Some may argue that Warwick achieved longer lasting glory and renown than either of the two Kings whom he served.

Warwick the Kingmaker lives on.

---

[543] *Warwick the Kingmaker* by Paul Kendall. George Allen & Unwin 1957. Page323. Leroux de Lincy Pages 159-173
[544] *Historical Poems of the Fourteenth and Fifteenth Centuries* edited by R.H. Robbins. New York 1959. Pages 226-227.

Bibliography - Primary Sources

Parliamentary Rolls Various. British Library.

"Warkworth's" Chronicle: A Chronicle of the First Thirteen Years of the reign of King Edward the Fourth John Warkworth edited by James Orchard. Halliwell Leopold Classic Library 2015. Written 1470-85.

History of the Arrival of Edward IV in England and the Final Recovery of the Kingdoms from Henry VI Transcribed by John Stowe. Edited by John Bruce. Camden Society 1838. Kessinger Publishing 2007. Written 1471.

Ingulph's Chronicle of the Abbey of Croyland: with the continuations by Peter of Blois and Anonymous writers. Translated by Henry Riley. Published by Nabu Press 2014. Originally published 1854. Written 1486.

Selections From the Paston Letters transcribed by Sir John Fenn. Edited by Alice Greenwood. London 1920. Forgotten Books.

Philippe de Commynes Memoirs, The Reign of Louis XI 1461-83 Published by Penguin Books 1972. Translated and introduced by Michael Jones. Written 1498.

Philippe de Commynes Warwick the Kingmaker Blackie's English Texts edited by W.H.D. Rouse 1908. Elibron Classics 2005.

A Collection of the Chronicles and Ancient Histories of Great Britain, now called England Bibliography by John de Waurin. Translated by Edward Hardy. Published by Forgotten Books 2015. Originally published 1891. Written 1445-1470.

Three Books of Polydore Vergil's English History by Camden Society. Edited by Sir Henry Ellis. Published by Forgotten Books 2012 Originally published 1844. Written 1510.

Hall's Chronicle: Containing the History of England, During the Reign of Henry the Fourth, and the Succeeding Monarchs, to the End of the Reign of Henry VIII by Edward Hall - Published by Forgotten Books 2018. Originally published by Richard Grafton 1548.

The New Chronicles of England and France by Robert Fabyan. Edited by Henry Ellis London 1811. Forgotten Books 2018. Originally edition by Pynson 1516.

Three Fifteenth Century Chronicles with Historical Memoranda by John Stowe. Edited by J Gairdner for the Camden Society. Published by Nabu Press 2012. Originally published 1881.

The Chronicles of The White Rose of York: A series of Historical Fragments, Proclamations, Letters and Other Contemporary Documents relating to the Reign of Edward IV Edited by James Bohn. Published London 1845. Paperback Version Reprint 2012.

Edward IV from Contemporary Chronicles, Letters and Records by Keith Dockray. Fonthill Media Limited 2015.

Henry VI, Margaret of Anjou and the Wars of the Roses from Contemporary Chronicles, Letters and Records by Keith Dockray. Fonthill Media Limited 2016.

Bibliography – General

Wikipedia

Warwick The Kingmaker by Charles W. Oman. First Published 1891. Ithink books. Lightning Source UK Ltd.

The Life and Reign of Edward the Fourth King of England and of France and Lord of Ireland by Cora L. Scofield. Volumes One and Two. Fonthill Media 2016. First Published 1923.

Warwick the Kingmaker by Paul Kendall. George Allen & Unwin 1957.

Warwick the Kingmaker by L. Du Garde Peach. Ladybird History Book. 1966.

Henry VI by Bertram Wolffe. Yale University Press 1981.

Edward IV by Charles Ross. First Published 1974. Yale University Press 1997.

The Lordly Ones, A History of the Neville Family and their part in the Wars of the Roses by Geoffrey Richardson. Baildon Books. 1998.

Warwick the Kingmaker by Michael Hicks. Blackwell Publishers 1998.

The Lordly Ones, A History of the Neville Family and their part in the Wars of the Roses by Geoffrey Richardson. Baildon Books. 1998.

Edward IV by Michael Hicks. Reputations. Hodder Headline Group 2004.

The Wars of the Roses; The Soldiers' Experience by Anthony Goodman. Tempus Publishing Limited 2005.

Warwick the Kingmaker Politics, Power and Fame by A.J. Pollard. Continuum Books 2007.

Edward IV and The War of the Roses by David Santiuste. Pen & Sword Military 2010.

Battle Royale; The Wars of Lancaster and York 1440-1462 by Hugh Bicheno. Head of Zeus 2015.

Blood Royale; The Wars of Lancaster and York 1462-1485 by Hugh Bicheno. Head of Zeus 2016.

The Nevills of Middleham by K.L. Clark. The History Press 2016

The House of Beaufort by Nathan Amin. Amberley Publishing 2017.

Richard, Duke of York King by Right by Matthew Lewis. Amberley Publishing 2017.

Henry VI & Margaret of Anjou by Amy Licence. Pen & Sword Books Limited. 2018.

The Brothers York, An English Tragedy by Thomas Penn. Penguin 2019.

Shadow King The Life and Death of Henry VI by Lauren Johnson. Head of Zeus 2019.

Battles

The Battles of St Albans by Peter Burley. Michael Elliott and Harvey Watson. Pen & Sword 2007.

Fatal Colours, Towton, 1461... England's Most Brutal Battle by George Goodwin. Weidenfeld & Nicolson 2011.

The Battle of Northampton 1460 by Mike Ingram. Northamptonshire Battlefields Society 2015.

The Battle of Edgcote 1469 by Graham Evans. Northamptonshire Battlefields Society 2019.

Where both the Hosts Fought... The Rebellions of 1469-1470 and the Battles of Edgcote and Lose-Cote-Field by Philip A. Haigh. Battlefield Press 1997.

Barnet 1471 Death of a Kingmaker by David Clark. Battleground Pen & Sword 2007.

Tewkesbury 1471 Eclipse of the House of Lancaster by Steven Goodchild. Battleground Pen & Sword 2005.

Tewkesbury 1471 The Last Yorkist Victory by Christopher Gravett. Osprey Publishing 2003.

Articles

The Earl of Warwick's Use of Sea-Power in the Late 1450s by Penny Tucker. Southern History Review. June 2022.

The Lincolnshire Rebellion of 1470 Revisited by Penny Tucker. *The English Historical Review*, Volume 136, Issue 578, February 2021.

Robin of Redesdale's Rebellion of 1469 by P. Holland. Northern History 58 (2) Pages 1-20 May 2021.

Battlefields Trust

The Battlefields Trust is a registered charity dedicated to the protection, promotion and interpretation of Britain's battlefields.

The Trust's Battlefields Resource centre is full of useful information for anyone wanting to visit or study a battlefield or even just find out more about these crucial episodes in our history.

New Members are most welcome.

www.battlefieldstrust.com

Northamptonshire Battlefields Society

Northamptonshire Battlefields Society is a non-political group originally formed to promote and protect the site of the Battle of Northampton 10th July 1460.

Its remit has been extended to cover the other battles and skirmishes in Northamptonshire including the battles of 1065, 1088, 1174, the three battles of 1215 and the 1264 battle. It also covers the medieval sieges of Rockingham and Fotheringhay, the battle of Edgcote and nationally important monuments such as Queen Eleanor's Cross.

New Members are most welcome.

www.facebook.com/groups/Northampton1460

Richard III Society

The Richard II Society was founded in 1924. In the belief, that many features of the traditional accounts of the character and career of Richard III are neither supported by sufficient evidence nor reasonably tenable, the Society aims to promote, in every possible way, research into the life and times of Richard III and to secure a reassessment of the material relating to the role of this monarch in history.

New Members are most welcome.

https://richardiii.net

www.facebook.com/RICHARD-III-SOCIETY-114452911904874/

About the Author

Steve Williams is retired after a working lifetime with Barclays and Santander. Married with 3 grown up children, he lives in Milton Keynes. He walks, reads and does jigsaws, but not all at the same time. Football is his passion, and he is a proud MK Dons season ticket holder since their first season in 2004.

A member of the Northamptonshire Battlefields Society, the Battlefields Trust and the Richard III Society, "Warwick the Kingmaker" is his eighth book. He obtained a scholarship to read history at Oxford but switched to law. He is a historian by interest rather than by training.

Other Books by the Author

Richard III
A Man of his Time

Richard III is perhaps the most well-known King of England. Many books have been written about Richard over the 500 plus years since he was crowned King. This book is based upon a review of all available sources.

Richard has been judged good, bad, evil even. Opinions have changed through the years. History has been written, rewritten and revisited so many times. Many questions have been asked and many answers given. Yet there is no certainty. Much is still unclear. The passage of time clouds the picture. New theories are put forward and old ones updated. Fresh research is conducted. Conclusive proof is lacking.

Richard is born on 2nd October 1452 to Richard the 3rd Duke of York and Cecily Neville. He is of royal blood and is descended from Edward III. As the youngest of four sons surviving past infancy, he is more likely to be destined for the church. Yet he becomes King.

Richard's father and a brother are killed. His eldest brother Edward seizes the throne. Twice he flees England for his life. His mentor and Uncle, Warwick, dies fighting against him on the battlefield. Another brother George rebels and is executed for treason.

The unexpected early death of his brother King Edward IV results in him being appointed Protector to his nephew Edward V. Richard is crowned King himself yet within two years he loses his wife and son and is killed on the battlefield at Bosworth.

Richard experiences the wheel of fortune like few others. His life is but a roller coaster of emotions. Events cannot fail to influence and shape Richard. Medieval life is harsh and brutal.

Richard is a man of his Time.

Richard III
The Sources

Richard III is known to us from school, books, plays, television, film, and most recently through social media. Our picture of Richard, as man and King, is our view based on what we learn from these **sources of information**. Richard has traditionally been portrayed as a bad King. Views have changed over the centuries.

Contemporary writings and records are primary sources. These are invaluable but secondary sources cannot be ignored and can provide a fresh perspective and a critical review of the evidence to help one arrive at one's own judgement.

It is important to understand the origin and nature of the sources in order to evaluate the information and to what extent it is fact or interpretation or 'colour' for a story. The intended audience and motive for writing helps to establish possible bias and prejudice. Reliability will depend on the writer and the source of their information. The account may be first hand or perhaps heard from those present and involved. It may be plagiarised from the writings of others or intended as pure drama.

The purpose of this book is to review the main sources for those who seek to study Richard III whether that be for education, enlightenment, entertainment or enjoyment. The sources are considered in chronological order.

Richard III is what we take and make of these sources.

William Hastings
Lord Chamberlain of England

The rise and sudden unexpected fall of William Hastings makes for a colourful story. Yet it is lost amongst the great tales told of Edward IV and Richard III. William rose from a mere Squire to be a Peer of the Realm, a great Landowner and Lord Chamberlain.

William was very close to King Edward IV and for many years perhaps the second most influential man in the Kingdom. He fulfilled many roles including politician, administrator, soldier, diplomat, businessman, landowner and lord. Everything he had was due to Edward who he served loyally for over two decades from 1461 to 1483.

William supported Edward at or after Mortimer's Cross, was knighted at Towton, commanded wings of Edward's army at Barnet and Tewkesbury. William was the Head of the Royal Household. William wined, dined and more with Edward and fell out of favour with Queen Elizabeth Woodville for so doing.

Edward IV died unexpectedly in April 1483. William suddenly found himself caught between the Woodvilles, and the future Richard III, with whom he chose to ally. William was executed for treason and was buried in the north aisle of St George's Chapel at Windsor alongside his lifetime friend Edward IV.

The Rising Sunne of York...
Edward IV becomes King

He is the eldest living son of Richard, Duke of York and is from the Blood Royale. King Edward III is his great, great, grandfather. His cousin is Richard Neville, Earl of Warwick, who some call 'the Kingmaker'. He is not the son of a King, but he becomes King.

Born in Rouen, he lives his early years in France, Ireland and England as he follows the undulating career of his father during a period of political instability and uncertainty in the reign of King Henry VI. Ludlow in the Welsh Marches is where he is brought up, schooled and trained along with his younger brother Edmund.

The wheel of fortune turns and turns again for his father and then him, as the Wars of the Roses break out. The York family is set against the Lancaster family. Soon everything is at stake.

The sun of York is rising.

History with Dialogue & Character.

The Sunne of York in Splendour...
Edward IV is King

He is the King of England, by right and by victory on the battlefield.

Former King Henry VI and Queen Margaret plan and plot to take away his throne. They are supported by Lancastrian Lords who have sworn loyalty to King Henry together with the Queen's French relatives and friends, and the rebellious Scots.

Treachery lurks closer to home as his cousin Warwick and even his brother George, Duke of Clarence, turn against him and he has to flee to Burgundy for his life. Yet he returns, reclaims his kingdom and is King once more.

The wheel of fortune turns, and turns again

Everything remains at stake but slowly, and surely, he strengthens his hold on the throne of England.

The sun of York is seen in all its splendour.

History with Dialogue and Character.

Things could be worse…
…but I very much doubt it

John Smith is a special detective assigned to the National Financial Crime Agency. Investigating a number of financial scams, he finds himself unknowingly on the trail of a modern-day Godfather who sits at the heart of the establishment.

One ordinary day starts well but a series of seemingly unconnected events turn his life upside down. His car is stolen. His bank account is blocked. His Facebook account is hacked. A routine visit turns non-routine. His colleague is shot dead, and he is a prime suspect. He only just escapes himself. His wife is kidnapped. He no longer knows who he can and cannot trust. Someone is trying to destroy him and all he holds dear.

Yesterday he was a happily married family man and a police officer. He was respected, trustworthy and highly regarded. Today he's a man on the run, in fear for his life and the lives of his family.

Things could be worse. He is alive, and whilst he's alive, he has a chance of finding those responsible.

Things could be better…
…but I'm not hopeful

John Smith is a Special Detective with the Financial Crime Agency. He is asked to investigate a pension scam on some MPs including a Junior Minister in Parliament when he is contacted by a young student journalist who has information about an old adversary and a possible link to the fatal shooting of a colleague.

John tries to speak with the journalist only to find he has gone missing. The Junior Minister is caught up in a personal scandal. John's manager at work has retired and been replaced by the boss from hell. His wife has left him and taken their teenage daughter with her. His finances are severely stretched from trying to support two households. His local football team has just lost three games in a row.

Things could be better, but he's not hopeful.

Printed in Great Britain
by Amazon